'Splendid . . . Laced with [...] days indeed, but exhilarati[...] to give up hope.'

'An evocative tour of the la[...] history through the eyes o[...] South Africa's most perceptive writers.'   THE STAR

'*Strange Days Indeed* shows why Shaun Johnson has become one of the fresh voices in political journalism . . . His achievement is that he has kept his journalistic sanity.'
                                                        CITY PRESS

'Underpinned by irreverence and humour . . . Johnson's skill is his clarity of writing.'   PRETORIA NEWS

'Invigorating and exciting.'   CAPE TIMES

'Evocative and resonant.'   AGGREY KLAASTE

'Shaun Johnson has acquired the reputation of being one of South Africa's most perceptive writers. Some of these pieces are nothing short of brilliant, others are sceptical. The book will rekindle our jaded hopes.'
                                                        HELEN SUZMAN

'Shaun Johnson not only sees the point in South African politics, he sees beyond it to its consequences. His writings are always sane, humane and shrewd insights of value to all of us, like myself, who read him.'
                                                        NADINE GORDIMER

'This book is a must if one is to understand the modern mosaic of South Africa.' SOLOMON 'STIX' MOREWA

'Beelde van stof en trane van die land.'   DIE BEELD

Author photograph © Peter Baasch

Shaun Johnson was born in South Africa in 1959. He grew up in Libode, Transkei, Witbank and Durban before moving to Johannesburg. He was educated at Hyde Park High School, Johannesburg, Rhodes University, Grahamstown and the University of Oxford, where he was a Rhodes Scholar. He received academic and sporting awards at both universities.

He was deeply involved in the development of the alternative press in South Africa in the late 1970s and early 1980s, writing the feasibility study for the New Nation newspaper and helping to found Saspu National. A former assistant editor of the Weekly Mail, he directed a training project aimed at black journalists.

He has written for a variety of prominent publications here and abroad, and is a commentator on television and radio stations around the world. He is currently Deputy Editor and Political Editor of The Star, Johannesburg, and is one of South Africa's most prominent political analysts.

STRANGE DAYS INDEED

SHAUN JOHNSON

BANTAM BOOKS

LONDON • NEW YORK • TORONTO • SYDNEY • AUCKLAND

TRANSWORLD PUBLISHERS LTD
61–63 Uxbridge Road, London W5 5SA

TRANSWORLD PUBLISHERS (AUSTRALIA) PTY LTD
15–25 Helles Avenue, Moorebank, NSW 2170

TRANSWORLD PUBLISHERS (NZ) LTD
3 William Pickering Drive,
Albany, Auckland

TRANS-SA BOOK DISTRIBUTORS (PTY) LTD
Gallo House, 6 Hood Avenue, Rosebank 2196

Published 1993 in South Africa by Bantam Press
a division of Transworld Publishers Ltd
Bantam Books edition published in South Africa in 1994
Copyright © Shaun Johnson 1993, 1994
The title of this book was inspired by John Lennon's song
Nobody Told Me (1984, Milk and Honey, *Geffen.*)

The right of Shaun Johnson to be identified
as author of this work has been asserted in accordance
with sections 77 and 78 of the Copyright Designs and
Patents Act 1988.

A catalogue record for this book is available from the British Library

ISBN 0553–408917

Typeset in 10/11pt Plantin by
Chippendale Type Ltd, Otley, West Yorkshire.
Printed in Great Britain by
Cox & Wyman Ltd, Reading, Berkshire.

SOUTH AFRICA
FROM INSURRECTION TO
POST-ELECTION

For Joan, my extraordinary mother, with love.

CONTENTS

FOREWORD

A political journalist who writes a regular column about the goings-on of a country, Shaun Johnson always manages to capture the flavour of a moment and save it for a time when we can revisit the past and try to understand it better.

He writes from May 1986 until now; a turbulent, traumatic and dramatic transition in South Africa's history. He writes with a cool, old head on young shoulders. He combines clinical analysis with passionate engagement, and his deep affection for the land and its extraordinary people is clearly evident in what he says. Yet he does so without sentimentality.

Anyone who wishes to understand and get a feel for the current dynamics of transition in South Africa can do so in a comfortable, easy and untaxing read of *Strange Days Indeed*. Shaun Johnson is a very good political journalist.

FREDERIK VAN ZYL SLABBERT, JOHANNESBURG, MAY 1993

PREFACE
A MONKEYS' WEDDING

My eyes are bloodshot, one's trained on the television screen, one ear's cocked in the direction of the radio, there's a chaotic mountain of paper on my desk, I'm suffering from severe sleep deprivation and the after-effects of an insanely-timed end-of-election journalists' party. I have to think twice about what day it is. And there's a big stupid smile on my face.

Our country has made it, messily but marvellously, through the greatest test of its history. We've done what the world believed we never could do. All of us have voted together, in an atmosphere of astounding peacefulness, and today we are waiting together, in an atmosphere of astounding patience, to be told what we have decided. So far, at least, we have confounded the doomsday prophets who insisted we would by now be at war. We have defied that imperative of human history which holds that people would sooner follow an irrational short-sighted path than do what is more difficult, and invest in the future.

As I write on this Sunday morning we don't yet know the results of this election that has been gestating for 350 years, the product of a process that took much too long to start and then happened too quickly. Somehow, strangely, the precise percentage points are secondary for the moment. We're still elated (a little surprised at ourselves if the truth be told) because we did such a lovely thing last week. Today we inhabit a nether world called

3

the nearly-new South Africa, but in a matter of days we will be in our new country.

Of course it is true that the real challenges for this nation we are about to invent lie ahead. They are giant challenges. All this will have been for nothing if the maltreated masses are not convinced that in time their lives will improve and – even more profoundly – that their children will be given the same opportunities as their compatriots. Many of us will not live to see all the challenges met, if ever they can be. But it has been good to be alive these past years, as our beloved country made its hesitant, argumentative, long leap of faith. Voting day saw the arrival on our African landscape of more than just a new flag, new laws and a new anthem – it saw an entire polyglot people begin to renew themselves, reinvent themselves.

For many years I have argued (out of faith as much as insight) that an unprecedented, seemingly impossible unravelling of our racial Gordian Knot was within our reach if we would only believe in it sufficiently and act accordingly. I suggested that our reformist revolution – for that is what it is – could be altogether less bloody and vengeful than most expected, and that if rationality prevailed among the politicians, we need not emerge concussed as a country but in fact revitalised and on the threshold of performing the greatest racial miracle the world has ever seen.

I have never spoken of a land of milk and honey, or of the convenient and immediate reversal of the political red tide of centuries. There will be much to be disillusioned about in the new South Africa; that is the way of the world and we have elected mere human beings to oversee our affairs. But how different, practically and psychologically, is the heterogeneous government we have just chosen. From now on the successes of South Africa will be the successes of all of us, and the failures too.

Looking back at the rollercoaster ride we have taken from the beginning of this decade, it is easier to understand why it has been so nerve-wracking and so shamefully expensive in terms of South African lives. When FW de

Klerk made his courageous and rational speech at the beginning of 1990, he unleashed a process which neither he nor his political opponents could fully control or predict. He, sitting in Tuynhuys, set out with the rather simple notion that if the 'right' blacks were brought into the running of the country, this could be done more or less on his own terms.

For its part the African National Congress in Lusaka and elsewhere thought it scented outright victory – a triumphal march into the capital in the manner of decolonising Africa. Both were wrong: the world had changed irrevocably, and the cliché about South Africa being unlike any other African country was a cliché precisely because it was true. It has taken all of these four costly years for the politicians to come to terms with the complexities that make us unique. The product is the multi-coloured government of national unity, a mirror in which each and every South African can find their own reflection.

There has been, for all the brutality, the raggedness, the inelegance and the ugliness, a noble compromise. It is a rational compromise, away from the irrational path of a Yugoslavia or Angola, and we should be deeply grateful for that. The leaders – almost every one of note – have applied the dictum of deferred gratification, which is not their natural instinct.

I have thought long and hard about a way to characterise this armistice between African nationalism and Afrikaner nationalism, which provides for all other South Africans the scaffolding within which to fashion fulfilling lives. The best I can do is this: we have reached an outcome in which one leader, De Klerk, has given more than he was forced to give, and another, Mandela, has taken less than he was able to take. That is as it should be between powers which have failed to defeat one another and have decided not to fight to a nihilistic end.

Our country is not going to be another Rhodesia, with its white population halving overnight. Nor is it going to be like a Portuguese colony, with the populations of

5

entire cities sailing away over the horizon in sad flotillas on the way to mother Europe. For the overwhelming majority of us here, there is only one motherland and that is our African continent.

The pages that follow make up just a book of journalism. It is interesting journalism (I hope) because of the extraordinary period, people and places it chronicles. Because it is just journalism, and because journalism is by definition written under ferocious pressure, in wildly differing circumstances, it lacks the beautiful, crafted and polished structure of a good novel or book of history. The pieces come as fully flawed as they came: chronologically, from the peak (or rather, trough) of PW Botha's State of Emergency in 1988, to the most unexpected event in our history – this peaceful, all-inclusive election at the end of April 1994. That is a short time in which to have travelled from the brink of civil race-war and total collapse to the edge of something new, young and unknown. It is a period that will come to occupy chapters in the history books much longer and more prominent than those we learnt by heart at school.

It will be overtaken, of course, and soon, by the yet more important journey on which we are about to embark. But I think these strange days we have shared are worth remembering.

I hope that two characteristics – the eyewitness immediacy and the unflagging thread of optimism in spite of the horrors – make this collection different at least. The first half or so of the book is more descriptive, telling the history as I saw it, while the later pieces become more prescriptive, offering analyses of the situation – as I saw it. If there is a balance it resides in the whole. There is also an imbalance, which I concede at the outset. I am an ordinary white South African, do not aspire to be anything else, and do not claim to speak on behalf of anyone but myself. If I have been able to play any minor subjective role, it has been in trying to persuade, realistically but emotionally, fellow white South Africans to stay in their country, becoming

6

gradually liberated from their own guilt and ready to throw their considerable energies into building a new country of which we can all be proud. The spasms of departure, taking decent and talented but fearful South Africans to foreign lands, are a tragedy. I pray the spasms are ending.

One of my favourite, weird South African phrases is 'a monkeys' wedding'. For no obvious reason it describes perfectly those strange days here in our home on the southernmost tip of Africa when the sun shines and the rain buckets down at the same time. I'm told it has equivalents in Zulu and in Afrikaans (*'Umshado wezinkawu'*, and *'Jakkals trou met wolf se vrou'*), which is appropriate, because no single language is adequate to describe us and our doings. This book is a bit of a monkeys' wedding, like the country. But today, as I look out of the window over Johannesburg, only the sun is shining.

SJ, JOHANNESBURG, 1 MAY 1994

WHY WE ARE DANCING

In 1986 the townships erupted, President PW Botha declared a State of Emergency, and the black youth - the 'comrades' - began to lead a wild and violent battle against the system.

THE BOY THRUST HIS HEAD THROUGH THE CAR WINDOW. He was talking across me, to my companion. 'I am commandeering this car,' he said, 'in the name of the comrades.' My guide was calm, debating in measured tones. He was fully 10 years younger than me, but schooled in township politics.

We were in Alexandra township, Johannesburg. It was the fifth day of what later became known as the six day war in Alex. The compact ghetto was in the throes of an uprising, local government had collapsed, and the army and police moved about the dusty roads in large numbers and fearsome vehicles, bristling with weapons.

In groups the youths of the township – the comrades – darted from street to street, hiding in shanties at the approach of a Casspir or Hippo, only to re-emerge and hastily construct tank-traps and roadblocks. They dug holes here, erected barricades of burning tyres and ghetto garbage there. Soldiers approached with guns; the children ran off to build another barrier in another street.

9

My companion was from what he called the Cuba Section of the township. He saw himself as a revolutionary press secretary. He had offered to take me into Alex to 'see what the *boere* are doing'. The other comrade at the roadblock still needed to be convinced about the role of the press however.

'We need this car to go to 17th Street before the *boere* get there,' he was saying. 'We have to fire X's house.' X was a black town councillor, accused by the children of being a puppet in collusion with the police. The young interlocutor held in his left hand a Richelieu brandy bottle, half-filled with a clear, pinkish liquid, and with a piece of torn cloth jammed into its neck.

'Come. He will drive,' he said, pointing at me. My escort carried on arguing, about priorities. Was it not important, he suggested, that the few pressmen who had managed to get into Alex that day be allowed to do their jobs? Could alternative transport not be found for the mission? The comrade was getting agitated. There were army vehicles rumbling in criss-crosses on the steep streets all around. Eventually he turned and blew a whistle. Out of the acrid smoke of the burning tyres there emerged 10 or so children, mostly younger than him. My companion hissed at me to produce my press card. It was thrust out of the window and handed around. Shortly the chief comrade's head re-appeared in the window. 'We are going to vote,' he said.

And so they did, amid the din of gunfire and shouting and the crackle of burning shanties and the growl of nearby armoured vehicles. After a brief, heated debate, the soiled press card was dropped in my lap. A gap was cleared in front of us and we drove through it and away as slowly as we could bear to.

'You see,' said my escort after some time, 'we are not all *abosiyayinyova* (lawless thugs). We are democratic. You must write that.'

I thought about that eerie roadblock a lot, later. Of the dark figure beneath the smoke and heavy Transvaal clouds, a mad hybrid of Dickensian waif and child-crusader, who represented something new and frightening. His shoes were bare flaps of leather revealing bare leathery feet; his jeans, now hanging in strips, absurdly still sported a fashionable label: Ronald Sassoon. His black beret, by contrast, was brand new, drawn rakishly across the head and tucked over one ear. A metal badge, pinned to it, showed a crude reproduction of a drawing of Oliver Tambo.

Percy Qoboza wrote: 'If it is true that a people's wealth is its children, then South Africa is bitterly, tragically poor. If it is true that a nation's future is its children, we have no future, and deserve none . . . For we have turned our children into a generation of fighters, battle-hardened soldiers who will never know the carefree joy of childhood.'

The songs the black children of South Africa sing these days are unlike the songs of children anywhere else. In Alex there is this one:

> *Do not believe them when they say it is far*
> *It is coming today, it is coming tomorrow*
> *The drought will be broken*
> *For us it will be that the rains have come*
> *Do not believe them when they say*
> *We do not know why we are dancing*

After the roadblock I spoke to an older man in Alex. 'These kids have changed many things,' Mr Linda Twala said, 'the truth is that. Like now we are not going to carry the *dompas* – it is because of the children. But there are some things I don't like. A child is a child. I am an elderly person. Children are right to battle for freedom, but they must respect older people. People's courts are not the right way. Children can't discuss their fathers' problems. These comrades, they need us too.

'We will pay if we misdirect them now.'

UNPUBLISHED, MAY 1986

11

DARKNESS ON THE EDGE OF CAPE TOWN

Violence spread to Crossroads near Cape Town, where black vigilantes - allegedly with the connivance of police - rampaged through the poverty-stricken squatter settlement.

————————

TWO WEEKS AGO THE CROWDED SQUATTER 'SUBURBS' OF Crossroads were disembowelled. Hands reached in and ripped the place's guts out. A lot of people lost their lives, and many, many more the places in which they had lived. Thousands saw things or had things done to them equal in horror to those violent cinematic moments that make you look away.

Something worries me, leafing through a bulky sheaf of cuttings recording the bloody days and nights of Crossroads. They read like any other South African unrest report. There is no sense, no texture of the unspeakable, specific human tragedy that took place. More than 50 dead and a thousand times that many homeless, uprooted, bewildered and bitter. The kinds of figures that emerge after the visitation of any self-respecting hurricane or earthquake.

We South Africans who are not facing bullets, teargas, sjamboks, pangas and 'necklaces', have become brutalized in comfort. Even those icons of our insanely vicious society prompt barely a *tsk tsk* these days. Yet they are as deeply a part of us, of our precious way of life, as *braaivleis* and Chevrolet. And just as much of our making.

We have consummated the principle of adaptation. We explain the horror to ourselves – blaming system or struggle depending on our politics – and don't have to confront its content, or smell the blood. I have some recollections of Crossroads on Monday the 19th of May 1986. I scribbled disjointed notes furiously during a few hours of the fighting that day. I draw a personal lesson from them: don't romanticize horror. If there is ever heroism in violence, it is inestimably ugly at first hand, and the people who really suffer through it will not thank us voyeurs of the revolution for laundering that fact.

There was a mothers' meeting in New Crossroads. About 30 women crammed into a house. 'My son has been shot this morning,' says one, 'we are gathered to do something. We cannot just sit and wait.' What were they doing? Brewing coffee in a giant vat, buttering brown bread. Feeding the kids who came in to rest before going back to the fighting.

Alongside Lansdowne Road there were rows of fires as the shanties burned. Hundreds of homeless people sat on bundles containing their salvaged belongings. There were a lot of mattresses. A woman stumbled out of the smoke as her shack went up in flames; she clutched a steel window frame and a bright orange plastic bucket. A Casspir sped into the grey smoke and disappeared, swallowed. The Sun Shine Cash Store, a tin shanty like all the others, had escaped burning, and its sign could still be made out: Ubisi, 48c pint.

There was a high roar of fear and running. Casspirs lurched in, police grabbed a man, bundled him in. 'They are going to kill that man,' said a middle-aged woman. She smiled with relief when the police tossed him out of the armoured car again. All around, men were carrying axes, some store-bought, some home-fashioned. A woman wanted to tell me how her shanty 'animal clinic' had been burned, with dogs and cats inside, but I was trying to hide and pulled away because the gunfire was so close.

Another Casspir careened into the square. Suddenly there was the thud of automatic fire from the shanty at my left shoulder. 'AK! AK!' the people shouted; they knew the sound. Long volleys shrieked around and hundreds of us ran headlong, pushing and falling, ending up face-down, mouths in the dirt. I was pushed into a still-standing shanty, and told to hide. An old woman was inside, eating brown bread in the middle of the battlefield. We were welcome to stay, she said, until we were caught.

Much later, having been duly caught – ordered out of the area in no uncertain terms by angry, frightened policemen – I passed a Red Cross tent on a rise, with its flag fluttering high. Inside was a young woman clutching a baby. She was in a state of profound shock. She said she was grabbed and had a 'necklace' put around her neck, which was lit 'to teach her a lesson'. She escaped but her whole body was still shaking spastically.

On the road, eventually, heading back to the unscathed city of Cape Town, I looked back through the car window at the Hiroshima-shaped cloud of smoke which hung over Crossroads. Then as the highway dipped, it disappeared, the invisible darkness on the edge of town. I fear a hideous human harvest in the children who have grown up with this limitless violence around them.

VULA MAGAZINE, JULY 1986

THE REGGAE REBELS

Unrest gripped the 'independent homeland' of Bophuthatswana, home of the Sun City gambling resort. A farcical coup attempt was bloodily put down by a handful of South African soldiers.

────────────

WHEN RADIO BOP ANNOUNCED THE BOPHUTHATSWANA coup on Wednesday, the rebels' 500-word proclamation was followed not by the usual martial music, but with a burst of reggae. The eccentric approach was typical of the fumbled 15-hour coup, one of the more bizarre political events witnessed by a sub-continent which has become used to them.

The automatic gunfire which woke the residents of the capital, Mmabatho, at 3am on Wednesday, started a strange day. President Lucas Mangope, dressed in his pyjamas, was held hostage in the VIP lounge of the local stadium. The soldiers – trained only to guard buildings – were ordered to keep watch, but were not warned to repel attackers. A few soldiers casually took control of the radio station, but omitted to do the same with the television station. So confused was the Bophuthatswana Defence Force rebellion that it is still not clear, days later, who the military leader was.

The eventual restoration of order by 34 South African soldiers left the populace thoroughly bemused. The fragility of the coup had become clear at 4.15pm, when three Puma helicopters flew over the horizon and began to circle the *Garona* and the Independence Stadium. No-one was sure whether they belonged to the rebels or the South African Defence Force – until it was pointed out that the BDF boasted only two (much smaller) Alouette helicopters. And no pilots.

A shaken rebel spokesman arrived at the *Garona* at 4.30pm, with a convoy of armoured cars heading towards the building. 'The SADF are coming!' he shouted. Rebel guards discarded their uniforms and fled across the open veld. At 5.15pm the Ratels drew up, and soon after two Puma helicopters in quick succession, disgorging South African paratroopers. The troops gathered behind a Ratel and other armoured vehicles as they set about breaking down a gate and then a steel door barring entrance to the stadium. An almost festive air prevailed: one reporter shouted 'What time is kick-off?' A single shot was heard from inside the stadium. A civilian woman shouted at me: 'How dare they do this? It is humiliating.'

Within minutes reporters had gained access to the stadium terraces through the main turnstiles, and were able to witness the closing stages of the coup from what were literally grandstand seats. SADF vehicles had churned up the stadium's turf, which was so moist that one Ratel had to be towed out. Directly below lay at least one dead BDF soldier. Another, seriously wounded, leant against a wall while a third stood with his hands up against a wire fence, guarded by a paratrooper. Mangope was ferried to the parliament building, where he prepared a television statement. On the field, a column of some 60 subdued BDF soldiers emerged, their hands placed on their heads. SADF soldiers ordered them to lie on the turf, face down. Within a short time the stadium was deserted, save for a single Bedford troop truck.

Two hours later, President PW Botha, who had flown in

to Mmabatho, was giving a press conference at the South African embassy. 'Well, we had these problems,' he said. 'But we are tonight back in full control . . . *the president of Bophuthatswana* is in full control.'

WEEKLY MAIL, 12 FEBRUARY 1988

ALL QUIET AT THE NEW NATION

The State of Emergency allowed the Pretoria government to shut down troublesome newspapers, leaving anti-apartheid journalists bewildered and temporarily neutralised.

GABU TUGWANA, ACTING EDITOR OF THE NEW NATION, leans back in a chair in his silent newsroom, reading a telex. It is a press statement from Defence Headquarters in Pretoria. 'They're still sending us this stuff,' he remarks laconically.

Then he laughs out loud. Tugwana no longer has a newspaper in which to publish it.

It is the end of the first week of the outspoken newspaper's forced closure under the State of Emergency regulations, and its offices in downtown Johannesburg are full of such evocative imagery. Most striking of all is the uncommon quiet, where the intermittent chatter of the telex is now the most distinctive sound in the room. Empty desks and blank-screened computers provide a visual complement.

Then there are posters, forlorn proclamations of an earlier time: 'South Africa's Voice of the Voteless – On Sale Now!' and 'Are you part of the big rush for the New Nation?' It is an arresting tableau, but the funereal atmosphere is also deceptive, because the New Nation story is far from being played out. How will it all end?

The editor-temporarily-without-portfolio is nothing if not defiant. It is clear, he says, that 'the voice of the emerging press has grown so fast that the State could not tolerate it any more. But in the end, justice and truth will win.'

For the moment New Nation will embark on in-house training for its staff, and publish a newsletter – not for sale, but 'as a memento'. Then it will start up all over again. Tugwana believes history is on his side.

WEEKLY MAIL, 31 MARCH 1988

THE MOSES OF ULUNDI

With the ANC and other liberation movements still banned in South Africa, Zulu Chief Mangosuthu Buthelezi steadily built up a power base - and struck out on his own political course.

'WE,' SAID THE SPEAKER TO THE 5,000 DELEGATES assembled in Ulundi, 'are following the Moses of South Africa.' Their throaty response rendered dissent unthinkable.

If there is a single word to sum up the atmosphere of Inkatha's annual general conference, that word is rapture. There are no prizes for guessing its object: the President of Inkatha and Chief Minister of KwaZulu. In Ulundi, Moses equals Mangosuthu.

Ulundi and, more particularly, Ulundi during the annual pilgrimage of Inkatha devotees, is both the shrine and source of Chief Buthelezi's 'national cultural liberation movement'. It may be isolated in KwaZulu's hinterland, but Inkatha at least has somewhere to sit pretty. Ulundi is a haven of a sort not enjoyed by other black political forces.

There is no sense of threat to the shrine: what security arrangements there are, are confidently cursory. Soldiers manning a roadblock at its entrance were safe in the knowledge that it would take a reckless 'comrade' indeed to venture into this enclave.

What Inkatha's power is, precisely, remains an enigma. But Buthelezi used this occasion to serve notice – unequivocally, even by his own lights – that rapprochement with other black movements is not yet critical for his survival, even if he pronounces it desirable. In spite of the tragic bloodletting in greater Pietermaritzburg, in which Inkatha has suffered losses just as heavy as those of its opponents, irrespective of persistent claims that Inkatha is losing support in Natal's urban areas, and notwithstanding allegations of vigilante activity, Buthelezi is manifestly not begging for a deal.

One can see why, in Ulundi. He heads an organization which, unlike the battered structures of, say, the United Democratic Front, has emerged relatively unscathed from successive States of Emergency. Its positioning has allowed processes of politicization and organizational entrenchment to continue unabated. Hence the huge, precision-tuned conference. And hence, given the ferocity of repression against its opponents, Inkatha's ability to scold and threaten them with impunity.

But the differential levels of State attack are not in themselves a sufficient explanation for Buthelezi's buoyancy. Inkatha is also sustained by its very (efficient) nature, and the conference reflected this. Inkatha's strength, Buthelezi said, 'is monolithic; it is granite-like; it is unshakeable.' His critics would probably agree, but would ascribe this to its strictly hierarchical structures, its patronage, and its strong-arm tactics.

Certainly, there is never any shortage of such symbols at an Inkatha gathering. At this conference, hardly a delegate did not sport some Inkatha paraphernalia: khaki safari suits, green, yellow and black ties, tricoloured epaulettes, black berets, Buthelezi badges.

But this is by no means unique to Inkatha. It is the more abstract, inescapable fact of the reverence in which Buthelezi is held that makes the strongest impression.

21

Shades of authoritarianism can be read into this cult of personality, of course, but its reality cannot be denied.

The adulation translates itself into the resolutions emerging from the conference. This is how it works: Buthelezi makes a long speech in which he sets out his analysis of events. In each case, he lets it be known what he thinks should be done about it. The delegates then debate the contents, impassionedly, through the day and most of the night. Resolutions emerge the following morning. They codify, sometimes using the same phraseology, the president's vision. The delegates' inputs are vibrant, but not material. In the beginning there was the word, and the word was what Buthelezi said it was.

The process of voting is a similarly graphic demonstration of the conformism of Inkatha. A resolution – invariably lengthy – is read out, translated, and delegates are asked: 'Now what is your response, dear comrades?' Hands are lifted, papers shaken in the air, approval is chanted. There is no such thing as a *nem con* motion at the Inkatha annual general conference. Nobody bothers to count: concurrence is absolute.

Who are the thousands, many of whom have travelled by the busload from outlying areas, and who derive such obvious pleasure from being part of the movement? They look, to the inexpert eye, to be mostly middle-aged, more of them women than men. That they are genuine devotees is beyond question. The drive along the King Dinizulu Highway to Ulundi's Unit A, where the conference is held in huge marquees on a dusty field, is clearly a profound experience for them. They are elected as delegates, in Inkatha's own words, by 'the poorest of the poor'. This is not representative of black South Africa, but certainly some part of it. Inkatha has moulded them into a political force they would not otherwise be.

Then there is a gentle, effective avuncularity in the way Buthelezi relates to these people, the fibre of his movement. In pressing them to distribute propaganda, organize meetings and generally agitate on behalf of Inkatha, he

22

coaxes, wheedles, smiles beatifically: 'Do you take these documents and put them in boxes at home and let them rot?'

'No, no,' murmur the faithful. There is a genuine wish to please the Moses of Ulundi.

WEEKLY MAIL, 8 JULY 1988

A VERY CLEVER BOY

Rumours of the imminent release of jailed ANC leader Nelson Mandela reached fever pitch, and there was renewed interest in the modest Transkeian village in which he had been born.

IF YOU'VE EVER DRIVEN THROUGH THE TRANSKEI, CHANCES are you've passed by – and even looked at – the birthplace of the world's most famous political prisoner. Qunu, the village in which Nonqaphi Nosekeni Mandela gave birth to Nelson Rolihlahla on July 18 1918, sprawls on a hillside in view of the N2 highway, some 30km from Umtata on the way to East London. Like most other such settlements in the overcrowded 'homeland' these days, it is hardly a village at all in the sense that one might imagine it. It has no defined entry or exit, no centre.

People who live there know where it is, of course, and there is a roadsign. But otherwise, it is just another cluster of thatched huts built on scrub and grassland, inhabited by old women, young children and animals. The hut which heard Mandela's first cries is not there any more. It was demolished after his mother died in 1969, because no-one was able to pay for its maintenance. It is identifiable only by its foundations, fighting a losing battle against a maize crop, in turn facing defeat by weeds. The hills, too, where the herdboy tended cattle, are overgrazed since the population explosion that came with 'independence' in 1976.

But there are still Mandelas in Qunu, plenty of them, and the famous son is well remembered. Agreneta Mandela, matriarchal widow of Mandela's younger brother Sidumo, is the chief representative of the clan. She points to a donkey cart-load of yelping youngsters heading down to the stream for water. Yes, they are all related to Mandela.

Then there is the Mandela cemetery: unprepossessing but carefully tended, marked by wooden crosses bearing the names of more relatives – Lulama Mandela, William Mazwi Mandela. Nephews or cousins, she says. Mandela left Qunu when he was about eight, says a wizened teacher who introduces himself as 'Mr S Njomane'. He had gone to school about five kilometres away from his home 'until he was taken away by our chief, Jongintaba Dalindyebo. He was born in this location, you know,' says Mr Njomane. 'He was a very clever boy, very good.'

Agreneta Mandela remembers her famous brother-in-law very well. She knew he was going to be a leader, she says, 'because even during the family gatherings he would say that black people are oppressed and they were being underpaid. Whenever he came home, other people from various kraals, tribal people, would come to see him. He was a very strict person. He insisted that all the children must go to school. If they went haywire, you could be sure he would correct them.'

Agreneta is not so sure that she will see him again before he dies. He sent a message to Qunu just before he was sentenced. 'Nelson gave us the message that no-one at home should worry. In my opinion he knew the tragedy he was facing, but he said nobody must cry. So we did not expect a life sentence for him. We thought it would be a few years.' Now she waits, in the poor, beautiful Transkei, hoping for the day that Nelson Mandela will pay his respects in Qunu again.

WEEKLY MAIL, 15 JULY 1988

THE PARTY POOPERS

In a show of defiance, Mandela's supporters arranged parties around the country to celebrate the prisoner's 70th birthday. The police overreacted - with some comical results.

THE BIGGEST NEWS IN SOUTH AFRICA LAST WEEKEND was the way Nelson Mandela's 70th birthday wasn't celebrated.

The forces of law and order were mobilized, mightily, to counter such acts of subversion as pop concerts, fun runs, football matches, *braais* and plain old birthday parties around the country. The powers-that-be were evidently convinced, following Aristotle, that civil confusions often spring from trifles. No potentially Mandela-linked gathering was too trivial.

Some of the events were specifically planned to mark the legendary leader's birthday; others were incidental. Very few of them happened. However, the gusto with which they were curbed engendered much more publicity than could ever have been commanded by the events themselves. It resulted in front-page newspaper treatment at home, prominent coverage abroad, and earnest reports to foreign governments from local embassies.

The most bizarre of all was the banning – on the grounds

that 'the public peace would be seriously endangered' – of a football match and party on a fenced-off private plot in Honeydew, near Johannesburg. This football match was manifestly not considered a trifle. This week the hosts and organizers, television journalists called Miranda and Roger Harris, were still wavering between bemusement and outrage. This is hardly surprising. The combination of an invitation-only surprise party for Winnie Mandela with a long-awaited football challenge between Soweto's 'Mandela Eleven' and the 'Delmas Dazzlers' (made up of treason trialists out on bail), had unimaginable consequences.

Stripped to bare details, these included the besiegement of the rustic smallholding and an urgent application in the Supreme Court. South African Police delivered a notice at 11pm on Friday prohibiting the gathering in terms of the Internal Security Act of 1982. An urgent appeal was prepared, and eventually heard on Saturday afternoon – two hours after the football match was scheduled to start.

Some 100 confused guests milled around inside the property. Outside, a contingent of police manned a roadblock on an access road about one kilometre from the gate, and others stationed themselves at the entrance, observing proceedings with binoculars. They achieved an uninterrupted view by perching themselves atop a latest-model armoured vehicle, dubbed the 'Casspir GTI' by onlookers.

The guests included prominent political and cultural figures, and diplomats. Their only obviously subversive action was to grumble in unison about the lack of refreshments. 'Could I open a beer?' asked a parched guest of Mr Harris, adding: 'I brought my own.' He was unquestionably articulating the popular mood. 'Absolutely not,' came the reply. Another dangerously dehydrated invitee recklessly ripped open a Diet Sprite. Realizing the gravity of his move, he quickly held it up for the police binoculars, label faced towards them. No shots were fired.

Reports began to filter through that many black South African guests – including celebrated photographer Peter Magubane – had been unceremoniously turned away.

Whites said they had been allowed through. Indians reported that the police had been ambivalent but, on balance, let them pass. There being no 'coloureds' in evidence, the racial assessment of the situation had to remain a tripartite one.

Wild rumours now began to circulate. The police had offered, so the story ran, to allow festivities to proceed subject to certain conditions. These were that everyone went inside, and stayed inside. Two people would be allowed to do the *braaiing*. Another could ferry the meat back and forth. The football match could go ahead, but no-one could watch it. Heat and boredom combined to produce a vociferous faction in favour of this option. Mr Harris said no.

Back at the court, Mrs Harris's senior counsel brandished a 16-page application, arguing that the banning was unlawful: 'It is intended to provide food and liquid refreshment in the form of *braais*, salads, and various other prepared foods as well as wine (in limited quantities), beer and soft drinks. All the invited guests have been told they are welcome to bring their children and it is anticipated that many will do so . . . '

The judge postponed the matter to August 9.

WEEKLY MAIL, 22 JULY 1988

PRETORIA'S UNRULY OFFSPRING

Ethnic 'homelands' - intended to be apartheid's solution to the problem of the disenfranchised black majority - began to turn on their creators, causing widespread instability.

COUPS AND COUNTER-COUPS; ASSASSINATION ATTEMPTS; sorcery; civil war; astronomical embezzlement and omnipresent graft; monstrous infringements of human rights; territorial spats; constitutional crises; messy succession struggles.

Upheaval in the 'homelands' has become commonplace and – at least for those not directly affected – invariably rather comical. But the turbulence, which is beginning to look like endemic instability, is more than a joke. In its geographical spread and persistence, it could signal real danger for pater Pretoria.

Until now, reaction to trouble in the homelands has been largely flippant. This is because it is perceived that what is happening is not real, in the sense that the actors are not masters of their own destinies. Coups and the like are sideshows which can be stopped whenever Pretoria decides they have gone too far. South Africa is the father and the homelands merely ethnic offspring, amusing but unimportant.

Countless vignettes can be invoked to symbolize this patrilineal image. Think of the 'Bop coup' in February – disconsolate, penitent rebel soldiers being made to lie face down in the mud by a handful of South African troops while a chastened Lucas Mangope offered thanks for his deliverance. Or remember a meeting in Bisho in April: South African government financiers chiding representatives of Transkei, Bophuthatswana, Venda and Ciskei for their profligacy. If they didn't behave like grown-ups, the statelets were warned, they'd lose their pocket money. And so on.

But if the homelands can indeed be seen as troublesome children, then it should be pointed out that they are now approaching their teenage years – a period notorious for unpredictable and even uncontrollable behaviour. It is perhaps time to recognize that they can behave in ways which Pretoria can neither fully predict nor control. The teen years are going to prove very troublesome indeed.

WEEKLY MAIL, 16 SEPTEMBER 1988

PIK IN THE CLOUDS ABOVE
THE CONGO

The promise of independence for Namibia opened doors in Africa for the Pretoria government. Veteran Foreign Minister Pik Botha seized the opportunity to head north with alacrity.

IF PIK BOTHA HAS A FAVOURITE CITY OUTSIDE SOUTH Africa, it's just got to be Brazzaville. It was in the first city of the People's Republic of Congo this week that our Foreign Minister made his bid for acceptance on our continent.

What Pik later described as 'one of the most memorable days of my life' began memorably for those of us travelling with him. He took over the public address system of the appropriately-named South African Airways Boeing 737 'Limpopo'.

'This is Foreign Minister Pik Botha,' he said high above the clouds which were high above Lubumbashi in Zaire. 'We are going to defect to Luanda.'

When shock gave way to laughter, he read out the historic peace protocol to be signed on arrival in the Congo. It would end South Africa's troublesome 73-year-old administration of Namibia. And the rest of the day's events served only to improve the humour of the Nationalist Party politician most insistent about his 'Africanness'.

The signing ceremony made diplomatic bedfellows of the most incompatible of governments, and it gave Pik a platform he could only have dreamed of before. He exploited it to the full.

Brazzaville was a fitting symbolic setting for Pik's intermezzo. Indeed, the city can lay persuasive claim to the title of Africa's capital of compromise. The laid-back, steaming francophone sprawl on the northern bank of the Congo River hosted the partial rehabilitation of Africa's most loathed government. Never mind that this had more to do with realpolitik than with a change of African hearts, it was an experience which Pik will long savour.

The stylish ambience of the Congo gave him the opening. Even the political banners which festoon the highway leading into the capital have a nonchalant air. One reads (in French): 'Apartheid is a scourge, and must be eradicated before the end of the twentieth century.' As a journalist was quick to comment, even the conservative countries of the Commonwealth set the time limit at six months.

When his turn came to speak at midday on Tuesday, Pik laid it on thick to the variety of African dignitaries at the signing ceremony. Pausing meaningfully between impassioned bursts, he gazed across the Palace of the People, an elegant, understated former French Governor's residence. 'This is fundamentally an African agreement,' Pik said. Looking at Congo's President, Denis Sassou Nguesso, he pleaded for co-operation among Africans. 'If we don't stand together,' he said, 'we will never catch up and the industrialized nations won't care. I predict it here today as your brother.'

Then he made his bid for acceptance. 'A new era has begun in South Africa. My government is removing racial discrimination.' The applause inspired him. 'We want to be accepted by our African brothers . . . And Mr President, thank you for this wonderful opportunity to be with my African brothers.'

Defence Minister Magnus Malan, towering above the

Angolan and Cuban signatories, remained impassive.

With the applause still ringing around the Palace, Pik strode purposefully up to the grim-looking Angolans and Cubans, and shook their hands. It was the first – and only – direct contact between the parties to the protocol, and Pik could claim it as his own. Someone next to me remarked: 'Bet he wishes there was a presidential election in South Africa next week.'

WEEKLY MAIL, 15 DECEMBER 1988

WELCOME TO THE LOS ANGELES HOT BOX LIFE CENTRE

In Namibia's northern territory of Owamboland, news came of the arrival of the United Nations. But Owambos said they would believe it only when the South African soldiers left.

THREE LOCAL LANDMARKS HAVE SURVIVED OWAMBOLAND'S 20 cruel years of war. They are the ubiquitous makalani palm trees, the scattered cone-shaped ant-heaps and – most memorable of all – the cuca-shops.

The cuca-shop is an allegory of Owamboland's uncomplaining, almost impish approach to suffering. In a reluctant war zone – the fulcrum of the fighting only because of the accident of its location – these unique Namibian shebeens have been social rallying points for a shattered community.

In the cuca-shops, Owambos have attempted to live as if their remote, sprawling region was what it used to be – Namibia's peaceful pastoral enclave. Within the garishly-painted and wildly-named matchbox structures which dot the roadside from Ondangwa to Ruacana, there is enough beer and loud music to shut out the incessant rumble of Casspirs and Ratels on Owamboland's single strip of tarmac. And, if the coast is clear of Koevoet, politics may be discussed. This is what was happening on a weekday night after the curfew, two months before the implementation of UN Resolution 435.

A grizzled patriarch from Ongwediva township held court. He was drinking warm Windhoek Lager (in the early 1970s it would have been the eponymous Cuca beer the Portuguese brewed in nearby Angola), and eyeing the visiting journalist.

'In-depen-dence?' he asked rhetorically. '*Ag*, don't talk to me about that. Come back when the *boers* have packed up their Casspirs and are half way back to Upington. Then we can speak of independence.' The rest of the clientele in the 'Los Angeles Hot Box Life Centre' concurred. The good citizens of Owamboland have seen it all. Known in the depersonalizing argot of the security forces as the 'PBs' (*Plaaslike Bevolking* – local population), they have played host to an ugly, vicious war which refused to leave them out of things. Ninety percent of the war between Swapo's People's Liberation Army of Namibia (Plan) and the combined SADF/SWATF/SWAPOL has been prosecuted here in Sector 10, Owamboland.

Now, with Swapo having declared a unilateral ceasefire, insurgency has come to a sudden stop. Koevoet members relax at their recreation camp on the banks of the Okavango River. The dusk-to-dawn curfew is about to be lifted. Having got used to life during wartime, Owambos are trying to adjust to creeping peace.

At the Human Rights Centre in Ongwediva, a call comes through to say the Lutheran mission, half an hour away, has been surrounded by soldiers. A frantic drive to Oniipa reveals no siege: just a relieved, vaguely embarrassed worker who says a column of 'about 80 Casspirs and Ratels' had drawn up outside the mission. It turned out they were stopping on their way to the outpost of Eenhana, just below the 'cutline', the strip of cleared bush that separates Namibia and Angola.

The false alarm was characteristic of the atmosphere in

Owamboland. The Lutherans' printing presses had been bombed before, twice. Now, although the war seemed to be stopping, they aren't taking any chances.

Neither, it would seem, are the security forces. There are still innumerable roadblocks, more or less rigorous depending on the unit involved. Koevoet still mans Oshivelo ('the gateway to Owamboland') and the counter-insurgency specialists are characteristically thorough. White travellers are grilled and searched; blacks have, in addition, to walk past a window covered with camouflage netting. Behind the glass sit captured and 'turned' Swapo guerrillas. Their task is to point out members or sympathizers of the nationalist movement. Everyone sweats when going through Oshivelo.

Koevoet's relative inactivity, as locals know, is small comfort. If a rogue guerrilla is heard of, the Casspirs will roar out of Oshakati once more. The omnipresence of Koevoet (which will live in the Owambo psyche for generations) is most graphically symbolized on a mountainside near Otavi. A huge white footprint, made out of painted rocks, stands out from the green slopes. It marks a cave from which Plan guerrillas conducted operations in the 1970s. The footprint announces that they were stamped on by Koevoet.

But if the black townspeople of Ondangwa and Ongwediva don't know what to think about the imminence of independence, many white soldiers choose not to think about it at all. In an army bar at Oshakati – the forward base that sustained several Swapo stand-off bombing attacks – ears prick up as a South West African Broadcasting Corporation news bulletin comes on. 'The Administrator-General said that Resolution 435 . . . ' begins a voice distorted by static. The mere mention of the United Nations independence plan is enough to cause a commotion in the bar. '*Sit daardie fokken ding af!*' (Put that fucking thing off) shouts a burly corporal to the black barman.

He obeys promptly, and the soldiers settle back into drinking, declining to contemplate their futures. And so the uncertainty of the war zone comes full circle, over glasses of beer.

Back in the cuca-shop, a story is causing much mirth. 'Do you remember when those cucas were painted in Swapo colours?', says a patron. Everyone knows the tale, but it is for my benefit, so they roar encouragement anyway.

'Well, when one cuca owner heard Koevoet was coming, he rushed outside with a pot of paint and started adding all sorts of colours to the walls to disguise it. Koevoet didn't notice that half the bloody paint was soaking wet!'

The laughter mixes with the faint sound of SWATF convoys, some going north, some going south.

WEEKLY MAIL, 10 FEBRUARY 1989

THE LITTLE, DEAD, GENERAL

Winnie Mandela's name was linked with the missing child-activist, Stompie Mokhetsi. His tragic life story showed what had happened to a generation of brutalised black youngsters.

IN OCTOBER 1987, AT THE AGE OF 13 AND THE HEIGHT OF less than four feet, Stompie Mokhetsi didn't think he would live much longer. 'They can come and get me at any time,' he remarked impassively to Peter Godwin, a British journalist who had tracked him down in Tumahole township. 'I'm likely to die in the struggle.' Stompie's predictions were proved accurate in a forensic laboratory in Pretoria this week. A single identifiable fingerprint taken from his badly decomposed corpse put an end to weeks of speculation about his whereabouts. His short life was extraordinary.

At the time he was speaking in Tumahole, the minuscule activist was arguably the best-known figure in the township. He was the little general to an Under-14 army of some 1,500 ghetto children. He had just resumed his command after spending a year on remand in prison, and being acquitted on public violence charges. The Under-14s, he said, were formed in 1985 – because 'other groups were all talk and no action. We formed an army to protect the people.' His youngest foot-soldier was eight. 'We're braver than the adults,' he said. The child army fought battles with the municipal police – Green Beans – and right-wing vigilantes known as the A-Team.

His followers affectionately called him *Tompana* – a Zulu/Xhosa diminutive equivalent to the Afrikaans word *stompie*. He'd inherited the nickname because of the contradiction between his slight physique and overpowering presence. A stompie, in this sense, is a hard, unyielding thing.

Friends – most of whom doubled as admirers if not disciples – tell of him forever discussing politics. 'What is the direction, comrade?' was his catchphrase. His personality touched people beyond Tumahole. Professor Mervyn Shear of the University of the Witwatersrand recalls being so struck by Stompie that he invited him to lunch. The pocket-sized activist addressed a mass meeting at Wits in 1987: he entered the hall and mounted the stage carrying a businesslike black briefcase. Shear recalls that after the meeting he saw Stompie 'enthralling a large group of students who gathered round to hear his oratory.' They stood with their mouths open as the boy recited sizeable chunks of the Freedom Charter.

Stompie had been living in the Orlando Methodist Church sanctuary, set up for children whose home environments were devastated by the prolonged State of Emergency. Aged 11, he had been the youngest Emergency detainee in the country. His twelfth birthday was celebrated in a cell.

The journalist who spent time with Stompie in 1987 said there was 'more to his personality than politics'. His last memory of the child was 'sitting reading newspapers at the table of a township cafe, his feet not reaching the floor. Asked what he wanted more than anything right now, his answer was a BMX bike, some new clothes that fit, and something to eat.'

WEEKLY MAIL, 17 FEBRUARY 1989
(WITH THANDEKA GQUBULE)

HISTORY'S DECISION

Winnie Mandela lost her status as the 'Mother of the Nation'. Many Sowetans turned against her, and the anti-apartheid movement excommunicated the jailed ANC leader's wife.

WINNIE MANDELA HAS BEGUN A TERM OF BANISHMENT and internal exile in Soweto much harsher than her eight years of isolation in Brandfort. This time it is not the Pretoria government, but her own people who have rejected her.

The reverberations of yesterday's unequivocal statement by the 'Mass Democratic Movement' will take time to be felt around the world. Winnie Mandela has been excommunicated by the very struggle of which she had become a revered and potent symbol.

She stands accused of abusing the trust of her people, of not subjecting herself to the advice – let alone the discipline – of the anti-apartheid organizations to which her husband Nelson has devoted his life. And, almost unthinkably, she finds herself linked to a police investigation into the murder of a 14-year-old activist, Stompie Mokhetsi.

The statement, presented in Johannesburg yesterday by the United Democratic Front and the Congress of South African Trade Unions, suggested that the substance of the

40

allegations against her is true. That it was issued with a sense of deep regret was clear. 'The Mandela name is very dear to our hearts,' said the UDF's Murphy Morobe, 'it is a very sensitive and painful matter.' Asked why leaders had taken so long to speak out on the issue, he snapped: 'Because it has not been an easy matter'.

He added later, quietly: 'History calls for a specific decision, and we have taken it.'

SOUTH CHINA MORNING POST, 19 FEBRUARY 1989

THE LIBERATION DIVIDEND

As had happened so many times before in Africa, pundits speculated the liberation movement might lose the election. A drive among the people of Owamboland suggested otherwise.

THERE ARE TWO BASIC POLITICAL GESTURES IN NAMIBIA: the raised, slightly crooked right-arm salute of Swapo, and the 'V for Victory' sign of the Democratic Turnhalle Alliance. The predominance of one or other of these signals in Owamboland has become a matter of great political importance.

Most of the Namibian population lives on these vast northern plains, and Swapo's election prospects hinge on carrying its traditional stronghold. Has the organization managed to do so, in spite of the debacle of the past fortnight? There are no Gallup polls in Namibia, but there are other ways of assessing the mood of the people.

There are always crowds milling around on either side of the road that runs from Oshivelo to Ruacana, bisecting Owamboland. At the cuca-shops and on the roadsides, the civilians reflect the political temperature of the inaccessible villages of the hinterland.

On Wednesday, with so many People's Liberation Army of Namibia fighters freshly buried in mass graves, and the United Nations still waiting for the survivors, an unscientific survey was conducted. From a moving car, the Swapo and DTA salutes were alternately given, and the response recorded. Swapo salutes were enthusiastically returned, while the DTA gesture drew at best disinterest, at worst derision. This is still emphatically Swapo country.

To the local people, the recent events differ from what went before only in their intensity – the South Africans have been shooting the freedom fighters in the same way. There are just more of them, and there has been more blood. As always, the villagers give the Plan guerrillas sanctuary, although they won't talk about it to strangers.

Says Swapo Youth League member Ananais Itana: 'You are talking to Swapo right here. Everywhere you go you are talking to Swapo . . . from Cunene to Ruacana, to the Orange River.'

It is often repeated by whites here that Swapo, unlike Robert Mugabe's Zanla, failed to 'liberate' even an inch of Namibian soil. This is true, as it is true that the last, tragic spasm of the war means that Plan commanders will have some day to explain to the families of 250 freshly killed guerrillas why their children had to die just when independence was within reach. But still the villages will vote for Swapo, make no mistake. It is called the 'liberation dividend'.

WEEKLY MAIL, 14 APRIL 1989

DANCE, BEFORE TOMORROW

Namibians reacted to their pending political revolution in their own unique style – they talked about soccer, and partied as if their lives depended on it.

TAKE THE BRAKWATER TURN-OFF ON THE OKAHANDJA Road, 10km out of Windhoek, on any night you like. At Alla Pergola, you will find young, dressed-to-the-nines white South Westers drinking and dancing as if their lives depended on it.

Then take the main road from Windhoek into Katutura – any evening – and at Club Thriller or Namibian Nights, you will find crowds of young black Namibians doing the same thing.

Last week the United Nations independence plan was in grave danger of collapse as thousands of armed men fought to the death in the north of Namibia. But the crisis found itself strangely reflected in the south. Since the fateful arrival of April 1, Namibia's date with destiny, it seems the population has been afflicted by a scarcely-contained madness. It is on display in clubland like nowhere else.

It is certainly on the faces of Alla Pergola's patrons, sashaying unsteadily but determinedly to Madonna. The discotheque looms out of the savannah, a luridly-lit,

44

pulsating enigma. It is a kind of Namibian Paris, Texas. Inside, through the miasma created by dry-ice machines and strobe lights, politics is exclusively sexual. Pick-ups are effected amid bellows – in Afrikaans, German and English – at black waiters for bottles of Windhoek Special. There is a huge computer screen near the bar. These words run relentlessly across it: 'Don't Worry! Be Happy! Let's paaaarty!'

Over at Club Thriller and Namibian Nights, the faces are darker and the dance music more esoteric. But the pursuits are similar. The sparingly-decorated Katutura buildings resound with the citizenry's efforts to have fun right away, and consider the wider world some time later. Here, too, the atmosphere is madly jovial. The finer details of the Geneva Protocol on Namibia excite nothing like the passionate debate over the defeat of the Namibian soccer team at the hands of the visiting squad from Huambo, Angola.

Namibians, it has been said, are a relaxed people – even in the face of tragedy. Their apparent dispassion probably reflects the widespread feeling here that outsiders always seem to make the decisions about their country's future. And so they dance, not out of unconcern, but resignation.

Namibia does not feel normal. It does not feel, for instance, like Zimbabwe did during its great transformation. Everything is too fragile and, for the moment, too crazy.

WEEKLY MAIL, 21 APRIL 1989

DOWN SEVENTH AVENUE

During the Emergency it was commonplace for township leaders to disappear into police cells for months at a time. Moses Mayekiso returned quietly to Alexandra township in 1989.

THE LAST TIME MOSES MAYEKISO WALKED DOWN Alexandra's Seventh Avenue, its squalid shacks were framed by dark, thick smoke from burning barricades. That was in 1986; the township was in turmoil, and Mayekiso was the man most residents looked to as their leader.

This week when Mayekiso walked down Seventh Avenue again, there were none of the tell-tale signs of incipient civil war. By contrast huge, freshly-painted blocks of flats formed a backdrop to the shanties. They were not there when Mayekiso and four of his colleagues were arrested and eventually tried – unsuccessfully – for treason, subversion and sedition.

The high-rise blocks symbolize the physical changes in Alex over the three intervening years. At the same time, Mayekiso's homecoming showed an underlying political continuum. Alex was identified by the government in 1986 as a key example of an urban black 'oilspot'; a township which could erupt into rebellion at any time. It became a testing-ground for the two-pronged response to this threat: the removal of 'troublemakers' like Mayekiso, coupled with upgrading, to alleviate the material hardships of the community.

Pretoria's planners would have been disappointed to see residents' responses to Mayekiso's tour of the township this week. After brief seconds of non-recognition – he had been away for a long time – passers-by broke into broad grins and shouted to catch his attention. One elderly man ran after him down the dusty street bellowing: 'Hey! Moss! Hey!' Mayekiso stopped. *'Sidinga ukukubona njalo lapha, Moss,'* he said. (We need to see you here more often, Moss.) At other points during the walkabout, matriarchs emerged from lean-to's to embrace him.

Standing in the yard of the house he used to live in – it has now been sold off – he said the government's upgrading programme could not remove the grievances of the people of Alex. The tiny rooms leading off the yard were home to 13 families, each with five or six children. There was no electricity and no sewerage. There was one tap and three portable toilets. Graffiti painted on corrugated iron on the roadside proclaimed 'Viva Mayekiso'. The surrounding area is still known as the 'Mayekiso Section' of Alex.

The population explosion is overwhelming. 'You see this new shack settlement?' Mayekiso asked. 'This used to be a people's park called Freedom Square. It was where the very first meeting was held in '85, where it all started.' Freedom Square is now, like all the formerly vacant lots in Alex, a dense warren of shanties, constructed from the unlikeliest rubbish-dump flotsam. There are fetid gullies running unpredictably through the shack-suburb, pouring out on to the street.

'Well, we are back,' said Mayekiso. 'And we will just have to start again where we left off.'

WEEKLY MAIL, 2 JUNE 1989

47

SHEBEEN POLITICS

They called it a 'general election', but black South Africans were mere spectators. September 1989 saw the last of the old-style elections, with momentous change just around the corner.

IN THE MILITANT BLACK TOWNSHIP OF ALEXANDRA, abutting Johannesburg, the nearest thing to election paraphernalia is the graffiti, spray-painted on the side of a shack. 'Why vote?' is written in small letters.

But someone has drawn a cross through the first word, replacing it with booming capitals. 'WHAT vote?'

Once again, this Wednesday, the blacks will be spectators as the whites, coloureds and Indians prepare to go to the polls in another of South Africa's curious 'general' elections. The response, in Alexandra at least, is to repair to the nearest township shebeen and swap jokes about the stupidity of the whites, as well as to talk about protest.

This duality in the black response to South Africa's colour-coded polls has become a permanent feature of our society. It merely intensifies with each successive election. In the end, of course, the protests will subside. Another small and inconclusive chapter in the South

African struggle will have been written. On the surface at least, not a great deal will have changed.

On Friday in an Alexandra shebeen a silly question was asked: 'If you could vote, who would you vote for?' The answer was silent and unambiguous. The men in the room, smiles turning to grim seriousness, raised their fists in the salute of Nelson Mandela's banned African National Congress.

It will be some time before they can openly mark their crosses next to the ANC on a ballot form. But they are prepared to wait.

THE SUNDAY CORRESPONDENT, 3 SEPTEMBER 1989

A SPRING IN THE STEP OF
THE PRESIDENT

No-one quite knew what to make of South Africa's new State President, FW de Klerk. A reformist with a conservative background, he baffled friend and foe alike.

THERE WAS A DISCREET BUT DISTINCT SPRING IN THE STEP OF President FW de Klerk when he emerged from his meeting with Archbishop Desmond Tutu and the Reverend Allan Boesak in Pretoria this week. Today, as thousands of black protesters gather for what could be the biggest demonstration in decades, we shall see whether his buoyant mood falters.

Mr de Klerk has strengthened his position greatly with his conciliatory moves, announcing the release of eight of South Africa's most important political prisoners at the same time as holding the extended meeting with the country's most influential churchmen. He has breathed new life into his reformist image (just in time for the Commonwealth Heads of Government meeting in Kuala Lumpur), and he has displayed a combination of political cunning and subtlety which was woefully absent among his predecessors. At the very least, he has confused Pretoria's most implacable foes. Mr de Klerk revealed much about himself in his performance this week. In one of the friendliest encounters ever witnessed between a leader of white South Africa and the local press corps, he submitted himself with unusual grace, even relish, to questioning. This new face has not only brought accolades – a rare commodity in the corridors of the Union Buildings – but has also had the gratifying effect of buying time for his government. Better still, the costs were relatively low. The prisoners had to come out sooner or later, and to charm rather than hector Tutu – while it might infuriate some diehard right wingers – effectively undercut what could have been a telling denunciation from the church leader.

It is difficult to equate the dapper, grey-suited Gorbachev-lookalike with the once dour, unforgiving, *Dopper* cabinet minister who for years railed against integrated sport, mixed marriages, trade union rights for blacks, and spearheaded a vicious attack on South Africa's clutch of liberal universities. He is a consummate politician. He has banter for Boesak and bonhomie for Tutu; he never loses his temper and seldom raises his voice. He engages, with smiling sincerity, even the most disingenuous of questioners.

It is not surprising that he is so tough to read, and that many still believe he is playing a devious and extremely dangerous bluffing game, utilizing a large stock of reformist goodies, spreading his beneficence over a long period. But he must also be considering the sobering lessons of history. PW Botha employed short-term diversionary tactics when seeking respite from internal and international pressures; he too released a senior ANC leader and deigned to talk to Archbishop Tutu. Once the initial excitement was over, however, he had nothing to offer and the usefulness of the tactic was soon exhausted. If Mr de Klerk is to retain his new-found jocularity, he knows he will have to make the concessions of substance, as well as style, that his predecessors showed themselves incapable of making.

THE SUNDAY CORRESPONDENT, 15 OCTOBER 1989

SOWETO'S SORT-OF LIBERATION

The strength of the wind of change in South Africa finally became clear when the ANC's 'Rivonia trialists' - with the exception of Nelson Mandela - were freed from prison.

STANDING IN FRONT OF A HUGE – AND PATENTLY ILLEGAL – flag in the vivid black, green and gold colours of the African National Congress, an elderly black revolutionary yesterday addressed a crowd in Soweto for the first time in 26 years. 'Well,' he said laconically, 'we have been in the struggle for a long, long time. Now we are back here, and we hope we can be of help to you. Thank you for coming to see me.'

The man was Andrew Mlangeni, 63, a leading member of the banned ANC and its military wing, Umkhonto we Sizwe, who had only hours before been released from prison by the South African authorities, along with seven other political prisoners serving life sentences. The response from the crowds that had gathered outside Mr Mlangeni's modest home in Ndlovu Street threw clouds of dust into the air, and Mr Mlangeni and his wife, June, smiled as the well-wishers sang and danced. 'Andrew Mlangeni, *akunaye ofane naye*,' they chanted: 'Andrew Mlangeni, there is no other like you.'

The walls of houses and shops nearby were daubed with freshly-painted slogans praising the imposing, bespectacled, slightly balding figure who had been classified as one of the most dangerous men in South Africa, and sent to Robben Island more than two decades before. The Springbok Supply Store's facade was turned into a colourful billboard, with 'Welcome home Comrade Mlangeni, the People's Leader' obliterating the customary advertisements for samp and mealie-meal. The shopkeeper did not seem to mind the disruption: he too was drawn into the rejoicing, and disappeared in a sea of ANC flags, fashioned out of any material Sowetans could lay their hands on at short notice.

Sunday's extraordinary scene in Ndlovu Street – made more striking by the complete absence of the South African Police – was being replicated at other poor houses in the labyrinthine township, sweltering in the first days of the Highveld summer. Hundreds jostled for a glimpse of 77 year-old Walter Sisulu at his home in Orlando West. Young black 'comrades', who had not yet been born when Nelson Mandela's deputy went to jail, fell silent as they studied the grey-haired seraph of their struggle. They sang praise songs in Kgaye Street for Elias Motsoaledi, who stood stiffly to attention in an ill-fitting suit, gripping the hands of two of his grandchildren. At Winnie Mandela's house on the opposite side of the township there was a reception for Wilton Mkwayi. The gigantic ANC flag flying from the roof acted as a magnet.

As news of the releases began to course through Soweto the carnival atmosphere spread. Groups, hundreds strong, did the toyi-toyi dance down the streets. The roads were filled with noisy motorcades; motorways became one-way streets.

The black townships around Johannesburg were 'liberated' yesterday, sort of. Usually, the activists who raise the ANC flag at protest meetings wrap scarves around their faces to hide their identities. No-one bothered this time.

THE INDEPENDENT, 16 OCTOBER 1989

THIS CHAP DE KLERK
IS A THINKER

Walter Sisulu, Mandela's confidant and an intellectual lynch-pin of the ANC, was the most important prisoner yet released. Lunch with him showed that jail habits died hard.

HALFWAY THROUGH A LUNCH OF MEAT AND RICE IN THE bedroom of his Soweto home this week, Walter Sisulu suddenly threw aside his knife and fork. 'Hey, let me just leave out these things,' he said, picking up a spoon. 'They're just wasting my time.'

The habits of a lifetime in prison didn't die easily, he agreed, but added quickly that in all other respects he was back in business. The 77 year-old ANC veteran, perched on the edge of his bed, has lost none of his mental agility. He was 'thrilled' by the discipline of the schoolchildren who had come to greet him. And what's more 'they took my message home. I told the youth about education, that they must pay particular attention to it whatever else they do.'

As he talked, Sisulu's bedroom door opened and closed as admirers and friends arrived to see him. Some just looked and smiled, others kissed him.

It was 'still guesswork' as to when Nelson Mandela would be freed, he said, 'but I do not think it will be this year. The government is excited about the situation. They have fears because they have seen the response of the people, they think that there will be chaos, riots, revolution.'

What did Sisulu think of the man who freed him? De Klerk was 'a little more balanced than PW Botha,' he said, 'who was, after all, merely an emotional agitator. This chap De Klerk is a thinker. Of course he's still a Nationalist, but there is a change of style in keeping with his diplomacy and personality.' Sisulu was 'impressed by the ability of De Klerk to control the situation' during the government's leadership crisis. 'He got the entire Cabinet behind him, and not only that, he was not small-minded. They were not petty – they praised Botha.'

He said the first he knew of the historic meeting between Botha and Mandela was 'on the 6 o'clock TV news', but that he would be trying to see Mandela again soon. He was hopeful about the future, and impressed by the younger black leaders.

'They are more organized than we were at the same age, more systematic,' he said, reaching for his dessert.

WEEKLY MAIL, 20 OCTOBER 1989
(WITH THAMI MKHWANAZI)

INCIDENT ON GREENMARKET SQUARE

It was the day no-one thought would ever come: the white president announced to parliament that the ANC was to be unbanned, and impromptu celebrations began in Cape Town.

───────────

THE MERCEDES, MOVING DOWN THE COBBLED SIDESTREETS of Greenmarket Square, found its path suddenly blocked by several hundred ululating black youths. They were leaping into the air, waving imaginary sticks, and pressing forward in a solid phalanx. The young white driver braked sharply, nose to nose with the crowd, and for an instant the menacing scene was frozen in the bright morning sunlight.

Then, smiling, a youth broke ranks and removed the black, green and gold bandana from around his forehead. He tied it carefully to the car's radio aerial. The Mercedes' four occupants began to laugh, and a young woman in the back seat lifted her hands through the sunroof, brandishing a copy of the just-published *Cape Argus*, whose banner headline read, simply 'ANC UNBANNED'. The crowd surged around her good-humouredly, shaking hands and singing. Bemused riot policemen looked on as the car drove off with the African National Congress colours fluttering gaily above its bonnet.

Cape Town on Friday, February 2 1990, was an extraordinary place to be. By just before midday much of the citizenry of South Africa's coastal capital seemed to have heard that State President FW de Klerk had taken the step no-one thought he was capable of. The demonstrators at Greenmarket Square were just one of many groups which had hived off from a previously-planned protest meeting on the Grand Parade; they weren't heading anywhere in particular, they were giving vent to their delight at the legalization of their movement after three decades. Their chance encounter with the wealthy young whites was among innumerable vignettes symbolizing the impulsive, unconditional goodwill of the moment.

Throughout the afternoon and into the night celebrations erupted in the townships and in the white city. With only the most minor of exceptions police held back, and those white bystanders who were not swept up in the mood kept their feelings about this oddly benign revolutionary activity to themselves. At St George's Cathedral, Archbishop Desmond Tutu giggled with wild optimism. 'Just wait till De Klerk sits down with Tambo,' he bubbled. 'They will be surprised to find how South African they both are. It's going to be nice!'

So enthusiastic were the participants in one chaotic cavalcade that when it reached Guguletu township – several miles distant – they turned around and did the whole thing again. On the return journey they simply flagged down and piled into any vehicles which happened to be driving along the Klipfontein Road.

By Sunday, unsurprisingly, the euphoria was losing its edge as the implications of what had not changed in South Africa began to dawn. The city reverted to its familiar summertime torpor. Winnie Mandela emerged from Victor Verster prison nearby to say that her husband would not be coming out until the State of Emergency was lifted in its entirety. Resistance leaders in South Africa realized that this week's historic events constitute the introduction, not the conclusion, to the slow saga of negotiating a political settlement. De Klerk has changed irrevocably the country's political culture, but its system remains intact.

A United Democratic Front official laughed when I suggested that the piles of unused placards on the Grand Parade, each bearing the legend 'Unban the ANC!' could now safely be thrown away. 'But we'll still be needing these', she said, handing me a pocket-sized pamphlet entitled 'Guidelines for demonstrators'.

'There's a long way to go yet.'

TIME OUT MAGAZINE, 7 FEBRUARY 1990

WHERE *KAFFIR* IS NOT
A SWEAR WORD

Mandela's release was now certain. Unknowingly, the white right gathered angrily in Pretoria while De Klerk, in Cape Town, announced that the ANC leader would be freed.

IN CAPE TOWN, NELSON MANDELA'S IMMINENT RELEASE was being announced. In Pretoria, thousands of Afrikaner Weerstandsbeweging supporters were gathered under a placard bearing a crude drawing of the African National Congress leader. 'Wanted for target practice,' it read.

'From today,' thundered Eugene Terreblanche in a voice which carried eerily through the empty streets beyond Church Square, 'Pretoria will never be the same. The hour of resistance is here. The *boer* nation is on the march. This is a revolution that De Klerk is bringing on.'

'Hang Mandela, hang Mandela, hang De Klerk,' screamed the crowd.

'In a short time the South African Communist Party and the ANC will open offices here in Pretoria, in the heartland of the *boer volk*,' said Terreblanche. 'Shall we allow the hammer and sickle to fly here?' A group of men just below the statue of Paul Kruger snapped to attention with Nazi salutes.

61

Saturday afternoon saw the first public gathering of right-wingers since President de Klerk's historic opening address to Parliament on February 2. It was also the most openly insurrectionary meeting the fanatical right had ever held. Reporters hardened to the bigoted, fire-and-brimstone atmosphere of AWB meetings sensed something was very different on Saturday in Church Square. The far right is in a snarling, frothing, dangerous mood.

There was more to it that just the usual chilling Naziesque paraphernalia. The violence of the movement – sometimes shrouded in euphemism, sometimes overtly stated – was seething close to the surface. 'How many Barend Strydoms are there here?' asked an Afrikaans-speaking passer-by before hurrying off in fright. Two huge, perspiring AWB stormtroopers stood in earnest conversation. *'As Mandela nou uit die tronk kom, is dit die laaste straw,'* said one. *'Ja, ons moet nou moer,'* said his partner. (If Mandela comes out of jail now, that's the last straw. Yes, now we must hit out.)

Besides those carrying pistols on their hips, there were several men brandishing pick-axe handles, clubs and batons of all descriptions. Self-styled *Boere-Kommandant* Dirk Opperman called on the crowd to act lawfully (*'Ons boere is wettig'* – We *boers* are law-abiding). Pretoria's chief magistrate had ordered that there be no inflammatory speeches, he said . . . 'But I was taught that *kaffir* is not a swear word.'

In his speech, the centrepiece of the gathering, Terreblanche appealed directly to the police who were present, all within earshot. 'Month by month the government has impoverished you,' he boomed. 'Black bullets have drunk enough blood from our people. Now this blood could be the higher fuel for the revolution we must fight.'

Anti-semitism was on display as never before. A Star of David flag was torn and then burned in front of television cameras (to cries of *'daar's hy, skeur hom!'* – there it is, tear it) and small children carried banners reading 'Jews are sucking the land dry' and 'Hitler was right. Communism is Jewish.'

It was difficult to tell, in the naked ugliness of the moment in Pretoria, just how dangerous a phenomenon the gathering represented. Four to five thousand people do not make a mass movement, but they do make a large crowd. The government has indicated by its actions that it believes the threat to be isolated and containable. This might be true – Terreblanche's threats against Namibian independence proved to be so much bluster – but Church Square on Saturday, on the day before Nelson Mandela was released, was a discomforting place.

A speaker on the podium made the point again. *'Wil julle skiet?'* he screamed. *'Dan skiet Mandela!'* (Do you want to shoot? Then shoot Mandela.)

WEEKLY MAIL, 12 FEBRUARY 1990

THE DAY MANDELA CAME HOME

South Africa came to a standstill. It was Sunday and Nelson Mandela, the world's most famous political prisoner, was about to walk out of the gates of Victor Verster prison, a free man.

———————

IT WAS, I SUPPOSE, WHAT THESE EPOCH-MAKING DAYS ARE supposed to be like. There was triumph, tremendous heart-soaring triumph, as Nelson Mandela stood to address the largest crowd I have ever seen, thus ending his 27 years of imprisonment. But there was also tragedy as parts of the crowd ran amok, leaving some celebrants dead and many more injured, and stores with looted, broken windows.

A hundred thousand people is as good a crowd estimate as any. It was a huge, unforgettable gathering, too big for the National Reception Committee to control.

The crowd on Cape Town's Grand Parade started building up early in the morning, and was big by 3pm, the scheduled time for Mandela to walk out of Victor Verster prison in Paarl. It grew more volatile and unwieldy as the blazing hot afternoon wore on and the delays continued. By 4.30pm, with no clarity yet on whether Mandela had emerged from prison, youths went out of control. Fear gripped the outer edges of the crowd as teargas fumes filled the air, along with the chilling, incessant reports of firearms.

But on the Parade, the sea of people made for a breath-taking sight. Against the colonial backdrop of City Hall – draped in ANC colours – a blur of faces milled and crushed. Ambulances snaked in and out of the crowds as organizers using a wholly inadequate public address system pleaded for calm and order. By 4.50pm the organizers were clearly worried, castigating 'elements causing unnecessary problems for us', but the news that Mandela was on his way calmed matters briefly. Rally organizers shouted at the youths, but to little avail. One said dolefully: 'Mandela may be out, but these kids are unemployed.'

Just after 5.20pm the Mandela cavalcade roared into the city. A huge crowd ran wildly alongside his car as it wound through the streets, beating on the windows and chanting. A group of women jostled and pushed, desperate to see the leader. They wept and laughed simultaneously. The press of the crowd slowed the motorcade to jogging pace and Mandela, in the back seat with his wife Winnie, looked out at the mad crush. He was impassive, his fist raised stiffly in salute. With helicopters – some belonging to the police, others to television networks – swooping over the square, the scene had all the elements of imminent battle.

Suddenly Mandela's whereabouts could no longer be ascertained. Some said he was trapped in his car in front of City Hall, others said he was in the building. United Democratic Front patron Allan Boesak warned, desperately, that Mandela would not speak unless there was order. 'No, no, no comrades,' he screamed, 'the police are firing teargas. Do not provoke.'

With the sun beginning to lose its sting, and still no sign of Mandela, a chant went up from a small group on the eastern edge of the Parade: 'We want Nelson!'

'Comrades!' shouted an organizer from the podium. 'He has waited 27 years for his freedom. We have stood here for five or six hours. Where is our patience?'

Mandela eventually spoke just before 8pm, and the

crowd quietened. He delivered a hardline speech. He had clearly decided that his first appearance was a time to reassure and mobilize his own followers, leaving overtures and initiatives aimed at his opponents for later. The speech was an opening thrust, carefully prepared and delivered strictly according to the text. In a strong, but strangely unemotional voice, Mandela said he stood before the gathering 'not as a prophet, but as a humble servant.

'I place the remaining years of my life in your hands,' he said to resounding cheers.

At the end of the long, historic day, supporters heeded the ANC leader's call to disperse with dignity, and left the Parade peacefully. Groups of youths dancing the toyi-toyi laughed and greeted groups of riot policemen and soldiers as they spread out into the night.

WEEKLY MAIL, 12 FEBRUARY 1990 (WITH GAVIN EVANS)

NUMBER 8115 VILAKAZI STREET

Nelson Mandela returned to his bungalow in Soweto, which he had fled in the 1960s. Calmly, in his matchbox-sized garden, he faced questions about the future to which he was central.

BEFORE LAST SUNDAY, THE POLITICAL PLACARD TIED TO the iron gate of 8115 Vilakazi Street, Soweto, proclaimed: 'Mandela is coming'. Now the message has been brought up to date: 'Mandela is back'.

On Thursday morning, the legendary African National Congress leader was sitting on his square of lawn at the tiny township house he left, to elude the police, nearly 30 years before. He was barely out of prison. Zwelakhe, activist son of Walter Sisulu, ushered me through the gate. It was more than just the culmination of a most extraordinary week in South African politics. It was, for a South African, the stuff of unreality – a moment I had thought would never come.

For many years, any snippet about Mandela had been seized upon in order to draw some mind-sketch of this near-mythical figure. But the man I met was human enough – tall, strikingly elegant, grey-suited with an avuncular smile, a ready laugh, and a strong, prolonged handshake. With the creases and furrows etched on his face, Mandela looks his age. But there is a curious, non-weatherbeaten quality about him, as if the cloistered atmosphere of prison has had an embalming effect. 'You must excuse me for a moment,' he said after warm greetings, 'I have something to do.' One of the young activists in attendance laughed: 'He is too old-fashioned to tell you he needs to go to the toilet.'

Having led the way into his living room, past bouquets from wellwishers and hundreds of telegrams from all over the world, Mandela settled down on the sofa and answered questions with rigour and intensity belying his 71 years. On the ANC's negotiations with the government, he said: 'If you are not prepared to compromise, then you must not enter into, or think about, the process of negotiation at all. Insignificant things, peripheral issues, don't need any compromise. You need to compromise on the fundamentals.' He called for generosity of spirit in allaying the 'understandable' fears of whites.

Mandela in person is a captivating, even awe-inspiring man. He repeatedly insists that he has no 'magic wand' and that it is wrong-headed, and dangerous, to believe he alone can cure the country's ills. If it is a cultivated charm, it is effective nevertheless. Mandela has already shown a keen eye for the telling, statesmanlike gesture. During the historic drive from Victor Verster prison to Cape Town, Mandela suddenly asked the chauffeur to stop. He had noticed a white couple with two small children on the side of the road near Paarl. The ANC leader stepped out, alone, and walked up to the couple. He introduced himself, chatted for 10 minutes, ruffled the children's hair, and then posed for a photograph.

For the moment Mandela is playing the role of conciliator. But of course he will soon need to provide substance, a much more demanding task, not least because it will involve pulling recalcitrant elements of his own community into line. It is then, perhaps, that the famed harder edge of Mandela's personality will emerge.

I caught a glimpse of that edge when Mandela was

asked what he thought of Afrikaners. His eyes flashed and, for an instant, the measured beneficence disappeared. 'Why do you ask that question?' he said rounding on the young Afrikaner reporter. 'For the last three years I have been negotiating with Afrikaners. The progress that has been made so far has been made with Afrikaners. That is sufficient comment on what I think of them.'

THE SUNDAY CORRESPONDENT, 18 FEBRUARY 1990

MK'S AMBIGUOUS VICTORY

The ANC won the political battle against the Pretoria government, forcing it to unban the organisation. But it never won militarily, leaving its guerrillas in a curious position.

BENT OVER A TABLE IN A FLAT IN JOHANNESBURG, A SMALL group of white radicals worked with mortar and pestle, grinding piles of permanganate of potash into a fine powder. Drawing on their experiences of the second world war, they fashioned timing devices from ball point pens, and made incendiaries by pouring acid into doctored bottles. Their efforts marked a key point in South African history.

The group, which included a youthful Joe Slovo, was manufacturing some of the first bombs for the African National Congress's new military wing, Umkhonto we Sizwe, the Spear of the Nation. A device was detonated successfully on December 16, 1961, thus launching the armed struggle against apartheid. Today, Umkhonto we Sizwe – known as MK – is enormously powerful within the ANC, and is thought to account for half the organization's external personnel and financial resources. Such opposition as there is to peaceful negotiations within the ANC appears to be grounded among the firebrands of

70

MK, the most elusive and secretive branch of the liberation movement. The influence of leaders like Joe Modise and Chris Hani is beyond question.

It was Nelson Mandela who, in 1961 after the crushing of a strike, asked: 'Is it politically correct to continue preaching peace and non-violence . . . have we not closed a chapter on this question?' He had no doubt about the answer, and when Slovo and his colleagues went to work with the crude explosives a few months later, it was at Mandela's bidding, with him as commander-in-chief. They underestimated the might of South Africa's security forces, but still a sabotage campaign carried out by ill-trained ANC loyalists began, and MK cells sprang up across the country. The remaining leaders worked on a strategy Mandela had first canvassed. To the bombing of pylons was to be added training of professional guerrillas, and arrangements were to be made to spirit recruits to Tanzania, Algeria, the Soviet Union and elsewhere. The MK high command's plan was ambitious. Operation Mayibuye (Operation Come Back) sought to infiltrate about 7,000 guerrillas – some to be delivered by submarine or aircraft – who would render South Africa ungovernable in preparation for an invasion by (unnamed) foreign troops. During this period the first MK cadres were captured and hanged, and Walter Sisulu took over from the arrested Mandela the task of issuing directives from the underground. The strategy collapsed at 3pm on July 11 1963, when police raided the high command in Rivonia. Slovo, on a mission abroad, escaped. While training continued outside South Africa, MK's internal structures were in ruin.

In the wake of the 1976 Soweto student uprising MK's activities began to increase. Still it was clear that the early hopes of revolution were fanciful, and MK – now under the direct control of the political leadership in exile – reorganized. At Kabwe, Zambia, in 1985 it was resolved to broaden the guerrilla strategy, with trained insurgents acting more like officers than combatants, passing on their skills to chosen sympathizers within South Africa's borders in preparation for a 'people's war'. The strategy increased MK's presence, but maverick actions were inevitable. The bombing of a shopping centre in December 1985 – a civilian soft target – drew sharp international criticism and put the ANC president, Oliver Tambo, in an invidious position. Nevertheless, it was estimated in 1987 that MK's troop strength stood at 8,000, with as many as 2,000 inside South Africa at any one point.

Since his release from prison, Mandela has urged an intensification of the armed struggle, pending the government's accession to ANC demands. Attacks have continued sporadically; the war of attrition persists. But now the spotlight has shifted, for the first time, to MK's political role. Only when Modise and Hani return to the country will there be an indication of whether the ANC's warriors have joined the organization's diplomats in seeking a negotiated settlement. The question then will be: can MK be satisfied with having broken the will of whites to resist change, rather than, as was hoped all those years ago, defeating them militarily?

THE SUNDAY CORRESPONDENT, 8 APRIL 1990

FEAR AT THE DINNER TABLE

After the euphoria following Mandela's release, middle class whites began to ponder the future under a non racial government. Most conceded fear, but only in private.

———————

FEAR HAS BECOME AN UNWELCOME GUEST AT SUBURBAN dinner tables and *braais* around the swimming pool; the honeymoon is over for President de Klerk's white tribe. 'If you listen carefully,' joked a young, rich, liberal, English-speaking businessman over dinner last week, 'you can hear the sound of bets being hedged all around this city.'

To determine the accuracy of this statement, you need do no more than drive along suburban Johannesburg's wide avenues. Each imposing wall of each fortified, sprawling property boasts a sign of one kind or another. Putative intruders are told: 'Beware! *Pasop!* Protected by 24-hour Immediate Armed Response Unit.' Home security – provided by 'First Force', 'Supercops', 'Loss Control', and any number of other such professional vigilante organizations – is one of South Africa's few burgeoning industries. But alongside these frank admissions of fear, more familiar signs are also appearing, these inviting rather than warning off visitors. 'For Sale', they read. The wealthy whites are waiting again.

The predictable, practical fear of those Afrikaans-speakers of the lower to middle classes, whose sheltered employment and statutory superiority over blacks seems threatened, has been joined by an all-pervasive, gnawing white terror of the unknown. It afflicts the grand homesteads of Westcliff, Parktown and Sandton, whose occupants voted years before the accession of President de Klerk for the kinds of reforms he has now set in motion. Then, the tiny liberally-minded parties of opposition had no prospect of implementing their schemes – now the Nationalist Party government has embraced and acted upon them. The higher-mindedness of South Africa's affluent, cultured class has been vindicated, but instead of celebration, the air is filled with anxiety.

Majority rule could prove to be more frightening a concept to whites – even the most sophisticated among them – than might have been expected. A middle-ranking manager of a large Johannesburg business set this out clearly last week. She, a longstanding Democratic Party supporter, believed President de Klerk was 'moving too fast', that he had 'lost control'. 'You must understand,' she said, 'that I really hate apartheid. But I have children. And my maid is convinced that when the ANC comes to power she will be given my house. Don't you think I should be considering leaving?'

But the mood is, above all, ambiguous. It oscillates from day to day, and inappropriate significance is attached to single events. Newspaper readership has risen sharply, and talk shows on the independent Radio 702 can hardly cope with the numbers of callers. Most of the whites phone in with questions; seeking reassurance rather than declaiming in the old way. There is a recurring refrain: 'I am not a racist. I believe that this country has got to change. But . . . '

President de Klerk is well aware of the white jitters: the restlessness of the 'natives' in townships across the country is being echoed, quietly but firmly, in the suburbs. It was this awareness that prompted him to take an uncharacteristically hard line in his address to parliament last Tuesday. Votes of equal value for all did not mean majority rule, he said. The government was not envisaging a handover of power, but rather a controlled process of sharing it out more equitably.

The Johannesburg manageress is not alone in giving serious consideration to flight. The number of passports issued by the British embassy here has risen sharply – to nearly 2,000 each month – and other embassies, such as that of Australia, say that enquiries about possible naturalization have taken a steep upturn. It happened in 1960 after the Sharpeville shootings; in 1977 after Soweto; and again in 1986 after the township uprisings.

'Every week there is a convoy of the prudent leaving town,' wrote the South African novelist JM Coetzee in 'Waiting for the Barbarians'. 'Those who depart are the sensible ones, the husbands and wives who lie awake in bed whispering, making plans, cutting losses. They leave their comfortable homes behind, locking them "till we return", taking the keys as a memento . . . Resentment builds up against those who go . . . Now there are families that simply disappear in the dead of night.'

And there is white resentment against the richer among them: the punitive exchange rate means that none but the most affluent and resourceful can consider 'taking the gap', as fleeing is referred to in the suburbs. And even then the departees know that they will not be able to replicate their lifestyles on foreign shores. The uncertainty resonates in the less affluent suburbs, too: in Yeoville, which is rapidly becoming a 'grey area', a graffiti artist has adapted the ubiquitous slogan 'Apartheid Rules'. He has crossed out 'apartheid' and replaced it with 'angst'. The chairman of one of South Africa's largest and most liberally-minded manufacturing concerns lamented recently: 'You'd be shocked to hear the private responses of the captains of industry to De Klerk's changes. They have always at least been seen to be to the left of the government – now they are galloping toward what they see as the natural state of things, where business is more conservative than the government of the day.'

Mood is a fragile and fickle thing. Confidence can come back for the slightest of reasons, and in the rumour-filled parlours of white suburbia, it tends to spread as quickly as gloom. The vast majority of whites is staying, whether by choice or circumstance, and they are waiting with ears cocked and eyes trained. The current episode of hysteria is not enough to make them pack their bags. They are still comfortable enough where they are, and therefore must be hopeful. White South Africans also have a peculiar, endearing attachment to their homeland – a sometimes fierce geographical patriotism. As Coetzee foresaw, 'no-one really believes, despite the hysteria in the streets, that the world of tranquil certainties which we were born into is about to be extinguished.'

THE SUNDAY CORRESPONDENT, 22 APRIL 1990

A TRULY SERIOUS MEETING
(TWO WORLDS COLLUDE)

Both sides had agreed in principle to negotiate a political settlement, but had no idea of its contents. It was time for the exiled leaders to fly home from Zambia and start talking.

THE WHITE SOUTH AFRICAN SECURITY POLICEMAN SPOKE earnestly into his walkie-talkie. 'Yes, Mr Lekota,' he said. Moments later, on specific instructions from the United Democratic Front official and former treason trialist, he chaperoned a group of journalists from the gate to the door of Somerset West's Lord Charles Hotel – straight into the care of waiting Umkhonto we Sizwe security personnel.

The representatives of regime and revolution addressed each other civilly, professionally, and with more than a small measure of curiosity. The task of the former was to screen all arrivals at the hotel; the latter to usher approved visitors into the presence of the African National Congress delegation. Their relationship symbolized the extraordinary nature of developments in Cape Town this week.

As the historic 'talks about talks' got under way at Groote Schuur on Wednesday, they had already been overtaken by the quiet, practical co-operation elsewhere. 'What's it like protecting Joe Slovo?' the security policeman was asked. 'It's just my job,' he replied.

From the moment that the Zambia Airways jet conveying the ANC team touched down at DF Malan airport on April 27, one of South Africa's most enduring psychological barriers crumbled. Policemen demanded 'ANC accreditation' from reporters, UDF activists hunkered down to make logistical arrangements with their former jailers, and an air of profound unreality descended. Govan Mbeki, sensing this, made the point in his welcoming remarks for the returning exiles. 'From Africa, always something new comes,' he said, beaming. 'Strange things happen . . . In the days before (the delegates) left the country, we could never have gathered like this. The gentlemen on the other side (the security police) would have been trailing us. It's a very different story today.'

Indeed it was, and the bizarre elements were driven home repeatedly in the run-up to the talks. At the happy, disciplined welcoming rally for the delegation at Mitchell's Plain, white traffic policemen studiously turned away those vehicles without 'ANC Press' markings. By the same token, ANC marshals courteously escorted representatives of the SABC into a reserved media enclosure.

Senior ANC delegates conceded that there was an air of perversity about it all, but they were philosophical. They had to be when they arrived at Groote Schuur on Wednesday morning. Adorning the front of the gabled Cape Dutch mansion – home since 1910 to successive South African premiers – is a bronze frieze. It depicts Jan van Riebeeck's first (unequal) encounter with the Khoi and the San. Nelson Mandela was quick to note that Van Riebeeck's arrival had marked the beginning of a 300-year history of domination of South Africa's indigenous peoples.

He said: 'This is the first time in 78 years that a truly serious meeting takes place between delegations of the ANC and the succession of white governments that have ruled our country. It indicates the deadly weight of the terrible tradition of a dialogue between master and servant which we have to overcome.'

As convoys of sleek luxury cars started ferrying in each of the delegations, it became clear just who the servants now were: shiny-suited security personnel hovering with walkie-talkies clamped to their ears. A television cameraman wanted one to move out of his shot, and shouted: 'Come on Van der Merwe'. 'I am Dippenaar, and not Van der Merwe,' riposted the security man with dignity.

State President FW de Klerk and then Mandela delivered brief addresses, their respective teams standing together behind them: Umkhonto we Sizwe commander Joe Modise next to Deputy Minister of Constitutional Development Roelf Meyer; Foreign Affairs Minister Pik Botha alongside South African Communist Party chief Joe Slovo. Whether they liked it or not, the negotiators found themselves occupying the new middle ground.

WEEKLY MAIL, 4 MAY 1990 (WITH GAYE DAVIS)

JUST GIVE ME YOUR OLD CELL, MENEER MANDELA

Longstanding right wingers were left on the sidelines as the ANC re-entered South African politics with a flourish. But that didn't mean they were prepared to keep their mouths shut.

————————

FATE MAY BE PLAYING A CRUEL TRICK ON ROBERT VAN Tonder, but the grizzled pro-apartheid campaigner has no intention of giving up his fight for the restoration of the old Boer republics in South Africa. Even as plans proceed for the establishment of a multi-racial suburb surrounding his farm in Sandspruit, Van Tonder and his followers are fashioning strategies to oust President De Klerk – by means of a *boer* rebellion, if necessary.

Ever since he wrote *Boerestaat* in 1977 – a book which became the ideological blueprint for the Afrikaner Weerstandsbeweging – Van Tonder has championed the seemingly hopeless cause of having the Transvaal, Orange Free State and Vryheid republics of the 19th century 'returned to the *boers*'. South Africa's myriad 'other nations' would have to be accommodated on agreed portions of the remaining land, so the theory goes.

The *boers*' third freedom struggle has begun, Van Tonder

said at his farmhouse this week, and the *volk* will rise up to put a stop to the 'madness' which has gripped South Africa. He is distinctive among right wing leaders because of his urbanity and articulateness, his insistence that racism knows no place in his political thinking, and his fearlessly subversive challenges to the 'traitorous' government. Sitting in his neatly appointed lounge, which is decorated with the *Vierkleur* flag of the Transvaal Republic and memorabilia of Boer War leaders, Van Tonder looked an unlikely firebrand. Sporting a blazer plus tie and ready laugh, he spoke quietly and earnestly about the plight of his *volk*.

'You must understand the seriousness of our situation,' he said. 'We lost the wars (against the British) and we lost when we rebelled against participating in the second world war. We could afford to lose then, but this is the last battle. If De Klerk persists, he's heading for civil war.' With a flagrant militancy that was previously the preserve of exiled black nationalists, Van Tonder speaks unfalteringly of the possibility of a coup d'état, a *boer* rebellion, or a national strike by white workers. 'I always say that providence made us poor in order to help us keep our country,' he says. 'You must realize that for railway workers, postal workers, coal miners – all *boere* boys – this is a matter of their very lives being threatened as never before.'

Van Tonder believes the government's plan is to hold a referendum rather than face a white general election. They'd get a 'sound whacking' in an election, he's certain, but in a referendum where rural consistencies would 'lose their clout', he's not so sure. 'If they win that referendum,' says Van Tonder, 'then we've had it.'

What if his cherished dream is not realized, and the ANC does indeed accede to power? 'Well, then all I ask of Mr Mandela is that when he puts me in prison, he gives me the cell he had.

'You know, the one with the swimming pool and garden.'

WEEKLY MAIL, 8 JUNE 1990

CHAOS IN THE HOUSE

President de Klerk had signed away the assets of the old parliament, on a stop order. MPs decided to make the most of the time they had remaining to them.

_____

AWARE THAT PARLIAMENT AS THEY KNOW AND LOVE IT will never be quite the same again, members made the most of the dying minutes of this year's session. The final debate was arguably the session's most rancorous and chaotic – which is to say something in a year which has seen previously unthinkable anti-apartheid legislation pass through the chamber.

Its ostensible subject? Whether or not parliament should adjourn.

The motion was put forward by the leader of the House of Assembly, Dawie de Villiers, who said: 'The house, at its rising today, will adjourn until February 1991, providing that during such adjournment, the speaker might accelerate or postpone the date for the resumption of business.'

Neither the Conservative Party nor the Democratic Party were going to let him have his way that easily. Jan Hoon (CP, Kuruman) initially stuck to the point at issue, blasting away at the government by saying that squatter problems and labour unrest, among other things, meant that it would be irresponsible for MPs to go home. This prompted a spirited comeback from National Party chief whip Keppies Niemann, by way of a non sequitur. Waving a copy of the *Vrye Weekblad*, he bellowed at the CP benches, challenging the opposition leaders – *'mal regses'* (mad rightists) – to repudiate reports about assassination plots.

Pandemonium ensued: 'Honourable Members must first calm themselves down,' pleaded the beleaguered chairman, Dr Helgard van Rensburg of Mossel Bay. 'The government are *mal linkses*,' (mad leftists) yelled a CP member before the chairman could finish.

'I can't accept this senseless screaming,' said Van Rensburg, prompting further senseless screaming. 'Is it in order for him (Niemann) to point a finger at this side of the house and then talk about mad rightists?' enquired another CP member in an injured tone. 'Which member referred to the government as mad leftists?' riposted the chairman.

'I did, just like he did,' piped up a voice from the CP throng.

'No', said the chairman, head sagging. 'I don't think the times in which we live allow us to play games like this in the house.' This was the cue for Harry Schwarz (DP, Yeoville). His party was the only one acting with any dignity, he said, to delighted jeers and catcalls from all around. 'If the public of South Africa could be here to witness this . . .' he lamented in schoolmasterly fashion. 'This just proves,' he went on, 'what an important role the DP has to play, bringing common sense into the political scene.'

The statement prompted very little common sense from the opposing benches, and a great deal of commonness. Finally, Schwarz advanced his party's reasons for wanting parliament to keep sitting. They had to do with the labour crisis and the economy. 'This exhibition we've had today,' he eventually shouted, 'is the clearest proof that this session of parliament hasn't achieved its objective . . . I'm trying very hard to get the CP to talk with reason . . . '

'*I'm* trying very hard to get order in this place,' said the chairman, by way of reminding members of his presence.

Deputy Minister of Planning and Provincial Affairs Andre Fourie was somewhat rhetorical: 'Does the honourable member really think if we extend this session and continue to talk to the CP, that any common sense will be achieved? *Agge nee man*,' (Ah no man) he added, before being drowned out.

The chairman said wistfully: 'I think we will end this session. I put the question.' At 4pm, it looked like he would succeed, and it would be all over. 'Uh-uh', said the CP's Koos van der Merwe, uncommonly quiet until then. He wanted to declare his innocence in the 'assassination plot' saga. 'He can't use the summing up to make personal statements,' said someone, on a point of order, from the NP benches. The chairman confessed: 'These points of order are coming so thick and fast that I can't make a decision.'

And then, suddenly, it was over. The NP majority prevailed on the crucial question of whether they could all go home. *'Voorspoed vir die nuwe jaar,'* (Good luck for the new year) said the chairman, with relief. As the session broke up and MPs dashed for the lobby, a senior CP figure explained the real reason behind the afternoon's unseemly fracas. 'Actually,' he said, 'we and the DP dragged it out because we knew all the Nats had booked early flights to Jo'burg. Now they've missed them, and we've got all the seats on the later ones.'

Then he winked.

THE DAILY MAIL, 25 JUNE 1990

THE SHOTGUN MARRIAGE

The 'Pretoria Minute' was signed in the capital. News of the ceasefire between the SA Defence Force and Umkhonto we Sizwe was not well received by militants from either side.

'SELLOUT!' SCREAMED THE YOUNG WHITE STUDENT ON THE campus of an intellectual cradle of Afrikanerdom, the University of Pretoria. 'Sellout!' snarled the young activist from one of black South Africa's founts of militancy, the Soweto suburb of Diepkloof.

Both were reacting to the news of a ceasefire between the white government and the guerrillas of the ANC. Momentarily, the two youths were making common cause by vilifying their leaders, FW de Klerk and Nelson Mandela. With the ink yet to dry on the historic 'Pretoria Minute', both leaders face an enormous task in selling the ceasefire to their constituents. Having nullified a canon of South African politics, and confused their followers deeply, they have a lot of explaining to do. The government swore it would 'never negotiate with terrorists'. The ANC swore it would lay down its guns only when the white power bloc had been destroyed.

These tenets, drummed into ears on either side since 1961, carry enormous psychological weight. Militant young whites and blacks, in particular, feel rudderless without them. It was for this reason that Mr de Klerk's first public appearance after the signing of the truce was made on the restless Afrikaner campus of the University of Pretoria. He delivered a brave, unequivocal speech, in which he said whites had 'no alternative' but to negotiate with the ANC, and he carried the majority of students with him.

For Mr Mandela the challenge is, if anything, even greater. To get his complicated message across, explaining the necessity for compromises and tactical interventions to a disparate audience of millions, is an unenviable task. On Friday, the ANC published advertisements in national newspapers ('ANC report back to the people of South Africa') in an attempt to explain the agreement.

It is important – no, it is vital – for both Mr de Klerk and Mr Mandela that they persuade at least the majority of their followers that they have done the right thing. And it is a new, curious corollary that each must do everything he can to see that the other succeeds too – the negotiating process will collapse if either side falters.

The effect of last week's agreement was to consummate a political marriage between the two men. A divorce, for whatever reason, will destroy both. Selling the ceasefire is the first test of the shotgun wedding.

THE SUNDAY CORRESPONDENT, 12 AUGUST 1990

INSIDE THE MIND OF
A NECKLACE KILLER

The 'necklace' murder - one of South Africa's most gruesome inventions - resurfaced in 1990 amid clashes between rival township factions. Youths justified the barbarity.

ON THE TARRED ROAD OUTSIDE JABULANI LAY A CHARRED object. It seemed like just another burnt-out barricade. A group of journalists was walking by . . . when they suddenly realized that the object was the still-smouldering body of a man who had been 'necklaced', perhaps only minutes before.

Radio France reporter Paskal Chelet first asked on-lookers what had happened, but they were too frightened to speak. Then a group of youths approached and claimed they were responsible for the killing. 'We had him', said one youth, who described the victim as 'prey'.

'They (Inkatha) have killed plenty of us . . . We also have traditional weapons – like the necklace.'

The youth was part of a group. He did not identify himself. This is how he explained his actions. 'This man came from the (Jabulani) hostel. These people broke our windows, they looted some beds, mattresses especially, they took some food from inside of homes, and then money . . . and then they went to the hostel.

'We told the police to bring our stuff. The police promised to bring our stuff. But these people still came to our location with spears, assegais, *knobkieries* and everything. They tell us it's their tradition, and they're going to march inside the location any time they want to. If anybody is in their way they will destroy him in any way they want to do . . .

'And so we made our vanguard. We feel that our things are gone and that this man is a threat. He can hit us or kill us because they even carry guns, AK-47s. And so we retaliated, and the guy is . . . out.'

The youth was asked: 'But this man from Inkatha is now dead, burned on the road. How did it happen?'

He replied: 'He is from the hostel, and so being from the hostel, since we've been waiting here, he was . . . prey for us. He was a target, and we had him, we finished him. We are also showing our anger, that we can also fight, that we can also protect our people. He was burned.'

But, he was asked, how do you do such a thing?

'How do we do it? We put a tyre around him. And that's it. We set it alight.'

And you will do it again?

'No. We will never do it again. But if we are provoked we can do it again, because there are so many of us. We are more than they. They are only a minority. They are probably less than 400, and we are over a million here.

'They provoke us. That is why we are doing what we are doing. Because they are doing what they are doing.'

The body was still smoking, arms sticking out sickeningly from the pile of newspapers covering the torso.

THE DAILY MAIL, 20 AUGUST 1990

AYINAMASONDO:
IT HAS NO WHEELS

*Less than a year after the reform process began, disillusion was
setting in amongst the poorest of South Africa's people, who
had been expecting a dramatic improvement in their lives.*

———————————

THE ZULU MIGRANT WORKERS WHO LIVE IN SOWETO'S
spartan single-sex hostels have a new word to describe
what the 'new South Africa' looks like from their lowly
vantage point. *Ayinamasondo*, they say, 'it has no wheels'.
An alarming number of their more fortunate countrymen
are beginning to agree with them.

A few short months ago, when President de Klerk first
spoke the words 'the new South Africa', many whites and
blacks alike embraced it as a promise of rebirth and of a
miracle that none had ever believed could happen. Few
use the phrase now, except as a sarcastic introduction to
the catalogue of disasters which have, since it was coined,
befallen the country. The disillusion that has set in runs
deep.

What is new in South Africa is that politics at the top
has changed beyond recognition, while life below remains
all too familiar. Violence in the townships is as bad as the
oldest resident can remember and the first jabs from an

oncoming recession have poleaxed the economy. Black humour abounds, especially in the white suburbs. 'What did the Zambians use before they had candles?' asks a young English-speaker, gesturing north to the Limpopo and black-ruled Africa. The answer, accompanied by bitter laughter, is: 'electricity'.

But what is happening now, a year after FW de Klerk came to power and six months after Nelson Mandela's release, was probably to be expected. Forty years of apartheid could not disappear without a shake-out, and underlying trends are more important than tremors on the surface. There is cause for cautious optimism. First, both De Klerk and Mandela say the negotiating process is still on track. Given the number of excuses available to each for crying foul and pulling out, this is an astounding indication of the depth and commitment of government and ANC to a political settlement. The view is becoming more widely accepted that the process has gone too far for either to turn back without destroying themselves. Also, while the stature of both leaders has been reduced by their inability to maintain full control during the early stages of transition, they have not been dumped by their constituencies, and pretenders to the left and right are nowhere near powerful enough to mount a challenge at this stage.

The trick, though, the real trick, has still to be performed. The ordinary people out there have to be convinced that the peace process 'has wheels' after all.

THE SUNDAY CORRESPONDENT, 9 SEPTEMBER 1990

NOT A NATION OF JELLYFISH

Pretoria's rehabilitation in world capitals saw President de Klerk travelling to the United States on an official visit. It made whites feel good about themselves again.

A CURIOUS THING IS HAPPENING IN SOUTH AFRICA THIS week. After years of mealy-mouthed apology for their birthplace, whites are suddenly flushed with national pride, and outwardly boastful. By contrast the blacks, who have always occupied the moral high ground, now seem somewhat confused, even shamefaced.

What has brought these changes about is President de Klerk's triumphal visit to the United States – the first, as the State-controlled radio and television never tire of telling us, by a South African head of government since Jan Smuts went there to help draft the founding tenets of the United Nations after the second world war.

It matters little that Mr de Klerk's current tour is much more about style than content. Even before he left for Washington he conceded that the visit would not result in the lifting of sanctions; what is beginning to be revived among the whites is a sense of national dignity and individual self esteem. White South Africans, in large measure a humourless and self-interested bunch, had forgotten how it feels to be liked by anybody beyond the Limpopo River. The *laager* mentality, immortalized in the challenge of former President PW Botha's government to the world to 'do its damndest', had become a way of life. The world was simply ignorant, and could go to hell.

In the 1980s, shrugs and fatalism met each new announcement of the refusal of landing rights to South African Airways, or the imposition of some punitive visa requirement by those countries that admitted South Africans at all. Even the *Spitting Image* sketch with its chorus of 'I've never met a nice South African' – which many whites here have seen – met with little more than a 'Well, what would you expect from them?' sneer.

Now, magically, whites have a leader of whom they can be proud, and, as a corollary, they are feeling proud of themselves. After Mr de Klerk's two-hour tete-a-tete with President Bush at the White House, an extraordinary and near-orgiastic bout of self-congratulation gripped the white suburbs. Radio talk shows were swamped with callers wishing to proclaim their South Africanness. A middle-aged woman who confessed to having 'wept when I saw on television the orange tail of an SAA Boeing on a runway in the US again' was by no means unrepresentative; nor was she being disingenuous.

There was a startlingly unusual meeting of minds among the nation's newspapers, including those that in the past have been most critical of government policy. In Cape Town the *Argus*, an evening paper, lost its head completely, bringing out a special morning edition and using its biggest type to proclaim across the front page: 'It's Thumbs Up'.

As always, of course, a hangover will follow the party. Whites will soon come to realize that although the door to international acceptance is indeed ajar, many things have yet to change before it swings open. These are things that will frighten them, particularly when 'foreign diplomatic breakthroughs' are no longer enough of a novelty to distract attention from the ANC's nationalization policy, preferential living standards and the like. Nevertheless, they are beginning to sense, as Nelson Mandela pointed out after his release from prison in February, that it need not be all give and no take for South Africa's whites.

This is an exceptionally timely development for Mr de Klerk, who will shortly have to move from grand declamatory statements about the future, to building a consensus among whites about tangible concessions. That is the moment for which the white right wing – which has so far turned in a desultory performance – is waiting. Its task will be made much more difficult by Mr de Klerk's symbolic triumph in Washington.

Why then are this week's events causing consternation in the townships? It is precisely because the old enemy, who could once be relied upon to display all the diplomatic sensitivity of a Jean-Marie Le Pen, is performing so well that black leaders are in danger of being wholly outmanoeuvred. Diplomatically at least, the ANC and its allies are used to taking the crude loudmouths of Pretoria to the cleaners; now they have a fight on their hands. There is also a sense, for some, in which the developments erode their certainty in the absolute correctness of their own positions. Quite simply, blacks – and black intellectuals in particular – fear that Mr de Klerk might sweet-talk the world into accepting him and his government, and then quietly renege on his promises. The fear is born of 40 years' bitter experience, from the likes of John Vorster, prime minister in the 1970s, to President 'We are not a nation of jellyfish' Botha, who began a reform programme but found it too hot to handle.

Thus many in the townships suspect that the world is being duped (in the cases of Mrs Thatcher and President Bush this is judged to be voluntary), and giving away the prizes before the competition is over. A small sit-in protest against the Washington visit at the US consulate in Cape Town was the product of precisely this kind of thinking. But it was no more convincing than a 300-strong protest outside the White House on Monday.

The white delight is beginning to find an opposite echo. One Agnes Mamoepa, an 'ordinary citizen' of KwaDlangezwa, wrote this odd, bitter message to her countrymen this week: 'To all my fellow black people who kill one another . . . I wish to say well done and keep it up! Prove to the whole world that we are just a bunch of savages who, without the white man's intervention, would massacre each other. But if in another million years we are still the doormat of the world, let's not blame anyone but ourselves. It really hurts me when men to whom we thought we could look up turn out to be just African butchers like Amin and Bokassa.'

Strong – and overstated – stuff, but unthinkable before the changes wrought by Mr de Klerk. While the whites exult and dream of Californian holidays as welcome guests, Agnes Mamoepa agonizes at home, and the starkness of the shift in South African political fortunes is on display. They will shift again in the unpredictability of the coming months, but the Pretoria government shows every sign of liking the feeling of shedding its pariah status. This is a warning to the diplomatic whizzkids of the ANC to pull their socks up.

THE TIMES, 27 SEPTEMBER 1990

BRAAI, THE BELOVED COUNTRY

South Africans were beginning to get used to the dramatically altered political script in their country, and the rapidly changing cast of characters. Some even laughed at themselves.

THE WEEK IN SOUTH AFRICA WENT SOMETHING LIKE THIS. The Natal rugby squad was welcomed home in Durban with a tickertape parade. Nelson Mandela said Oliver Tambo was coming home too. Denis Worrall said he wasn't going anywhere as ambassador, and Afonso Dhlakama, the Renamo leader, said he was going down the tubes if South Africa didn't start supporting him again. The rains came. The Ivory Coast became very friendly. The PAC didn't.

De Klerk and Mandela met for the umpteenth time and appeared to make peace, as always. By nightfall they were at it again. Spareco sacked all 683 members of its staff. It was agreed that Madagascan ships would soon start arriving in South Africa, and South African planes would start landing in Kenya. It was unseasonably cold.

A mob wielding knives stolen from a curio shop stabbed holidaymakers on Durban's beachfront. Men armed with automatic weapons shot up a bus near Inanda, killing six passengers. The 'Soweto Friendship Month' rugby match between Northern Transvaal and the SA Barbarians was called off because 'the safety of the players could not be guaranteed'. Captain Dirk Coetzee, in London, said salt did not weigh the same as poison and refused to submit to a bizarre test concocted by counsel for General Lothar Neethling. A Black Consciousness Movement of Azania training camp was discovered in Botswana, and Foreign Minister Pik Botha was sworn in as Acting State President of South Africa . . .

I will repeat that last item for those of you who missed it the first time around. As we speak, Pik is President of South Africa. I myself saw FW hand over the ceremonial *kruithoring* at a little low-key ceremony at Jan Smuts airport on Thursday night. How many times have we asked ourselves: I wonder what would happen if Pik was president? Well, now he is. Anything is possible. He might just decide to sort the whole place out according to his own tastes before FW comes back next week. He might offer Thabo Mbeki a deputy ministry. Then again, he might just go hunting and leave us to get ourselves into a mess without the help of the government. This is exciting stuff. I would suggest that anyone who feels strongly about a dramatic change or two should give Pik a ring at the Union Buildings first thing Monday morning.

Alas, though, there is very little intrigue involved in Pik's elevation. His spokesman explained that the reason the ranking senior cabinet minister had never stood in as president before is that he's always gone on the trips with the boss. It's different this time because FW has been invited to address the Young Presidents Organization aboard the QE2, and there wasn't a berth for Pik. It seems he decided (sensibly enough) that rather than kick his heels in Southampton waiting for FW to dock, he would stay at home and have some fun. His spokesman warns that this is unlikely to happen again, so we'd better enjoy it while it lasts.

President Pik was the high point of the week. Indescribable, wholly irrational violence was the low. People are more frightened than I can remember. 'Change is pain',

Mzwakhe Mbuli's evocative phrase, has never been more apposite. At the risk of sounding like an ostrich, it seems to me that a bit of forced optimism – emphasizing the good over the bad – is in order if we are to approach the rest of the year in a state other than that of delirium tremens. So: curfews are being lifted, Magnus Malan can sing *Nkosi Sikelel' iAfrika*, and Adriaan Vlok has learnt the ANC's wrist-clasp handshake, which the minister tried quite deftly on a bemused Soweto resident when he popped in to see how Operation Iron Fist was coming along. (Can this approach be described as assault and flattery?)

I insist this is all progress. Despite an imminent bloating of the petrol price, medical charges, and a tax every time you so much as look at an airport, things could be worse. And there is still the country's talent in the matter of high-class graffiti. The latest *cri de coeur* from Yeoville is: '*Braai*, the beloved country'.

And may the *wors* be with you.

SATURDAY STAR, 13 OCTOBER 1990

THE AK BAZAARS

The new year began badly amid reports of spiralling violence. Successive government attempts to restore law and order had little effect, save to intensify criticism of the police.

THE INFANT 1991 HAS TAKEN ITS FIRST FEW HESITANT STEPS. It is not a pretty or a temperate child. In the 96 hours since Monday midnight, the AWB defended the ethnic honour of another picnic spot, in Vanderbijlpark, by thumping black members of the 'Voices of Healing' ministry. Cape Town hospitals resembled battlefields on Tuesday morning after hundreds of South African revellers wished each other Happy New Year with bottles, daggers and knuckledusters.

Law and Order Minister Adriaan Vlok thought he would cheer everyone up a bit with the announcement of Operation Sentry, an 'anti-terrorist' blitzkrieg not wholly distinguishable from those we came to know and loathe in the pre-FW epoch. The best that can be said for Operation Sentry is that it is not quite as idiotically named as Operation Iron Fist and its ancestors. But the question must be put as to whether this one's focus and motivation is altogether called for. No-one doubts that a concerted anti-crime campaign is long overdue, but who exactly are the boys in blue looking for here? There is a reward, for example, of R3,000 for every RPG-7 rocket launcher which is handed in or pointed out. To my knowledge, RPG-7 rocket launchers have not featured prominently in the arsenals of the bank robbers, car hijackers, rapists and assorted brigands who have reduced our country to something resembling Hobbes' state of nature.

Rather, the only people who are likely to have a couple of RPGs lying around the house at the moment are Umkhonto weSizwe guerrillas – and they're ostentatiously not using them, in deference to the Pretoria Minute. The fate of Umkhonto's weaponry, as opposed to that of the nation's army of *tsotsis*, is the subject of delicate negotiations in a joint ANC/government working group. An indelicate frenzy of indiscriminate raids will, to say the least, ensure that not much work takes place in the working group.

'Sentry' also offers tremendous entrepreneurial opportunities to the likes of General Jonas Savimbi. Stuck in Jamba with a surfeit of AK-47s and a cash flow problem, the wily Commandante will surely be tempted to go into the export business. His 'AK Bazaars' up north will fetch R6,000 per unit down south; given that the weapon can be had for something like US$100 elsewhere, this is not a bad profit margin in anyone's book. A rough ride beckons South Africa this year. Kipling's hopes for the country, set down in 1903, are no less resonant in 1991:

And when we bring old fights to mind
We will not remember the sin
If there be blood on his head of my kind
Or blood on my head of his kin
For the ungrazed upland, the untilled lea Cry, and the
fields forlorn:
The dead must bury their dead, but ye –
Ye serve a host unborn.

SATURDAY STAR, 5 JANUARY 1991

THE APARTHEID PARABLE

A year had passed since the speech that changed South African history. Now, in his opening address to parliament, President de Klerk had to set out a timetable for dismantling apartheid.

ON FEBRUARY 1 THIS YEAR, A YEAR ALMOST TO THE DAY since his seminal speech which changed irrevocably South Africa's political landscape, President FW de Klerk will rise to open parliament. It is a moment of great historical import, and some pathos: Nationalist leaders will be undoing the cherished work of their forefathers. This parliamentary session is a climax in a long and painful story; in its own way, a spectacular allegory.

Imagine apartheid as a giant building, the pieces put together painstakingly and deliberately over 40 years and more. The structure grows quickly and sure-footedly at first. Its bricks are acts of parliament, its fancy balustrades and sweeping arches the attendant actions of the mighty construction company. It will be unique, say its architects, it will be magnificent in its scope and cohesion.

It will last forever.

As it gets bigger it gradually begins to take on the look of the baroque – and the architecturally unstable. The builders and engineers grow worried: buttresses are called for, but still the structure becomes more rickety. More plaster is added, and the architects begin to concentrate on preserving what has already been created, rather than constructing new floors. They die, still engrossed in their toil of attempted restoration.

The descendants of the original designers decide eventually that some of the more elaborate components of the building might be done away with, without changing its shape. They chip away, pulling out bricks and pillars here and plastering over cracks there. The building's enemies, meanwhile, attack it in the dead of night, causing damage but not collapse.

Repair work is a constant activity, and eventually it takes its toll. It is time to hand over to a new generation of builders. These builders look carefully at their forefathers' creation; they study it from every side. They look, for the first time, at the foundations, which are rotten and weak. They begin to tear from the top; still the structure groans and creaks and they fear it will fall down upon them. They confer in deadly earnest, and finally agree. It cannot be saved. It is condemned, to be demolished as soon as possible. The new architects promise they will call in the wreckers, and will supervise the work until nothing remains.

Where the old building stood, they say, a new one will be built – this time with the help of those who hated the old. And this one, they say, will last forever.

THE STAR, 24 JANUARY 1991

A KING RETURNS TO ABDICATE

The last of the exiles, and the best known of them all, was to return to South Africa after thirty years. But Oliver Tambo was already an ailing man, adding to the pathos of his homecoming.

————————

THE MIDDLE-AGED BUSINESSMAN PEERED OUT OF THE airport terminal, open-mouthed. At that moment a great roar went up, accompanied by the thundering of thousands of feet on the vast piazza outside Jan Smuts airport. 'Tambo, Tambo, Viva OR Tambo,' bellowed the crowd. '*Liewe hemel*' (Good heavens), said the man under his breath.

He had happened, with hundreds of other unsuspecting white commuters, upon one of the most extraordinary scenes yet witnessed at Johannesburg's dour international airport. The piazza and walkways were crammed; phalanxes of riot policemen formed a human barrier between 5,000 toyi-toying celebrants and the international arrivals hall. Oliver Tambo was coming home after thirty years in exile.

The return of the ailing ANC president was the only event which could compete, in terms of emotion, spectacle and historical import, with the earlier release from prison of Nelson Mandela. Like Mandela, Tambo was the stuff of ANC legend, ineradicably part of the iconography of black South Africa. Although physically debilitated by a stroke in August 1989, Tambo-as-symbol drew what is believed to be the largest welcoming crowd ever seen at Jan Smuts – larger, even, than that which gathered to greet Hendrik Verwoerd on his return from the Commonwealth conference in 1961.

And so charged was the atmosphere on Tambo's day that even 'ordinary' commuters – the incidental tourists who certainly did not regard the man as their leader – lingered for hours, drawn by the power of history in the making. They watched as, at 10.50am, an animated and excited Nelson Mandela emerged from an anteroom in the terminal. A burly police officer complained about the throngs of reporters which besieged the ANC deputy president, Tambo's lifelong alter-ego. 'But we don't control the press,' smiled Mandela gently, 'they control themselves.' Then he disappeared, to find a more reflective spot in which to await the return.

By 11.15, a quarter of an hour before Tambo was scheduled to arrive, the piazza outside was filled with restive, rumbustious celebrants. Black, green and gold banners waved in the sharp sunlight. As Tambo's name was incanted over and over in song, the barking of police dogs provided an odd, edgy chorus. The South African flag flapped incongruously above. By 12.25, an hour late already, the blazing heat was getting to the crowds and there was anger and impatience for the first time. Exchanges with police threatened to spill over into open clashes. *'Ons soek water, ons soek water'* (We need water), chanted the 30,000 and the braver among them broke through the police cordon in search of taps. ANC marshals hissed urgently at one another, struggling to keep their arms linked and trying to hold the perimeters of the crowd in some order. 'Comrade chain,' shouted one to a youth sweating next to him, 'please do not let us break apart.'

At 1.05 good humour returned for no apparent reason, and the crowd began to applaud and sing for Tambo once more. It turned to anger again as the wait continued; the young riot policemen looked jittery and fragile. There was the sound of breaking glass, the first victims of dog bites were taken away for treatment. A tourist bus passed between the police and the crowd, its occupants goggle-eyed and plainly terrified.

At 2pm precisely, Nelson Mandela's red Mercedes-Benz swept along the first floor slipway. Mandela and Tambo sat still, briefly, in the back seat. Tambo stayed longer in the car, his grey hair visible, his fingers fiddling nervously with his familiar, heavy tortoise-shell glasses. At 2.05 he was lifted out gingerly by aides, his frail legs placed on the ground. His gaunt face, with grizzled white beard, split into a grin of the purest joy as he caught his first sight of the welcoming throngs below. They roared. He waved his left hand awkwardly, clenched his fist and grinned. It was a long moment of communion, without a word being spoken.

'Our president wishes to say he is happy to be home,' said Mandela. Tambo was driven to Soweto as the crowd dispersed. Two years before, in London, Tambo said he would live to see the collapse of apartheid. 'That moment will come in the lifetime of Nelson and myself,' he said then.

THE ARGUS, 1 FEBRUARY 1991

IT'S PARLY TIME

The right wing realized that parliament, though declining in influence, offered a public platform from which to denounce the 'traitorous' government. The exchanges were fierce.

THE SESSION TO END ALL SESSIONS IS UNDER WAY. ONCE again, the corridors and chambers of the tricameral parliament reverberate to the sound of the low-flying mixed metaphor. It's parly time. Let the history books show that there has never been an opening of parliament quite like that of Friday, February 1 1991. The president's address, traditionally heard in respectful if not sepulchral silence, was met briefly and ingloriously by a Conservative Party caucus doing a convincing impression of Rag Day at the University of Potchefstroom. It happened thus.

'Legislation is to be tabled shortly for the repeal of the Land Acts of 1913 and 1936 . . . ' began President de Klerk. 'You don't say,' boomed SP Barnard (CP, Hercules), on his feet. 'Order', growled the Acting Speaker, Dr Helgard van Rensburg. ' . . . and the Group Areas Act of 1966,' persisted the president. 'You are a traitor, man,' came the voice of J Chiole (CP, Pretoria West) from the distant backbenches. 'Hangman of the Afrikaner,' added PJ Groenewald (CP, Stilfontein), helpfully. Things were beginning to warm up.

'The honourable member for Stilfontein must immediately withdraw that remark and apologize,' said the acting speaker in tones of sharpened gravel. Having made it quite clear that apologizing was the very last course of action he would consider unless severely tortured, said honourable member found himself on his way out of the chamber, while the president waited to get on with his speech. 'The state president is a traitor', yelled the honourable member for Pretoria West again, either because he thought nobody had heard him the first time round, or as a gesture of solidarity with his departing colleague. 'Who said that?' snarled the acting speaker. Pretoria West soon followed the way of Stilfontein. There was by now a marked lack of gravitas in the chamber, as CP honourable members fell over each other in the rush to leave. Peter Soal (DP, Johannesburg North), thought this an excellent idea. '*Loop! Loop!*' (Walk! Walk!) he shouted at the remaining Conservatives. Koos van der Merwe (CP, Overvaal), leaning his considerable frame sideways out of his bench, yelled 'You have no mandate to do what you are doing.' This to the president, now an almost lonely, mute figure on the podium. '*Loop!*' giggled Mr Soal, delirious at the prospect of parliament being turned into a CP-free zone.

Honourable members for Losberg, Kuruman and Hercules obliged, as did most of the northern Transvaal and a sizeable chunk of the Free State. The president battled on gamely. Eventually Dr Andries Treurnicht decided it was no good staying in the front benches when you have no backbenches left, and scarpered himself. By the time Mr De Klerk got to the bit about the 'disappearance of the last remnants of apartheid', the last remnants of the CP had disappeared too. 'The good news is that the CP has walked out,' said a senior NP official. 'The bad news is they'll be back on Monday.' The *hoor hoor's* sounded like an intensive bout of hiccups.

THE STAR, 7 FEBRUARY 1991

106

THE SITUATION IS VROT WITH DANGER

The opening sessions of the historic parliamentary sitting were reminiscent of a tough, and not always clean, sporting contest. De Klerk's men outplayed their right wing opponents.

THIS WEEK, THE GOVERNMENT WENT INTO WHAT DR VAN Zyl Slabbert might call the 'Last Grey Parliament' on what Americans would call 'a roll'. This was a National Party team brimming with confidence not seen for a long time. The Conservative side was never in with a chance.

Top goalscorer FW 'Dazzling' de Klerk kept up the form of last season, forcing opposing skipper AP Treurnicht to resort to persistent, if desultory, fouls. De Klerk's three cheer-leading troupes, led by Zach de Beer, Allan '*Hoor Hoor*' Hendrickse and JN 'Ever' Reddy, were transported with delight as the first half got under way. Referee Helgard 'Hath No Fury' van Rensburg seldom had the whistle out of his mouth. Also on form was 'Dazzling's' forward line, comprising ageless veterans Gerrit '*Flinkdink*' Viljoen and Pik '*Potjiekos*' Botha. Dr Viljoen made a valiant effort to stick to the sporting motif of the session, describing the ANC's insistence on a constituent assembly as being like 'putting the goalposts at the start of the race'. For all his other attributes, commentators noted, the minister cannot be described as metaphor-friendly.

Potjiekos Pik's finest moment came when he read out a lengthy testimonial to the National Party squad from Mr Edson Arantes do Nascimento, otherwise known as Pele. Well, known to some. It was marvellous that 'this famous football player' had taken the time to write, enthused Potjiekos, 'and I say from my side that he is welcome to visit South Africa. What a wonderful day it would be if this famous sportsman could attend the first international soccer match between South Africa and Brazil.'

The Conservative Party benches were thoroughly non-plussed by all of this. They didn't know who on earth Pik was talking about. By way of stark contrast, the men from the House of Representatives responded with an impromptu Mexican Wave. This, one assumes, is exactly what the CP means when it talks about irreconcilable cultural differences.

There was a distinct air of unreality about proceedings in parliament this week. For, once the president had delivered his speech, the game was all over bar the shouting. The National Party's reform measures will go through the house as surely as day follows night. Then the real politics will get under way outside parliament. There will be a great deal of sound and fury in the chamber and it may go on for several months, but we know the result already. Ministers are much more interesting to talk to about their dealings with the ANC than they are on the subject of *broedertwis* with the CP, so far has the wheel of South African history already turned. In other words, as a Labour Party MP remarked: 'The situation is *vrot* with danger.'

SATURDAY STAR, 9 FEBRUARY 1991

THE HOUSE OF HENDRICKSE

A sideshow to the main political drama of the South African transition was the gradual and inelegant demise of the 'coloured' and 'Indian' houses in the tricameral parliament.

FOR WHAT IS ARGUABLY THE FIRST TIME IN SEVERAL YEARS, the House of Representatives has been debating an important question. The question is: 'What are we doing here?'

As the politically aware reader will know, others outside the tricameral parliament have been wanting this answered since 1984. Now they are getting some satisfaction in the Reps' twilight days. The formal topic for discussion was the Budget, but the interleaving theme was 'Our Relevance'. (Research reveals that the word 'relevance' was used in the House this week as often as most prepositions. Indeed, it was frequently used as a preposition.) 'All the signs are that if we do not now act with resolve we will be written off by history,' declaimed Jac Rabie (UDP, Reiger Park), at the time of writing the Leader of the Opposition. His proposal to the majority Labour Party (Proprietor: Hendrickse and Sons), was that all the Reps should stop their silly debate and 'march to Tuynhuys to deliver our demands to the state president'.

It was not immediately clear what these demands were

109

– besides the overarching issue which is concentrating the mind of the nation: Will the Reps get full pensions when the playhouse is abolished? Nic Isaacs, (DRP, Bishop Lavis), until a week before himself the Leader of the Opposition, was also all for walking out. 'There is no more honour in this House,' he said, inviting an obvious question.

Some Reps sat firm. Arthur Roper (LP, Alra Park) went straight to the point. 'Who will profit more financially (from walking out) than that honourable member?' he demanded. 'He has been in parliament since time immemorial. It is now the golden opportunity for him to get a golden handshake.' Mr Roper was touching on a crucial issue.

Those Reps who have been in the system from the beginning already qualify for full parliamentary pensions, while more recent arrivals do not. Hence the consuming interest in matters which might otherwise appear to the casual observer to be somewhat parochial, selfish and – dare we say it – irrelevant. It is a hard fact that the Reps have close to no influence whatsoever in parliament in these pre-new South Africa days. Thus the house sees out its autumn in a state of lazy chaos, contemplating its collective navel and convincing itself of the urgent need to continue doing whatever it was it was doing in the first place, which no-one can quite remember for the moment.

While the South Africa outside changes beyond recognition, the men in the House of Reps (irreverently known as the House of Reprobates, or House of Hyperbole) stay much the same. The heroines of Hansard carry on filling in party affiliations in pencil, because they change so often. The intensity of insult is raised to an ever higher plane. The Speaker, like the boy with his finger in the dyke, barely manages to avoid scenes of epically unparliamentary proportions.

THE STAR, 7 MARCH 1991

CHILD'S PLAY

An incident of innocence, played out guilelessly by children of different races in Cape Town, contrasted sharply against the hatred and vitriol prevalent throughout the country.

EARLY ONE MORNING ON A PICTURESQUE STREET CORNER AT the foot of Table Mountain, a timeless South African scene was unfolding. A white man was shouting, for reasons not immediately apparent, at a black man. His vocabulary relied heavily on six-letter words beginning with *k*. The black man was in a silent fury, eyes flashing and fists balled.

Around the corner, suddenly, there appeared a boisterous group of toddlers in school uniform, off on an outing under the supervision of their teacher. The children's complexions ranged from the bright pinks of Camp's Bay to the deep ebonies of Guguletu, taking in the beiges of the Bokaap along the way. They stopped and stared uncomprehendingly at the malevolent tableau. They were all (for safety's sake, presumably), holding hands.

The two men turned to look at them. There was a long, sepulchral pause as the representatives of the old South Africa – filled to the gills with all the familiar hatreds, grudges and prejudices – were confronted by those of the new, who had not yet mastered any of these keystones of our culture and simply did not know their meaning.

The new triumphed, totally. The children began to laugh, as they would have in earlier times at a Punch and Judy show. The men felt ridiculous and, chastened, allowed the hostility to evaporate. The children gambolled on.

SATURDAY STAR, 16 MARCH 1991

THE OTHER CHRIS HANI

Chris Hani, chief of staff of the ANC's guerrilla wing, became one of white South Africa's most hated figures. But beneath his tough talk, he was committed to a peaceful solution.

———————

THANKS IN LARGE PART TO THE EFFORTS OF THE Government's warlike minister of defence, Chris Hani has replaced Joe Slovo as white South Africa's *bete-noire*. The latest slanging match between General Magnus Malan and the Umkhonto we Sizwe chief of staff – sparked by Mr Hani's remark that a continuing ANC ceasefire depended on 'the behaviour of the regime' – has yet again reinforced Mr Hani's image among whites as that of the man to be most feared in the ANC; the dark side of the new South Africa.

Mr Hani is presented as an unremitting militant, a man of violence by preference, and leader of a powerful 'anti-negotiations faction' waiting in the ANC wings. In the white public perception, a peaceful solution seems possible only if the 'Hani-ites' are defeated.

In fact, while Mr Hani's swaggering, toyi-toying style and his chosen political office (he is a ranking member of both the ANC military wing and the SA Communist Party) certainly conform – probably intentionally – to

113

his radical chic image, the conclusion is highly questionable. The current spat with General Malan is the clearest case in point. General Malan reacted furiously to a single sentence culled from a lengthy interview given by Mr Hani in the Cape. Malan warned the MK chief of staff that his indemnity from prosecution was 'only temporary', and Hani responded with the political equivalent of an invitation to jump in the lake. Rational debate gave way to bravado and bellicosity.

It is worth revisiting what Hani said in order to make a more serious assessment of his role in the negotiating process, and his likely place in the future South African polity. First, the offending statement. It was, in fact, swathed in qualifications. Hani's actual words were: 'It would be wrong to say that there is no possibility of going back to armed struggle. Our dear wish is that we don't have to go back, but it doesn't depend on us – it depends on the behaviour of the regime.' This is commonplace ANC dogma, and it is little different from the government's insistence that it will not hesitate to use force if one or other negotiating partner reneges on the agreed rules. Hani's observations on broader questions affecting the negotiating process (and on the performance of the Mandela leadership) are much more revealing about the man and his mission.

They show, in stark contrast to Hani's public image, a commitment to the peace process, pragmatism and democratic accountability. Hani defended Mandela's right to 'take certain initiatives' without consulting the membership on every issue. (Including the suspension of the armed struggle.) Everyone should 'accept the dynamism of our struggle. So many things are happening in our country, so fast. Much as it would be desirable to send (key issues) to the regions, I think that it is always important to come out with something fresh, because we are not only addressing ANC members.' He argued that the leadership required latitude: 'We shall be in trouble if we stick rigidly to positions in a dogmatic way'.

On the matter of ethnic and ideological differences with other groups, Hani was also conciliatory. 'No groups should feel ignored or left out,' he said. 'We cannot brush aside easily the national question . . . We should not just generalize about everyone, because that would be papering over some of the objective conditions that exist among these racial groups.' Peace with Inkatha required the ANC to 'moderate our language' because 'it must not bring about a situation that the other side feels vilified or maligned. We should feel free to criticize Inkatha and the PAC, in the same way as they should feel free to criticize us. These are healthy tendencies. Once you accept that you are going to have a multiparty system, then criticism should be tolerated and accepted as a norm of democracy.' Hani accepted that the integration of MK and the SADF might have to wait some time, and did not rule out the possibility that some ANC members could begin to operate in an effective interim government before a new constitution has been finalised.

In the current situation, therefore, Hani is clearly on board the ANC negotiations bus being driven by Mandela. Even high-level government sources say that while he is a tough negotiator, Hani is a very effective, serious participant in the joint working groups, and they get on well with him. Why then is General Malan acting as publicity agent for Hani as romantic revolutionary, simultaneously striking terror into whites and endearing Hani to young black militants? It could be that the minister simply did not read what Hani said, and reacted out of habit. Or, the two 'hard men' of the ANC and the government could be aware of the usefulness of having each other to bash, while leaving the broader peace process intact.

The situation carries attendant dangers: Hani might become so demonized that when the time comes to convince whites that he is 'OK' after all, their fears might be too deeply etched to be removed.

THE STAR, 4 APRIL 1991

WE ARE ALL ENTITLED TO OUR REVERIES

Mandela and De Klerk were wooing the world, but back home their special relationship had deteriorated considerably. Many felt it was their duty to present a united front in public.

IN A WELL-SYNCHRONIZED 'SEPARATE BUT EQUAL' international tour, two talented South African acts roared abroad this week. I like to think of our latest attempt at cultural invasion as a series of sepia-coloured polaroid snapshots.

There's one of Our President reclining in his Dublin hotel suite. His eyes are closed, he's kicked off his Cabinet-issue grey shoes, and there is a beatific smile on his face as the strains of his beloved Vivaldi – piped in by the thoughtful Mr Haughey – wash over the presidential countenance. He is a happy man. The important people he has been meeting like him a lot.

He is dreaming of applause, and of fruit and vegetables, of the shiploads of *nartjies*, nectarines, kumquats and butternuts which will soon be filling Irish bellies again, just like in the old days. His country is going to be great, he has told everybody, and they seem to be convinced.

Down the N1 (the one in Britain, which is open, as

116

opposed to the one in Johannesburg, which seldom is) there stands our Deputy President. He is enjoying his triumphal journey from the Orient to the Occident. Just a day or two earlier we had seen his winning grin in Japan, this time sandwiched between two geisha girls in Kyoto. He, too, has the look of a gentle dreamer. His brow softly creased rather than furrowed, his dark-suited, pencil-thin, towering frame is the object of curiosity and wonder to all who look on. He has told them that his is going to be a wonderful, blessed land, and they believe him.

These two are, surely, South Africa's greatest ever drawcards, outshining even the Kruger Park, Table Mountain, and freshly sliced biltong. And tours to foreign shores bring out the benign best in them. They emphasize hope and reconciliation, prosperity and peace and, what is more, the world listens with an attentiveness that few other politicians enjoy.

But alas all is not so rosy.

The 'special relationship' between Mr de Klerk and Mr Mandela has been cruelly battered in the year-and-a-bit of its duration. It is true that when abroad, our leaders tend to spend less of their time at each other's throats – supporting the growing perception that we are all of us savages best left to our bickering fate – and more trying to convince people that this shambles we call home can actually work out in the end. It is true that when they are on the international stage it seems to matter less that back at the ranch, the dull thud of the panga is competing with the deathly rattle of the AK-47, that deadlines are looming and graft is spreading as quickly as water hyacinth. For brief moments it doesn't rankle so much that economic growth is a distant memory, or that banditry is reaching levels undreamt of even in the days of Wells Fargo. It is a good feeling, to have hope triumph over experience for a while.

But does it have to last such a little while? I imagine another snapshot. The tours have been combined; the solo stars are on the same bill. It is rather like watching Lennon and McCartney play together for the first time. They sing the same song, having penned the lyrics together. Everyone at home is unbearably proud, and there is an outpouring of neighbourly goodwill.

Foreign fans, captivated, fall over each other to support the society which has produced such a unique partnership. The twosome is photographed, finally, at a concert back home, taking a deep bow, against a backdrop of smiling, well-fed, bright and excited faces . . .

Ah well, it was just a thought. We are all entitled to our reveries.

SATURDAY STAR, 27 APRIL 1991.

STOICISM IN THE MOUNTAINS

After a lifetime in prison, Nelson Mandela faced another intolerably cruel blow. His wife, Winnie, was convicted of maltreating the child-activist, Stompie Mokhetsi.

NELSON MANDELA SAT, ERECT, ON A SOFA IN A CHARMING Cape Dutch *voorkamer* set on the slopes of the mountains outside Stellenbosch. He was smiling and, save for the incongruous surroundings, it looked like one of the more ordinary days in his and the country's political life.

In fact, the moment was of potentially epochal importance. Barely ten minutes before, Mr Mandela had been informed by telephone that his wife Winnie had been sentenced to six years in jail. If he rejected Mr Justice Stegmann's verdict, he rejected the existing legal system, and the entire negotiations process might collapse.

The irony of the situation, too, was palpable. Who could have imagined, little more than a year ago, that a free Nelson Mandela, having just addressed a gathering of Afrikaans students, would be called upon to comment on the possible imprisonment of his wife? There is surely no adequate precedent, anywhere, for this unfolding South African saga.

In the event, the strange moment in Stellenbosch will

be remembered as being placid, rather than explosive. A composed Mr Mandela read out a short, hand-written statement, drafted in a room upstairs only minutes earlier. Its contents were clipped. His voice sounded heavy, but not querulous. He said: 'My wife was sentenced to six years this morning. I have never believed that she was guilty of assaulting anyone . . . I believe she did not know about the assaults. We trust that soon her name will be cleared completely. The last word on this issue has not been spoken.' Then he repeated the statement in Xhosa and sat back, graciously inviting questions. Had he now lost all confidence in the South African legal system? Mr Mandela would not be drawn. 'It is premature,' he said, 'to deal with that point now . . . Once an appeal has been made, it is proper to leave the matter in the hands of the court.'

How had he felt when he heard of the sentence? 'Well,' he said, 'in the light of the judgment delivered yesterday, the sentence passed was not unexpected. But only in the light of the way in which the learned judge handled the matter.' It was clear, almost immediately, that the moment of potential crisis had passed. Mr Mandela tacitly accepted the sovereignty of the courts – it would have been easy enough for him to denounce the white-centric legal system – and he resisted what must have been a burning temptation to unburden himself of all the anger, frustration and confusion he felt as a result of the ghastly situation in which he found himself. He stressed what he found positive in the judgment. If ever a politician behaved in a statesmanlike fashion at a critical point, it was surely this one.

Mr Mandela went further. As he was being chivvied away by aides, he stopped to joke with journalists – and in doing so made a crucial off-the-cuff statement about the effect of the Winnie Mandela saga on the broader peace process. 'The case itself has no direct relevance to negotiations,' he said. He then shared some light banter with those thronged around him. He promised to do an interview in Afrikaans at a later stage for the SABC ('It's difficult now, you know, *my kennis van Afrikaans is swak*' – my knowledge of Afrikaans is poor), and left. The resilient South African negotiating process had negotiated yet another moment of truth.

THE STAR, 16 MAY 1991

CHILDREN WITH EYES EIGHTY YEARS OLD

Massacres of unimaginable brutality and barbarism were now occurring regularly in South Africa. The psychological effects on the children of the townships were clear, and chilling.

THE IMAGE THAT STICKS WITH ME MOST DOGGEDLY AFTER this week of high political drama is not one you might expect. It is not – riveting though that was – the picture of a convicted Winnie Mandela descending courtroom steps with the radiant smile and clenched fist of one just acquitted. It is not of Nelson Mandela, sitting dignified in Stellenbosch, riding another blow in a lifetime filled with them. It is not, either, the snapshot of Mrs Thatcher receiving her belated heroine's welcome from white South Africa, when her world and ours had long since turned topsy-turvy. It is not, in fact, any of the other pictures of our familiar 'newsmakers' caught in the alternating eddies of fortune good and ill.

The image I cannot shake off is of someone we've never heard of. It is a young black child, unnamed, staring glazedly into space from behind a woman weeping over the defiled, dead body of her husband. They are residents of a forsaken place called Swanieville, and the man has been gouged and hacked and torn to death in a way that doesn't bear thinking about. The man has no hands any more. The child has the eyes of an eighty year-old.

It is a picture that makes all the others seem somehow trivial and irritating. It makes nonsense of the importance we attach to them. I cannot stop trying to imagine how that boy can possibly grow up as anything resembling 'normal', after what he has seen. Moreover, he is but one of tens of thousands of children who have witnessed such barbarous horrors in the long, convulsive labour pain which has attended the pre-birth of the new South Africa.

For every two, or six, or twenty-seven dead South Africans we read about each morning, it is chilling to consider how many more saw what happened, were related to those bodies, or were nodding acquaintances at the local cafe. Leave aside for a moment those who did it or had it done to them – think of all the others who are inescapably affected, forever.

The Swanieville massacre is not comprehensible to me, viscerally. I was not there and I don't care to think about the screams and the smells. But intellectually, it seems to raise a blindingly obvious question. Newspaper reports described how a group of some 800 head-banded men was seen making its way back to a hostel after the blood orgy. Why, in the name of everything decent we say we still believe in, was that hostel not immediately surrounded and everyone inside it arrested? Why were each and every one of that marauding band not put in cells and interrogated until the planners and participants in this monstrous crime were identified? Why were the white suburbs silent on the subject?

South Africa's policemen face one of the least enviable tasks in the world. There are many, many, individuals among them who are trying heroically to fulfil it. But where is the political will? The ghastliness of what happened in Swanieville demanded an instant, unequivocal response – ordered, if necessary, right from the top in ministerial offices in Cape Town. The township victims needed to be shown that the government shared their horror, and would act with the enthusiasm, skill and ruthlessness it used to deploy against 'terrorists'. The township murderers needed to be shown that they dare not repeat their brazen brutality without paying a terrible price. Instead, Swanieville becomes another statistic. And the next massacre is awaited.

What must be done is surely obvious. The government acknowledges ultimate responsibility for the safety of all citizens. The carrying of any dangerous weapon in public must be banned right now, and the ban must be enforced at all costs. There must be no more posturing. We must stop the killings, or we shall all die, physically or spiritually. If we do not stop it we need not wait for the barbarians any longer. We will have found them in ourselves.

SATURDAY STAR, 18 MAY 1991

NATS TO THE LEFT OF ME, NATS TO THE RIGHT

The march toward obscurity of the tricameral parliament prompted hilarious scenes as MPs scrambled to join parties they thought might have a chance of surviving.

THERE ARE BLESSED TIMES IN PARLIAMENTARY LIFE WHEN us Gallery scribes are rendered all but redundant. Hansard says it all. The Hansard people, as you know, perform the Herculean and hair-raising task of recording each and every syllable uttered in the various houses. These screeds are then published for the historical record. When things get as hot and bothered as they have in the past few days (what with the unseemly stampede of Labour Party members to become 'brown Nats'), the verbatim transcripts need very little improvement. But a bit of background.

It was Monday in the Chamber of Parliament. The Abolition of Racially Based Land Measures Bill was being debated. Many coloured MPs – the numbers kept changing – were making their first appearance as 'brown Nats', and seating arrangements had not yet been altered to allow for them to sit with the white Nats. There were Nats all over the show, as Dave Dalling, DP chief whip, pointed out. 'Mr Speaker,' he said, 'I must admit that I

125

feel the atmosphere in this chamber today is just a little claustrophobic.' Then he launched into what sounded like a passable cover version of the old Steeler's Wheel hit 'Stuck in the Middle with You'.

'I have Nats to the right of me,' he sang, 'Nats to the left of me, Nats to the front of me, Nats behind me, New Nats, Old Nats, Coloured Nats . . . '

The DP had clearly decided that with every Tom, Dick and Hennie wanting to join the Nats, mockery was the best policy. In fact, the trouble had been started earlier by Jannie Momberg (DP Simon's Town), who had asked in the House Of Assembly 'whether it is permissible that Honourable Members of the same party do not sit on the same side of the house?' The Chairman said this could be sorted out later by the Speaker, but by then Tom Langley (CP Soutpansberg) decided that he really, *really* wanted to see the multi-coloured Nats sitting together and he wanted to see it now.

'May I suggest,' he asked the Chairman unctuously, 'that you adjourn these proceedings and seek the opinion of the Speaker? We are busy with serious matters here. In this house deliberations take place according to order and defined procedures.' The Chairman was not impressed.

Then, with emotions running dangerously high, things careered off the subject entirely. 'Honourable members are not allowed to sleep in here either,' yelled an honourable member. Now if there is one thing Tom Langley hates, it is being accused of sleeping in the house. The reason his eyes are closed for long periods, say his colleagues, is that he concentrates better that way. The accusation sent him off the deep end.

'I will begin to talk about people whose hands are dripping with blood,' he growled viciously in the direction of the interjector. 'If they want to talk about such things (his allegedly soporific approach to debates) we can talk about adulterers, people that shoot other people dead, and of wife beaters and all that sort of thing.' The brown Nats were all but forgotten in the storm of white acrimony

126

this occasioned. The Chairman battled gamely for order. 'Was the honourable member referring to members of this House?' 'I didn't name names,' said Mr Langley. 'I said we can talk about it if they want to talk about it. I am not scared. I am not scared.'

'You are a coward,' bellowed the NP's JJ Vilonel. 'Mr Chairman,' said Mr Langley 'that drink-befuddled honourable member wants to call me a coward.' 'Who called him a coward?' asked the beleaguered Chairman. 'I did,' yelled Mr Vilonel, 'and I repeat it – he's a big coward.' Mr Vilonel had to withdraw the remark that Mr Langley was a big coward. Mr Langley had to withdraw the remark that Mr Vilonel was a big drunkard. And so things went on.

Need some light bedtime reading? I'm prepared to loan out my Hansards. At a price.

THE STAR, 30 MAY 1991

MEAN-SPIRITED CONVERTS

The legislative cornerstones of apartheid were being rapidly bulldozed in parliament, but without apology from the politicians whose party put them there in the first place.

IT'S NICE TO SEE AN OLD JOKE HAVE ITS DAY, AFTER YEARS of faithful service. Back in the mists of time, when Nelson Mandela was still the world's most famous prisoner and his wife the unsullied mater of the nation, we used to quip that the only time Winnie would visit Tuynhuys would be when she was measuring up the curtains.

This week she did indeed take tea in Tuynhuys, and had ample time (five and a half hours, to be exact) to cast a practised eye over the interior decorating of the pied-à-terre she could still come to occupy, Mr Justice Stegmann notwithstanding.

An encouraging aspect of the meeting between the ANC Women's League and the President, at least according to senior government chaps, was that Mr de Klerk's solicitousness and patience in dealing with the women's carefully-presented demands was such that they at the last minute called off an earlier plan to stage an embarrassing sit-in in his office. The older women in the delegation, I am told, prevailed upon the more militant youngsters to leave at the appointed time and via the appointed exit.

Would, though, that FW could have transmitted this generosity of spirit to the rest of his National Party. To me the single most extraordinary and distasteful thing about watching the legislative demolition of the pillars of apartheid, is the total absence of joy surrounding the occasion. The repealing taking place in parliament is a taciturn, mealy-mouthed and mean-spirited affair. The government cannot (with some honourable exceptions, like Deputy Minister of Foreign Affairs Leon Wessels) bring itself to say it is happy to have the opportunity of righting a wrong it has itself perpetrated for more than 40 years. At most, it speaks of its universally despised policies having turned out to be unworkable, or as failed experiments. In this case unbridled arrogance, rather than love, means never having to say you're sorry.

It is thus not surprising that neither the Labour Party nor the Democratic Party (never mind the ANC) can bring themselves to throw their hats in the air and shout hallelujah, and thank you for your courage. The jaw-jutting posture of what is today an unbearably smug National Party is just too offensive. It seems a tremendous pity. What could be an opportunity for an unprecedented surge of across-the-board optimism and reconciliation is being frittered away.

And if there is bad blood between the relatively like-minded sectors of the parliamentary system – at least they agree on the basic ideals for the new South Africa – the latest mood swing of the Conservative Party is downright frightening. From Wednesday onwards, the CP implemented a clear decision to flaunt one of the fundamental rules of parliament: that no member may call another member a traitor, or accuse them of treason. One by one, with calculated venom, CP speakers did just that. Dries Bruwer (Lydenburg), Cehill Pienaar (Heilbron) and Dries Oosthuizen (Smithfield) were the first to conclude their speeches on the repeal of the Land Act with direct accusations of treason.

Mr Pienaar said the CP would 'deal' in due course with the traitors of the Afrikaner nation. 'I regard you (Nats) as traitors,' said Casper Uys (CP Barberton) later. 'Blood is going to be spilled.' To this Louis Stofberg (CP Sasolburg) added with naked hatred: 'You are the ugliest traitors in South Africa's history.' More CP MPs followed, each of them in turn being 'named' by the Speaker – a form of censure not invoked for more than two decades and one which results in a five-day suspension from parliament.

It has been an unedifying spectacle. What we need is more tea-taking, not blood-talk.

SATURDAY STAR, 1 JUNE 1991

A HOLY AND UNHOLY PLACE

Robben Island, South Africa's Alcatraz and long-term home to the country's most famous political prisoners, was finally opened for scrutiny. Mandela's tiny cell breathed pathos.

THE ISLAND IS VERY FLAT. THE BOAT COMES UPON IT QUITE suddenly: there it is, through the fog and the towering swells of the Cape of Storms, an undistinguished stretch of green and brown which looks as if it might be submerged at any moment. There are no jagged cliffs, no impenetrable jungles, just waves washing kelp prettily up against the shoreline. This island is a legend not because of the doings of nature, but of man.

I went to Robben Island this week. I found there a place of some wildness and beauty. But most of all, I felt the haunting mystery of history. What a curious life this isolated oval slab of our land has led.

It has always been assumed by those in power to be a natural repository for South African outcasts of one kind or another. Van Riebeeck banished his troublesome Khoi interpreter 'Harry' there in 1658. Political prisoners have followed ever since. The Prince of Madura, a Muslim holy man, died on Robben Island in 1754. The Xhosa prophet Makana was ferried to non-existence across

Table Bay in the 1800s. And there were lepers and luna-
tics too, through the centuries.

This hard history culminated in the 1960s, when the
men who are now negotiating South Africa's future with
a man much younger than they, President de Klerk, were
banished to the island's maximum security prison for life.
Their presence there has ensured that Robben Island will
be a myth to conjure with for generations. It was the
innards of this South African secret that I had really come
to see.

The sprawling stone monolith of the prison is empty,
the last eight political prisoners having been transferred
to the mainland little more than a week ago. The ghosts
are fresh. In some communal cells, tattered posters are
still secreted behind locker doors, and Bibles (carefully
inscribed: 'BJ Bogale', 'RB Mpondo', 'M Nyandeni') have
been left behind in the rush. In the courtyards there are
sculptures, lovingly painted by the prisoners. The main
door is of steel, big and heavy. It shuts with the expected
terrifying, echoing clang. The corridors, labyrinthine, are
clean and insipid, the glossy paint of institutions the world
over reflecting the harsh light of bare bulbs.

There is an office for 'Records' and one for the 'Cen-
sor'. The outer walls are thick – 45cm – and the window
bars so sturdy that an adult's hand cannot easily close
around them. In short, it is an old prison, like other
old prisons. Except, as I say, for who has been inside
it.

Nelson Mandela's cell, in 'Section B', is three paces wide
and two-and-a-half paces long; a small space in which to
spend nearly two decades. It has a wooden door on the
outside, and a barred steel door inside. Its walls are cream
and there is a small pine bookshelf above a steel bed. A
high window looks on to a gigantic wall; if you stretch
up on your toes you can see the exercise yard between.
There is nothing in the cell to commemorate its occupant.
A warder who knew him says he never hung things on the
wall anyway, he just had some books around.

There are pigeons in the yard, and under an ersatz, home-made pergola, a bench for sitting and talking. Curiously, there is a chilli plant growing in the corner. Nearby, and offering a perversely spectacular and maddeningly enticing cross-water vista of the Cape peninsula, is the quarry in which Mandela and so many others broke rocks with pick-axes all those years ago. Only the gulls sing here now. The island is deeply affecting.

What will happen to this strange, holy and unholy place we have created? Visiting the prison felt like putting a hand into an open wound. As far as nature conservation and historical preservation are concerned, the government is doing admirable work. But surely it cannot decide alone on what to do with the prison. Just as much as Afrikanerdom has the right to decide what happens to, say, the sites of the Boer War's concentration camps, so the island jail's victims must choose its fate.

SATURDAY STAR, 8 JUNE 1991

THE INTERREGNUM

The transition to democracy moved forward apace, but proved to be a slower and more tortuous business than anyone had expected. South Africans found themselves betwixt and between.

THE OLD IS DYING, THE NEW HAS YET TO BE BORN. To what do we cling in the meantime? If ever the difficulties and dangers of South Africa's unique transition period – in which the old regime is still in control although the pretenders to power are visible – have been on display, that time is now.

One of the final tasks of this parliament is to vote on the Interim Measures for Local Government Bill. As has been the pattern throughout the year, the measure will be supported by all parliamentary parties save the Conservatives, and it will be viewed with deep suspicion by those, such as the ANC, who are still on the outside looking in. It will become law, because what the National Party says still goes. But will it serve the country? The ANC and its political soulmates believe the Bill is preempting the national negotiation process by attempting to establish a system unilaterally. The government, for its part, argues that the Bill is merely a legislative facilitator:

it will allow representative structures to evolve through negotiation. The alternative is stasis, so the reasoning runs – better this than nothing.

The arguments and details are complicated, but the underlying problem is not. The real reason for the foundering of efforts to get local co-operation off the ground is that there is a lamentable, overall lack of trust and goodwill between the two principal political actors. None of the disagreements is insoluble – but neither side accepts the other's bona fides. It seemed, for a brief moment after February 2 1990, that the government and the ANC were going to pull together to overcome this sort of difficulty; but what little trust there was has eroded alarmingly.

In local government, as in all areas of South African life, there is no substitute for *saamwerk*. If it is not forthcoming, the best we can hope for is to shuffle forward, snarling and spitting at each other along the way.

THE STAR, 17 JUNE 1991

CONTAINERS BOUND FOR
THE NORTH

*The end of the parliamentary session was followed by the annual
political trek from Cape Town back to Pretoria. Legislators
knew parliament would never be the same again.*

THE SIGHT OF ROW UPON ROW OF CONTAINER TRUCKS
parked on the cobbles of Parliament Street yesterday
signalled the start of the annual Great Trek away from
the Cape of South Africa's legislators. It is one of the
traditions – like the wearing of hats in the house for the
last sitting – which has, over the years, marked the end of
another parliamentary sitting and the beginning of another
long recess. But this was not just another session, and this
will not be just another recess.

The closure of parliament shortly before midday yesterday brought to an end an era of South African politics.

Never again will parliament in this form be the focal
point of the nation's politics. To be sure, everyone will
be back again next year – but it will be in the role
of managers, not policymakers. As far as this parliament is concerned, it has done what it needs to do –
it has cut the Gordian Knot of legislated apartheid –
and in the business of fashioning a new constitution, its

136

members will be participants rather than overseers.

The legislative backbone of social apartheid has been broken in parliament. Political apartheid will be dead only when the first black voter places a ballot paper in the box.

SATURDAY STAR, 22 JUNE 1991

THE EDITOR, THE MINISTER, AND THE COMMUNIST

An ethos of press freedom had struggled to survive under successive National Party governments. Now there were worrying signs that it might come under threat in future, too.

HERE IS THE STORY OF A SMALL SOUTH AFRICAN TRAGEDY. It happened the other day in Cape Town. Its principal characters were a cabinet minister called Adriaan, a communist called Tony, and an editor called Guy. Let me tell you something about the editor.

His full name is Guy Berger. He was a one-time lecturer at Rhodes University who was sent to prison in the 1980s for 'furthering the aims of the ANC' (remember that crime?), and who went into exile in England after he came out of Pretoria Central. This year, at last, he could come home and – better still for him – there was an opportunity to put his considerable journalistic skills to use. The Cape-based left wing journal *New Era* needed an editor, and he was appointed. But Guy had gone to jail for his political principles, and he also held some pretty strong journalistic ones. He had withdrawn from party politics and wanted a magazine that pulled no punches, that wasn't afraid to probe even those groups it sympathized with and, most of all, that was zesty enough to make people buy it out of interest, not duty.

His first issue was a big hit. It carried a tough and very knowledgeable interview with Chris Hani, which most other publications had to follow up. Fired by this success, the editor began planning his second edition. He came up with a fascinating idea: why not carry an interview with minister Adriaan Vlok, with a difference? The interviewer would be Tony Holliday, ANC and SACP member, former long-term security prisoner and exile. The two men had last met when the minister visited the communist in his cell in 1982. After much to-ing and fro-ing, the minister agreed, and the interview took place. The editor typed it up and gave it to his colleagues at the magazine. Then the tragedy began to unfold. They refused to allow it to be published, because they thought the minister came out of it 'too well'.

The editor argued that that was journalism: you take your chances, and let the readers decide. They said no, and as a collective had the power to enforce their decision. This was direct democracy in action. The editor said they couldn't do that; he'd be forced to resign. 'I was told that the idea I had of an editor was a Western concept,' says Guy. 'I felt like saying: Did you see those eastern European editors? I had to step down.' The second edition came out, with no minister being interviewed by a communist. The editor is an ex-editor.

The moral of the tale is, of course, that in the matter of press freedom, many among the government's left wing political opponents appear to have a lot in common with the unlamented Stoffel Botha. And if that isn't an awful irony, I don't know what is.

SATURDAY STAR, 29 JUNE 1991

ONE *AMANDLA* PER SPEAKER, PLEASE

The ANC marked its re-entry into formal politics with a high-profile national conference in Durban. The former underground liberation movement indicated it was ready for the switch.

A POLITICAL MEETING AS IMPORTANT AS, SAY, THE SAND River Convention got going in the sultry surrounds of Durban yesterday. It differed from said Convention in style – for starters, most of its participants were black – but it will come to occupy no shorter a chapter in the country's history books. Passers-by (and there were many on the University of Durban-Westville's campus as the ANC's historic National Conference began) stopped dead as they walked past the cavernous sports hall.

From without they could hear, quite clearly, Nelson Mandela's voice echoing eerily over the fields and beyond. Disembodied thus, it sounded strangely celestial. 'During the few days ahead of us we will have to take very important decisions,' he boomed. 'Decisions which may very well decide the fate of this country for many years to come.' Portentous words, but not under the circumstances an undue exaggeration.

The scene inside the hall was enough to induce instantaneous cardiac arrest in any crypto-securocrat. It was probably the best-organized subversive gathering ever held in this country. Phalanxes of delegates from all over South Africa (2,000 of them) sat in military orderliness, beneath 22 propaganda banners large enough to make Jonas Savimbi envious. The delegates did not shuffle, though it was hot. They did not smoke, though the speeches were long. They at least were convinced that they were there to decide the future of the country.

The conference was an altogether more businesslike affair than last December's preliminary, consultative gathering. Sloganeering was kept to a minimum (one, or at most two, *Amandlas* per speaker), as were delays. There were all sorts there: different colours, different ages, different sexes. Urbane Westernized intellectuals squashed up against farmhand populists – the former listening to the speeches in English, the latter using headphones for translations. Chairman Walter Sisulu, in the manner of an experienced continuity announcer, informed the faithful that Sesotho could be located on channel 1, Zulu on channel 2, Xhosa on channel 3, and Afrikaans on channel 4 – the last for the benefit of 'the Western Cape delegation'.

The delegates faced a punishing week, long and weighty. The first day's performance suggested they were up to it.

THE STAR, 3 JULY 1991

THESE GUYS ARE SERIOUS

Those who believed the once-impregnable government now faced oblivion underestimated the tenacity of the party that ruled South Africa for decades. The NP had plenty of fight left.

SOMETHING OF A CONSENSUS APPEARS TO HAVE EMERGED among non-governmental political pundits that the National Party's constitutional lego set – its recently unveiled model version of the new South Africa designed by Dr Gerrit Viljoen – is somehow not to be taken seriously, even by the Nats themselves. The general idea is that the NP mandarins are concealing a completely different vision by first offering up a complicated and absurd red herring. Experts reason that the plan was for internal NP consumption – and we all know that the NP faithful has consumed plans before, only to have them radically reinterpreted by the leaders.

In addition there is in ANC circles (very senior circles, I might add) an abstruse theory which holds that FW failed to persuade his colleagues to go with a plan closer to standard majority rule, and therefore agreed to forward this one in the knowledge that it would be blown out of the water . . . thus allowing his original plan to make a comeback.

I am thoroughly unconvinced by these lines of reasoning. I believe the NP's opponents are doing themselves a dangerous disservice by not taking the Viljoen proposition seriously, and by not accepting that this – give or take some fat – is actually what the NP wants, and what it will fight for, very hard. The detailed merits and demerits of the NP proposals are not the issue here. It is one thing to be convinced that the overriding NP objective is to retain levels of white political power out of kilter with white electoral power – this seems to me an entirely plausible conclusion to draw – but it is entirely another to say the NP has no right to pursue such an aim, and to conclude therefore that they expect to give it up at some point.

The NP does not accept as gospel that sooner or later this country will have to conform with models, like standard majority rule, which have enjoyed currency elsewhere. When the NP says it is not in the business of transferring power, but intends rather to strike a unique power-sharing deal, this is precisely what it means. And ominously, it has let it be known that it has the 'capacity to block' anything which strays too far from such an outcome.

All of this is to say, simply, that those who view the NP proposals as odious or ridiculous, and believe therefore that their collapse is immutable, are in my view underestimating the party which has ruled this country with an iron hand for many of our lifetimes. The NP's war plan is to give some ground in constitutional negotiations, but certainly not to vacate the battlefield.

Proponents of classical majority rule will also, in their battle of wills with the NP, have to contend with the fact that ANC leaders themselves have in the past not always been averse to 'uniquely South African' compromises. Consider this courtroom testimony:

'The government might say, "Gentlemen, we cannot have this state of affairs – laws being defied, and this whole situation created by stay-at-homes. Let's talk." In my own view I would say yes, let's talk. And the government would say: "We think that the Europeans at present are not ready for the type of government where there might be domination by non-Europeans. We think we should give you 60 seats . . . we will leave the matter over for five years and then review it."

'We would then say: "We will suspend civil disobedience, and we will then devote the intervening period for the purpose of educating the country, the Europeans, to see that these changes can be brought about, and would bring about better racial understanding." Then at the end of the five year period we will have discussions and, if the government says "We will give you again 40 more seats", I might say "That is quite sufficient. Let's accept it", and still demand that the franchize should be extended, but for the agreed period we should suspend civil disobedience.'

'That is the view I hold.'

The words were spoken, in the treason trial of 1960, by Nelson Mandela.

SATURDAY STAR, 14 SEPTEMBER 1991

A REVOLUTION, DID YOU SAY?

The writing was well and truly on the wall: white rule was coming to an end. But there was a curious lack of interest among many whites, particularly young English-speakers.

THERE IS SOMETHING EERIE ABOUT WHITE SOUTH AFRICA today. You don't need to be a visitor from Mars to feel this. We are living through the early-to-middling stages of a full-blooded revolution – political, social and economic – and most people are acting just as they always have, as if nothing was different.

To be sure, our revolution has been less dramatic, visually and viscerally, than those of, say, the Romanians or the Russians. It is among other things more controlled and more complicated. The old regime is not teetering and discredited – rather, it is fighting hard to become the new regime. There are not permanent barricades in the streets. And there are not vigils, hundreds of thousands strong, outside the Union Buildings every night. Still, its profundity is equal to the experience of eastern Europe, and that makes the national quietude all the more astonishing.

A western European businessman visited our country last week. He is an intelligent, sensitive man, but otherwise unexceptional – he could be taken for a middle-class South

African professional, save for his accent. His business here took him to innumerable northern suburbs dinner parties and springtime *braais* around the pool. The experience shocked him to the core. The conversations, he said, could have been taking place in Paris or London, Munich or Madrid.

Besides the occasional wry or bitter joke about Mandela and the ANC, there was little to suggest that his hosts were living on the southern tip of Africa, at a climactic moment in its history. Money, cars, gadgets, property, skiing holidays, islands . . . the focal points of the Nineties were intact, almost entirely independent of the nuance of the setting. If these people were thinking about the fact that the country in which they had grown up was soon to change beyond recognition, he said, they disguised the fact. Where he came from, discussions raged through the night and into the morning about the meaning of developments in eastern European countries, far away from where they lived.

The people he met here acted as if they too were at a great remove, but were markedly less interested. He could only shake his head in incomprehension. Was the businessman missing a point? Were his hosts presenting a facade to disguise fear? Probably not. More likely, it was genuine ignorance and complacency. And that is fearful.

SATURDAY STAR, 5 OCTOBER 1991

WAIVING THE WHITE FLAG

The simmering tensions within the white community had hovered below boiling point for months. It took abstract issues - like the country's flag - to bring them out into the open.

FLAGS CAN BRING OUT THE BEST, AND THE WORST, IN people. White South Africa is demonstrating the latter truth. The hysterical and ugly backlash against the use of neutral, temporary symbols for our re-entry into world sport does not only threaten to poison a monumental moment for which we have been waiting decades. It also sends a message of limpid clarity to black South Africans: most whites, far from being changed people, are not close to considering real change – even in the realms of symbolism. If there is acknowledgement that we are in the middle of a period of fundamental transition, it exists only at the level of abstruse theory: heaven help anyone who takes it literally.

Dr Treurnicht aside, politicians who should know better have behaved shamefully on the question of Olympic iconography. Minister Louis Pienaar, at his most churlish, says the introduction of temporary symbols is a slap in the face for the majority of South Africans. His definition of 'South African', in this construction, is presumably

Verwoerdian. Either that or his arithmetical skills are lamentable.

President FW de Klerk, who deserves so much of the credit for the process leading to our reconciliation with the outside world, turns joy to rancour with the palpably ludicrous claim that the ANC has hijacked the Olympic return. Then he compounds the error with the contention that the Springbok emblem has 'nothing to do with apartheid'. Those of us who were around at the time of John Vorster and Basil D'Oliviera may be excused for gasping loudly at this statement: there is certainly an argument for letting bygones be bygones, but you cannot simply deny what has gone by.

The National Olympic Committee of South Africa has in fact acted with sensitivity. It should be hailed for demonstrating to other groups that with goodwill, progress can be achieved during the transition process, without hurting anyone's feelings and without prejudging issues which need to be resolved jointly, when the time is right. There is no suggestion that the rather lacklustre flag Nocsa has produced, and the rather overused anthem it has borrowed, are intended to become a permanent part of South African life. Nocsa has simply realized that it would be equally divisive at this stage to utilise the old, or to impose the new.

To listen to the government's ill-considered outbursts, one might imagine that Nocsa had proposed the ANC colours – with crossed Kalashnikovs – as the flag, and *Viva Umkhonto* as the anthem. The government is right to the extent that it says no-one can unilaterally devise symbols for the nation. It is regrettable – and sadly characteristic – that it should fail to apply this sensible dictum to itself.

I would guess that South African cricket fans of all pigmentations will forget, within about 10 minutes, about the colours Clive Rice and his men are wearing in Calcutta tomorrow when they take the field. They will be much more concerned about the taking of Indian wickets. A salutary lesson of the VAT strike was the fact that consultation is essential in the new South Africa. I still believe that the moving force behind that strike was not the minutiae of the tax system, but the feeling of angry humiliation at having had it unilaterally imposed. And I would be prepared to place a modest bet on the prediction that, if the matter can be discussed in a calm, friendly and egalitarian fashion, black leaders might well agree that the Springbok emblem should be retained as the symbol of sporting excellence in South Africa.

This hope is threatened by the vituperation of the past few days. A Ukrainian proverb has it that 'when the flag is unfurled, all reason is in the trumpet.' I hope minister Pik Botha heard it on his recent travels in that area.

SATURDAY STAR, 9 NOVEMBER 1991

CROCODILE TALES

The erstwhile strongman president, PW Botha, had gone into self-imposed internal exile. Now a frisson of excitement swept the country as he hinted he might soon publish his memoirs.

IT'S BEEN DIFFICULT, OH SO DIFFICULT, TO CONCENTRATE ON serious political matters this week. The reason of course is that the *Groot Krokodil*, who had been hibernating away quietly on the seashore for months, has started slithering around again, swiping passers-by with that tail. Worse still, he is threatening to tell tales.

PW Botha is, after a fashion, our equivalent of Princess Di. He doesn't really mean a lot any more, but if he so much as burps over his coffee and rusks in the morning, this is news. We'd had enough of him by the time he was shafted; now we can't get enough of him. Confirmation that the old croc is supervising the writing of his memoirs has sent interest-levels off the scale; potential publishers are rubbing their hands in expectation of merchandise which could dislodge Wilbur Smith and Jackie Collins from the bestseller lists. (On the subject of the forthcoming crocodile tales, it is to be hoped that biographer Dr Daan Prinsloo will record for posterity one of PW's unique contributions to world politics: the invention of the political-scandal-per-fax. South Africans will never forget PW's resignation speech, which went something like this: *'FW de Klerk het my gefaks, en ek het hom terruggefaks'* – FW de Klerk faxed me, and I faxed him back.) He was at it again this week. FW faxed him on Tuesday, he said, with the clear implication that he was gonna fax him right back all over again.

But there are in fact more important things on the go in the Republic today than these reptilian roisterings. There is, for instance, the imminence of round-table negotiations which will mark the belated beginning of real change. A measure of public confusion – not to mention boredom – has quite understandably set in on the subject of the all-party/multiparty/congress/conference, because the run-up to the darn thing has been so messy and protracted. As Churchill might have said, anyone who claims they know exactly what has been going on is clearly confused. But it is going to happen, as surely as night follows day.

It is likely to be called, for easy future reference, something like the Convention for a Democratic Future. But what will happen there? A certain early indication is that the round-table talks (I use the term figuratively; there might still be major debates about the shape and style of the furniture), will not have the benefit of a great deal of public participation unless we insist on it. In other words, what you and I think is not going to be high on the agenda. For this reason, if you have any suggestions you would be well advised to get them in quickly. I have a proposal for starters.

It seems blindingly obvious that the wave of political violence, and the deadly breakers of common crime accompanying it, cannot be contained under present circumstances. The situation is going to get worse. The police are still undermanned, and still viewed in the townships as the iron fist of the *boere*. Now we are told that one item on the all party talks agenda is the role of the international community in South Africa's transition. There are tremendous sensitivities – especially in the Union Buildings

151

– about letting meddling foreigners gain even a toe-hold in the sovereign state on the southern tip, but the fact remains that some *uitlanders* with money and goodwill would get involved if asked.

I propose the immediate dispatching to South Africa of a Commonwealth police force. This force, paid for by the Commonwealth's member states, would report to a special directorate set up by the multiparty conference. It would have specific responsibility for the monitoring of and enforcement of order at political gatherings, widely defined. This would leave the SAP free to throw all its resources into combating common crime, thereby altering its image – and the security situation – dramatically. The Commonwealth is appropriate because South Africans of all hues can identify 'friends' among its members. It is also interested in playing a role, as secretary-general Emeka Anyaoka made clear on his recent visit.

So how about it? And, I would like to know from the negotiators: if not, why not?

SATURDAY STAR, 23 NOVEMBER 1991

THE NP LOSES ITS VIRGINIA

White by-elections, an anachronistic hangover from the old system, gave the right wing a chance to flex its muscles. The warning lights shone bright for De Klerk and his reformists.

IT WAS A WEEK OF ROMANCE AND RANCOUR IN NEW-SOUTH African politics. In other words, things were entirely normal. The National Party, reluctantly and after many years of defending it, prepared to lose its Virginia. The moment approached not without a struggle, but psychoanalytical opinion concurred that the trauma would not cause a change of behaviour in the blushing, politically deflowered ones.

Far away from this all-white clinch, the venue was being prepared for political intercourse which would have had the architects of the old Immorality Act swooning in horror. In a hotel near Jan Smuts airport (chosen to facilitate dramatic departures?) leaders of every hue gathered for the talks to end all talks (about talks). This time around, as opposed to the last national convention in 1908, the blacks in the conference room were not there just to serve the tea.

Precisely because of this, many white people whose ancestors had participated in 1908 declined to attend in

153

1991. National conventions, in their view, had deteriorated markedly in the intervening years.

The build-up was spiced-up by a furious tiff between a recently engaged couple called PAC and ANC. ANC had been cheating on PAC, the aggrieved party fumed – and with a deadly rival (called NP) at that. The engagement was not summarily called off, but several soothing candle-lit dinners were called for.

Meanwhile, in the thriving metropolis of Phuthaditjhaba, the strangest relationship was blossoming. AWB supremo Eugene Terreblanche joined hands (*skande!*) with Chief Minister TK Mopeli of QwaQwa, and the two emerged from their soiree to say they had found 'considerable common ground'. This was a most astonishing statement, leading to immediate speculation that the problem of where to put the *boerestaat* had finally been resolved – although it was not quite clear as to what was in it for the QwaQwanites. 'QwaOuTransvaal' did have a certain ring to it, though.

The onset of real, as opposed to play-play, negotiating politics this week has brought many chickens home to roost, turned some worms and let several cats out of various bags. Now that the real thing is getting under way, people are having to get real. The time for being more-radical-than-thou (on all sides of the political spectrum) is rapidly passing, and soon there will be those who are on the negotiating train, and those who are left at the station. This explains some of the contortions through which, for example, the PAC and the Conservative Party are going. In terms of multiparty negotiations the PAC is on the inside looking out, and the CP is on the outside looking in. There are powerful factions in both parties which would like to see the situation reversed: left-wingers in the PAC who want the organization to pull out, and '*verligtes*' in the CP who want the party to pull in.

The internal power struggles are now under way in earnest, and will continue for a long time. This could lead, in the new year, to factions peeling off from both the

CP and the PAC. They will pass each other, one lot heading in and the other out, in the corridors of the conference centre. This is a good development, and it is of course not confined to the PAC and the CP. All parties face a year of tough decisions and compromises. Those who are not really serious about a negotiated settlement will watch from the wings, and those who stay inside will have to show stamina – and thick skins. The fact that the near-farcical series of dramas which preceded Friday's meeting (Mandela's pre-emptive announcement of the date, Inkatha's quibbling, De Klerk's *kragdadig* outbursts, the PAC's conspiracy theories) did not succeed in scuttling the whole thing is an indication that the fragile negotiations process might be developing some useful callouses.

SATURDAY STAR, 30 NOVEMBER 1991

THE ODDEST LOCALE

*Formal constitutional talks were about to begin - and a location
had to be chosen for South Africa's latter-day national convention. The venue selected was unorthodox.*

DO YOU REMEMBER PRESIDENT DE KLERK ANNOUNCING
the unbanning of political organizations at the very moment that unknowing protesters prepared to march on
parliament to demand . . . the unbanning of political
organizations? Nelson Mandela being late for his own
release? We're a crazy people, and this makes for crazy
political events. The Convention for a Democratic South
Africa seems set to top them all.

The venue for this monumental occasion is an anything-
but-monumental building within ear-plugging distance of
Jan Smuts airport; a building that looks from the outside
like a Rainbow Chickens hatchery, and from the inside
like a low-budget version of the Sun City foyer. It is a
World Trade Centre that has seen precious little world
trade, and this is its big moment.

With 24 hours to go before the start of Codesa, the
scenes inside the World Trade Centre are extraordinary. In
the murky half-light one is confronted by figures teeming
and shuffling around in amiable confusion. Many of those

156

one bumps into are recognizable (Ah, Dr Viljoen, Mr Ramaphosa, Mr Rajbansi) and many are not, although they speak importantly into two-way radios. The aural backdrop is an interesting mixture of hammering, vacuuming, furniture-shifting and mumbled 'leaking' from political figures to hovering journalists. A large South African flag, memento of some less momentous occasion, is being bundled into a storeroom.

Behind a pair of wooden doors which look surprisingly like the entrance to a lavatory, the steering committee under the chairmanship of Dr Zach de Beer is meeting. He is patient with those who enter by accident, with other business on their minds.

The focal point in the cavernous complex is a gigantic debating pit, ringed by a viewing platform. It is rather like an ersatz Superbowl, red-and-blue checked carpeting, ghastly chandeliers and all. This is where the delegates will sit and make up their minds about the kind of country we should live in.

Off to one side, glass-fronted offices have been (and in some cases are still being) constructed for each of the 20 12-person delegations and their helpers. To find them, one must negotiate one's way through several fashion boutiques, unaccountably still operating. A shop manageress is bemused when asked for a list of her delegates to Codesa, but politely refers all inquiries to the office of Intando yeSizwe, cunningly concealed amongst the lingerie. Nearby, a man with a computer is sitting in a shop window, surrounded by summer fashions, typing up a political press statement. The offices in between the boutiques have been fitted with thick black linen curtains, producing an effect not unlike that of Von Wielligh Street escort agencies. The other offices, for administrators, are not so coy, and the passing observer can peer through the glass to watch Codesa Security, Codesa Administration and Codesa Travel at work.

The big boys – the National Party and the ANC – have roomy accommodation, complete with sofas and, in the

NP's case, an ethnic sculpture. The Dikwankwetla and Solidarity Parties are not so fortunate, being stuck at the end of a very long corridor in rather less salubrious surrounds. Delegates' aides have entered into the spirit of the times: a zealous Ximoko Progressive Party devotee has stuck a hand-drawn sign on his office window. *'Hi komba ndlela'*, it reads, 'we show the way'. And the XPP helpers are as good as their word, showing the way smilingly to the nearby Inkatha Freedom Party office. The IFP office sports on its door a large poster of Chief Mangosuthu Buthelezi. Above the leader's portrait is a slogan: 'Come share the feeling'. Below it is another: 'Come feel the thunder'. The door is closed, leading the casual visitor to eschew both invitations.

The South African Communist Party is situated surprisingly close to the Ciskei government (*'Ag*, but this is what *toenadering* is all about,' says a friendly SACP staffer) and the Transkei government is even closer. The mood is benign, however, with no signs of an immediate resumption of Kei-versus-Kei hostilities. In the canteen – which, as a colleague points out, is a foretaste of the dining hall of the new South Africa's parliament – nationalists, democrats, communists and exponents of most imaginable political 'isms' queue for appropriately unremarkable food. The juke-box and pinball machine in the corner are in constant use. The choice of music available is highly appropriate: among the songs on offer are 'Everybody wants to rule the world', 'Many rivers to cross', 'Change', and 'I still haven't found what I'm looking for'. 'With or without you', another option, seems as appropriate a ballad for the PAC as could be asked for, and 'Don't stand so close to me' says a lot about current feelings between the ANC and IFP.

Murphy Morobe, the amiable and able man in charge of arrangements for Codesa, is unruffled. It will be ready by Friday, he says, and he will get a bit more sleep thereafter. He surveys the bizarre hive of activity with some pride and fondness. The World Trade Centre, Kempton Park, is surely among the oddest locales ever chosen for a nation's date with its destiny. But it has its place in the history books now, and no-one can take it away.

THE STAR, 19 DECEMBER 1991

A FIGHT THEY HAD TO HAVE

In a heart-stopping moment at the end of the first crucial round of talks, Nelson Mandela savaged FW de Klerk in public for the first time. The peace process survived the catharsis.

NO-ONE WHO SAT IN THE CHAMBER OF THE WORLD TRADE Centre on Friday evening, transfixed by the sight of a black leader speaking to a white leader as a South African head of state has never been spoken to before, will forget that half hour. When the confrontation between Nelson Mandela and FW de Klerk was over, delegates, dignitaries and journalists sat in silent stupefaction. It is little wonder that they did so. Now that the shock has passed, the realization is dawning that what we were watching was the baring of South Africa's – our own – tortured psyche. For every South African present, of whatever political stripe, the exchange was excruciatingly painful. We listeners were like children witnessing the first deadly, vicious argument between our parents. We had known for a long time that there were terrible tensions beneath the surface, of course, but we had never expected them to burst out in this way. And now that the nausea of our first reaction has lifted, and we discover that our home is going to survive the trauma after all, we are beginning to feel the benefits of catharsis.

Septuagenarian Nelson Mandela's verbal savaging of the younger FW de Klerk was a product of something much deeper than a disagreement over the status of Umkhonto we Sizwe and the Pretoria Minute. It was a warning from black South Africa to white South Africa. It was a warning that will live with white South Africa, and influence its actions from here on. Friday, December 20 1991 – as opposed to February 2 1990 – marks the moment at which black South Africa came of age. It did so on its own terms.

President de Klerk made a fundamental error on December 20. He insulted Mr Mandela's dignity. Mr Mandela is in many ways an old-fashioned, traditional man. One treats Mr Mandela's dignity cavalierly at one's peril. Mr de Klerk used the crucial final speaking opportunity, granted to him magnanimously by the ANC leader, to hector and threaten the ANC in the tones of a headmaster admonishing an errant child. He did so in spite of the fact that other leaders – including the NP's own Dawie de Villiers – had intentionally adopted conciliatory stances in their Codesa speeches. Mr de Klerk did so in the knowledge that Mr Mandela had, the very night before, overruled his own angry executive and agreed to sign the Codesa Declaration of Intent – because the president had convinced him that this was the honourable thing to do. He did so despite Mr Mandela's earlier assurance of flexibility on the question of MK. He did so in front of the entire world – and paid the price.

The issue on which he chose to 'discipline' Mr Mandela – and the fact that he expected to get away with it – showed just how shallow remains the understanding by white South Africa of black. The existence of MK is not primarily a military or security issue. It is a matter of pride – indeed dignity – above all else. Aside from isolated acts by ill-disciplined individuals (and these have occurred in the SAP and SADF as well), MK has not launched any attacks since the armed struggle was suspended. It can be argued that it was, in any event, ineffectual before that. MK's recent anniversary celebrations were a sign of how weak, rather than strong, the organization really is. No-one seriously believes that MK is capable of launching an armed insurrection.

But MK is, for much of black South Africa, the symbol of its own resistance to apartheid. No-one should underestimate the shame that still exists in the townships, a shame at having impotently succumbed to discrimination for so long. MK's existence, irrespective of its efficacy, makes many black people feel better about themselves. Mr de Klerk underestimated the power of this symbolism. He also underestimated the anger the ANC feels when government spokesmen declaim about the political process from a position of assumed superiority – as referee in a game in which they are merely players. This is why Mr Mandela snarled: 'De Klerk must forget (the idea) that he can impose conditions on the ANC . . . he doesn't represent us. He can't talk to us in that language.'

When Mr Mandela spoke the words 'I am gravely concerned about the behaviour of Mr de Klerk today', he was delivering his message about dignity. He was saying, in blunt effect: You are treating us like picannins, and I am going to have to hurt you in order to make you stop. He did hurt Mr de Klerk, badly. There were many present who found it distasteful, felt Mr Mandela had overstepped the bounds of acceptable political debate, that he became too personal in his attack, that it was too long, that it strayed into improper areas – like the NP's loss of support to the Conservatives. There is truth in each of these allegations, but not enough to overshadow the fundamental issue. Mr Mandela's anger was genuine, and his opponents will not forget it in a hurry. They will think twice before trying to pull a similar procedural trick. This was a growing pain of the new South Africa, it had to be gone through.

But once the error of judgment had been made – none of this would have happened had Mr de Klerk simply noted his concern about the MK issue and left it for another forum – how did the president fare? Under the circumstances, very well, and for this the whole nation

162

should be grateful. He took the harangue on the chin. He did not walk out. Although visibly upset, he had the strength to take the podium and defend himself. He wisely avoided a personalized counter-attack. He ended off with a ringing appeal for goodwill and solidarity in Codesa. He ensured that what could have been a humiliation – and that would serve only the right wing – ended up as a sharp disagreement between two strong-willed men. One shudders to think how PW Botha would have reacted under the circumstances.

And so in the end the painful, discomforting experience might actually help South Africans in their search for a fair compromise that will stick. The bottled-up grievances have come out; decades of apartheid could not be wiped from memory in the course of an historic parliamentary speech.

THE STAR, 23 DECEMBER 1991

THE DOOMED THREAD IN OUR HISTORY

As negotiations entered their second year, the historical parallels with an earlier period were irresistible. The shadow of Oom Paul Kruger fell over the country, a century on.

———————

SO MUCH HAPPENS IN 12 SHORT MONTHS IN SOUTH AFRICA these days that it becomes difficult to look forward or back for a context: the present is overwhelming, our faces are shoved up against it, noses squashed against the pane, visibility a matter of inches. This brief political hiatus at the beginning of a new year is thus a special opportunity to draw back from the window and look around to see where we're standing.

It is a place very different to any we have stood at before. There have been other new years that promised great change: change under Smuts, change under Malan, Verwoerd, Vorster, Botha. But the change under De Klerk is unique, because we do not know its limitations. A thread of history which has wound its way unbroken from 1652 to 1992 is soon to snap. White rule as we know it is to go. It is a concession, after centuries of experimentation, to the fact that this is an organism which cannot survive forever in Africa. Whatever the complexities – and they are manifold

– of the government's plans for the future, they are no longer aimed at making blacks disappear, politically.

The year also marks the end of an historical cycle, filled with pathos. A century ago, Paul Kruger was in the *Volksraad* in Pretoria. He faced a problem, a version of which is only now approaching resolution. The politically privileged group he represented was coming under pressure from disenfranchized citizens, and that pressure was growing too harsh to bear. His solution to the 'racial problem' (it was *Boers* versus Britons then, blacks weren't considered) was a revealing forerunner of the tricameral parliament and other debacles to which we have been subjected.

In his memoirs, Kruger wrote of the time: 'It was evident to me that some means must be found to give the *Uitlanders* a voice in the representation of the country. I believed that I had discovered this means by the institution of a Second *Volksraad*, and it was my own idea that to this body might be entrusted the discussion of all the questions which were mainly of interest to the new arrivals.

'In this manner I endeavoured to open the way to the new population for the legal representation and remedy of their grievances . . . This proposal met with lively opposition, as some members of the *Volksraad* were of the opinion that it gave too many rights to the *Uitlanders*. The *Uitlanders* (themselves) contended that the Second *Volksraad* was of no practical use.'

Change '*Uitlander*' to 'black', change 'Second *Volksraad*' to 'tricameral parliament', change 'questions mainly of interest to the new arrivals' to 'own affairs', and see how strong is the doomed thread in our history. It has been tried in every possible way, by men of intellect and determination, but it was hopeless from the time of Paul Kruger. As we stare into this present, we should remember, so no-one is tempted to try it again. We are witnessing the end of *Oom* Paul's impossible dream, one hundred years of solitude later.

SATURDAY STAR, 4 JANUARY 1992

WHEN THE ONLY TRANSPORT IS A TIGER

The right wing was steadily gaining ground among whites, threatening President de Klerk's authority to continue negotiations. It was clear a referendum would be called.

WHEN THE REFERENDUM COMES, AS IT SURELY WILL, WILL whites vote 'yes' for a transitional government? Will we thereby surrender voluntarily the grip on exclusive power we have enjoyed since the day we were born? Will we confound the lessons of history and all we know of human nature by making a rational, visionary decision, based on the principle of deferred, rather than immediate gratification?

I doubt we have ever been asked a more important question. What will we do when that momentous day is announced? Throughout 1990 and into 1991 I clung to the notion that as whites gradually got used to the implications of President de Klerk's Great Leap, they would warm to the morality of it. In other words, fear of the (black) unknown would begin to dissipate and people would start to say: Yes, this is the right thing to do. We will have to face many tough changes, but at the end of it we will be cleansed of guilt and rescued from our pariah status in the world. Now, in 1992, I accept that was hopelessly naive. The referendum will not be fought on any such rarefied moral level.

The whites I see around me, be they industrialists, professionals, or struggling blue collar workers, are sullen and angry about current and future change. You need not scratch the surface too vigorously to discover that they would just as soon rewind the tape of history to the days when the only thing they knew about the ANC was that it was banned, and the only thing they knew about Mandela was that he was in jail. The latest HSRC survey tends to confirm this: a meagre 15 percent of whites believe life will be better in the new South Africa. So: given the obvious fact that a 'yes' vote in the referendum – no matter how the question is phrased – is a vote for the right of Mr Mandela and others to take their places in the government of this country, why should we believe that whites will display such unselfishness?

Well, I believe the majority of whites will vote yes. They will do so not for altruistic reasons. When the count is finally made, we will have a result that stems not from conviction, but survivalism – a negative endorsement, if you will. What many seem not to realize is that President de Klerk will not be asking whites to applaud all he has wrought and cheer him on to the next stage. He is not so naive. What he will be telling them is that there is simply no alternative that stands the remotest chance of working. His case will be greatly strengthened by the fact that the white right wing, in both its civil and uncivil forms, will not have been able to come up with a plausible plan for replacing the process embodied in Codesa. The racist dogmatists are lost, anyway; the referendum will be decided by the largely apolitical mass of whites in the middle. These people will not be interested in ideology: they will ask themselves, on the balance of probabilities, which course of action is likely to do their lives the least damage. And they will elect to ride the tiger, because it is the only means of transportation available.

There are some other, related factors. The conservatives will be cleaned up in the campaign itself. By the end of it, the proponents of a 'yes' vote will constitute an irresistibly representative grouping, offset against the fragmented and fractious peripheries. Then there is the traditional respect (some might say slavishness) towards authority figures which still exists in Afrikaner society. President de Klerk is still, for the moment, the authority figure for the majority.

It is sad to think that this country's rebirth is likely to be endorsed in a selfish mood. But that is the best scenario I think we can hope for – that whites will do the right thing for the wrong reasons. When Pik Botha, the wily old survivor, was pressed earlier this year on why he believes whites will go with the government, he gave a very honest and incisive answer.

'I don't believe they have a death wish,' he said. And that says it all.

SATURDAY STAR, 15 FEBRUARY 1992

MAN'S MALIGNITY

The Conservative Party recorded another by-election victory, placing further pressure on the reforming Pretoria government to demonstrate it still carried the majority of whites.

SO THE PARTY THAT OFFERS ONLY WAR AND DRESSES UP THAT pathetic futility as a policy has won itself another seat in the House of Assembly; a house in which there will soon be nothing left to assemble for. To South Africans who did not enjoy the dubious privilege of voting, the white burghers of Potchefstroom have delivered their mean message. This was not the noblest moment in Potchefstroom's history. William Hazlitt's resigned conclusion, 'I believe in the theoretical benevolence and practical malignity of man', resounds far, far away, one and a half centuries later.

It is no longer a question of whether a majority of whites actively supports the process of just reform that is taking place. It is clear they do not. It is a question, rather, of whether the opposition can be translated into votes for a last-ditch halting of the process. I have argued before that upon this rock the right wing will surely falter. President de Klerk will not be asking in his referendum for enthusiastic endorsement, he will be presenting a proposition to which the alternative is truly too ghastly to contemplate. Potchefstroom is in this context a nasty, sad, futile cry in the wilderness. It will change little except to confirm for black South Africans the fact that whites will not change because they want to, but because they have to. What a wasteful pity.

But to understand that the Potchefstroom by-election does not presage a nationwide white uprising against reform, one need only visit the remote villages of the stark and beautiful southern Cape coast, whence this is being written. Potchefstroom has not set Gansbaai or Franskraal alight, there are no blackshirt vigils at midnight. Life goes on here. There is a comforting side to this apathy. These are hardy people, much closer to the elements than we in the cities. Their day-to-day lives are of far more interest to them than the intricacies of constitutions and transitional governments. If pressed they would not, to be sure, say they much like what is being negotiated in Johannesburg – but they will ride it out and survive, as before.

The cities and towns are the crucibles of the new South Africa, and therefore a different matter. Whereas the term 'Codesa' has as much practical relevance for the Overbergers as *nouvelle cuisine*, it is clearly beginning to have a negative resonance among the shaken white masses in the urban areas. Herein I believe lies a great danger, and one which should be addressed before it is too late.

The most obvious problem, to my mind, is the alien location of the political bazaar in which our future is being traded. Johannesburgers might not be all that enthusiastic about what is going on at Codesa, but at least they know it is happening somewhere comfortably close by. By contrast, there is a distinct feeling of unease in other metropolises. People in Cape Town, Durban, Bloemfontein and elsewhere describe the negotiations as taking place 'up there'. There are obvious budgetary advantages attached to utilizing an unprepossessing warehouse within jogging distance of Jan Smuts airport for our latter-day national convention, but it does nothing

170

to imbue South Africans with the feeling that Codesa belongs to and is a part of their lives.

Some observers have expressed concern that Codesa has already cost R3-million. Frugality is an estimable characteristic in the current economic environment, but the criticism is not realistic in this case. The homelands system – the undoing of which is but one task faced by Codesa – cost billions, as did Mossgas. If we have to spend on Codesa now, then spend we must. Codesa's working groups should continue to meet near Johannesburg, but the plenary sessions should be held in different towns and cities. Potchefstroom should also be considered – it is not too far gone.

In Gansbaai, however, Codesa can probably leave well enough alone.

SATURDAY STAR, 22 FEBRUARY 1992

THE NEWS, READ BY PRESIDENT TREURNICHT

The make-or-break white referendum was duly called, and intensive campaigning began. It was an opportunity to consider what might happen if President de Klerk lost.

****** BULLETIN – SAFRICA – EMERGENCY URGENT PRETORIA, REUTER – South African State President Andries Treurnicht today declared a national State of Emergency and curfew as the death toll in riots and clashes around the country rose to more than 1,000. Minister of Law and Order Moolman Mentz said white males under the age of 60 who failed to report for military service within the next 24 hours would be court-martialled.

In a statement read on South African television, President Treurnicht appealed for 'calm and courage'. He expressed condolences to the families of the many white soldiers and policemen who have died in the fighting. Major metropolitan centres, including Johannesburg, are still paralysed by a 100 per cent stayaway of black workers. All businesses are closed, and most whites have barricaded themselves in their homes in the suburbs.

Police and South African Defence Force (SADF) soldiers are fighting pitched battles on the outskirts of the cities with small groups of black protesters, some armed with AK-47 assault rifles and RPG rocket launchers. Large crowds have begun to gather at township sports grounds, but it is not clear whether they plan to march into the cities. There were reports of continuing desertions from the security forces because of the 'shoot to kill' orders. At least three Nyala riot control vehicles were abandoned on the Soweto highway.

Trading on the Johannesburg Stock Exchange was suspended 'until further notice', and the building was evacuated and sealed last night. Foreign banks and financial institutions announced the immediate cutting off of credit lines, and South African assets have been frozen in several countries. All border exit points in South Africa have been closed and there are chaotic scenes at Jan Smuts airport, with thousands of people attempting to board flights out of the country. All air traffic has been halted.

Foreign governments are meeting in crisis sessions to discuss the possibility of evacuating their nationals from South Africa. The United Nations security council is expected to announce its unanimous decision to impose 'mandatory sanctions . . . including the option of military steps' in New York later today. The whereabouts of former President FW de Klerk and his Cabinet is still unknown. An undisclosed number of politicians is under house arrest, while ANC leader Nelson Mandela, in hiding, earlier urged 'all patriots' to realize that there was no choice but to 'resist the illegitimate regime with their lives'. He called for 'massive' international retaliation, saying black South Africans were ready to make 'whatever sacrifices were required' to prevent a return to apartheid.

President Treurnicht was unable to get to his office in the Union Buildings this morning, as overnight explosions had destroyed major access roads. He read his statement from Defence Headquarters in Pretoria's Potgieter Street. Yesterday Inkatha Freedom Party leader Chief Mangosuthu Buthelezi rejected President Treurnicht's offer of a seat in a 'temporary government of national unity'. Other homeland

173

leaders have also turned down President Treurnicht's plea for urgent discussions.

Unconfirmed reports said the '*Ystergarde*' (Iron Guards) – the paramilitary wing of one of the government's coalition partners, the Afrikaner Weerstandsbeweging – were going on 'black-killing sprees' in the Transvaal. The South African cricket team is stranded in Barbados after the summary cancellation of their tour by West Indian cricket authorities. In terms of the Emergency regulations announced by President Treurnicht, all communications with the outside world will be severed at midday today, for an unspecified period.

Dr Treurnicht's right-wing coalition government precipitated the crisis with its announcement yesterday that negotiations at the Convention for a Democratic South Africa were to be cancelled with immediate effect. This followed incidents of racial violence in the wake of the shock 'no' result in the referendum last month, and the violence-marred white election which followed it. – Reuter/SAJ

Fanciful? Fantasy? Fallacy? Perhaps. But do you fancy taking that chance on Tuesday? A frightening number of whites seem to have very short memories. The matter is quite simple. Just two years ago, our country was staring total ruin, both moral and physical, right in the face. Miraculously, brave politicians have sought mutual salvation, however traumatic and imperfect that process has been and will be. Whites can undo this work, and then proceed to learn their lesson all over again. It will be much quicker and more painful this time around. Or they can vote 'yes', as if their lives depended on it.

SATURDAY STAR, 14 MARCH 1992

A PLEIN STREET TABLEAU

The referendum was won, resoundingly, by FW de Klerk and his allies, renewing his mandate to reach a settlement with Nelson Mandela, and dealing a crippling blow to the right wing.

PLEIN STREET, CAPE TOWN, WEDNESDAY, MARCH 18 1992, just after 2pm. There they were for an instant, in frozen tableau: all the elements of the great unfolding South African drama, all visible within one sweep of the eye. Journalists were in the HF Verwoerd Building of the parliamentary complex, struggling to keep up with and interpret the results of the referendum in which whites were in the process of voluntarily releasing their grip on exclusive power.

Suddenly, outside the windows of the auditorium, a great mass of black faces pressed up against the glass. They were chanting and singing about the power that was coming their way. The journalists looked for a moment like a crowd at a tennis match: their heads turned rhythmically from the final doings of the old South Africa on the right, to the debut performance of the new on the left. A line of policemen separated the two worlds, and the reporters occupied the nether space between.

President de Klerk said later on that jubilant, unforgettable day that the decision by the whites – more even than his historic initiative two years before – marked the birth of a totally new, unrecognizable South Africa. Addressing a few hundred people gathered in the gardens of Tuynhuys – many of them weeping through broad smiles – he made a speech that will find its place in history alongside other famous summations of a people's destiny. The acrimony and politicking of the referendum was forgotten in that short interlude beneath the architectural symbol of old white power. Mr de Klerk and his allies stood brimming with pride; pride that instead of having been whipped into immoral defeat, they were standing and staring their chosen future in the face.

But now the celebrations are winding down. And questions must be asked. There is no doubt posterity will record that white South Africa made a choice of astounding courage on Tuesday. But it was not, in the first instance, a choice in favour of those eager black faces at the window, waiting for the police to move aside and let them in. It is on this issue that the real war to change white hearts and minds is just beginning. I wonder, sadly, what would have happened if the referendum question had simply asked whether or not they wanted a non-racial government – in other words, if the alternative of a Conservative Party in power had not been part of the equation. As it played out, the referendum campaign assumed apocalyptic qualities, and eventually came down to a straight choice between De Klerk and Treurnicht. And in the event, Treurnicht proved unsaleable.

While many white South Africans know what they voted against, they are not so clear on what they voted for. The challenge facing Messrs de Klerk, Mandela, Buthelezi, de Beer and others is to convert the rejection of the white right into active support for the colour-blind future.

SATURDAY STAR, 21 MARCH 1992

TEARING DOWN THE STATUES

With a non-racial South Africa drawing ever closer, the question was asked as to what would happen to the country's place names - which reflected centuries of white power.

IT IS THE NEW SOUTH AFRICA, CIRCA 1995. STATE President Nelson Mandela is at DF Malan airport, awaiting the arrival of an important foreign dignitary. Mandela, together with members of his coalition cabinet, is planning to take the visitor on a whistle-stop tour of the country. On the itinerary are stopovers at the JG Strijdom airport, the Hendrik Verwoerd Dam, John Vorster Square, and PW Botha airport.

Does anything about this scenario strike you as odd? It should, because it would be so incongruous – despite the fact that it is normal right now, in 1992. One might well add that the VIP visiting the all-new non-racial South Africa will travel the Ben Schoeman Highway, pass the Andries Treurnicht Park in Vanderbijlpark, stop off at the Willem Cruywagen Hospital in Germiston . . . But now let's approach the matter from the opposite direction. Let's say our hypothetical VIP is met in 1995 by President

Mandela at John L Dube airport, stops over at the JT Jabavu and Yusuf Dadoo airports, visits the Albert Luthuli Dam, Moses Kotane Square . . . I don't think either of these descriptions will fit the reality.

The national nomenclature has to change, and is going to change. As regards scenario number one above, the sooner whites accept and prepare themselves for this, the better. But the more interesting question that arises is exactly how this change is going to take place – in a punitive or an amicable fashion. Post-colonial history is brimful of examples of the former (statues being torn down, road signs vandalized); after-liberation-satisfaction was as often as not expressed by replacing the names of the vanquished with those of the victors. In our case things will not be quite so clear-cut, to say the least, and I think there is reason to believe we can do it differently.

The ANC has established a committee, quaintly named the 'Commission on Museums, Monuments and Heraldry', to look into the national iconography. I think this is an extraordinary initiative. A way is being sought, pre-emptively, by which wrongs can be righted with sensitivity. I believe plans are being hatched now – and negotiated compromises will follow – whereby excluded black culture can be given its rightful symbols, and white culture can retain that which is most dear to it. This means we are unlikely to see mobs pulling down Paul Kruger's statue the night after the first elections.

All of this raises another matter: the capital. It seems the Pretoria-Cape Town arrangement is unlikely to survive. My considered prediction (which pains me, as a passionate devotee of the Mother City's charms), is that Cape Town had better start making plans to fill the gap which will be left by parliament. The new government won't be able to shell out the enormous sums required to move parliament seasonally, and Cape Town will be regarded as too far out of the way for the rest of the country. I believe Pretoria will remain the capital. And its name? Mametoria? Pretolodi? Who knows?

SATURDAY STAR, 28 March 1992

AN ALLIANCE IN EMBRYO

Change was so quick in South Africa that the previously unthinkable happened regularly. So it was that some black leaders petitioned the government to slow down on reform.

IN THESE TIMES, WE SOUTH AFRICANS SHOULD MAKE A point of pinching ourselves at least once a week. This would serve to remind us that the changes of the past two years have been so astonishing that we tend to accept the extraordinary as ordinary, the previously unthinkable as commonplace.

It would have been difficult to believe, as the 1980s drew to their bitter close, that within a few years we would be in a situation whereby the firmest brakes on political change were being applied by black leaders. And yet this is precisely where we find ourselves today. We have the unlikely triumvirate of Chief Buthelezi, President Mangope and Brigadier Gqozo travelling to Cape Town to petition President de Klerk on the subject of Codesa. The plea is not that the government should stop its stalling on interim rule – but that it should slow down the transition from apartheid to democracy. This beggars belief – black leaders in effect demanding that power remain for longer in white hands.

The objections of these leaders – and Chief Buthelezi is

much the most important of the three – cannot be ignored. They will inevitably impact on the speed of the transition; indeed, they have already impacted, and the heady predictions of interim government by mid-year are being modified and scaled down by the day. Expectations about Codesa 2 are being dampened accordingly. In his submission to President de Klerk, Chief Buthelezi makes many valid and serious proposals regarding power devolution, electoral law, bills of rights and the like. These are precisely the sorts of issues which must receive a proper hearing at Codesa. But many of these arguments are undercut, in my view, by the document's undercurrent: that whether they like it or not, the three homeland leaders come out looking as if they are scared of the voters.

There can surely no longer be any doubt in any South African's mind that interim government is not only an inevitability, but an urgent necessity. Without interim – or, as the government prefers it, transitional – rule, there can be no real constitutional, economic or social progress. We are burdened with a government-on-hold; in vital areas a lame duck by definition. Every day that South Africa remains stuck in its violent time warp costs us; it reduces the prospects for success at the other end.

Until there is representative power-sharing there will be no major injection of foreign funds. There will be no resolution of the violence so long as the security forces are seen as the white man's tool. Moreover, there is no moral justification for the continued exclusion from government of the vast majority of the population.

Why, then, are political actors like Buthelezi, Mangope and Gqozo applying the brakes? It is surely fair to ask whether they have not calculated that when the time comes, the electorate is likely to treat them badly. In the cases of Mangope and Gqozo, in particular, this is a real probability. Their support is wholly unproven. Mangope runs a 'democracy' in which opposition parties can't contest the presidential elections, and Gqozo's 'popular mandate' comes from the barrel of a gun. The logical tactic, therefore, is to exercise as much influence as possible from one's extant power base, before one's claims of support are put to the test.

I think we might be seeing, in embryonic form, a conservative alliance in the making. What is most surprising about it is that Chief Buthelezi (who unquestionably has a genuine following although its size is uncertain) should choose to identify himself so closely with the other two. There is an almost poignant paragraph in the document submitted to the state president: 'We appeal to Your Excellency and your government to make sure that in the (negotiating) process, you do not fall into the error of treating friends as enemies and enemies as friends.'

This is the language of petitioners, reminiscent of the earliest, least assertive days of African nationalism in South Africa. It is also hard to imagine that it is the kind of language which will appeal to the millions waiting impatiently to be enfranchised.

SATURDAY STAR, 9 MAY 1992

ON THE BRINK OF A BREAKLOCK

Negotiations were frustratingly complex and inconclusive, confusing an already bewildered public. There were plenty of opportunities for poking fun at the politicians.

IT MIGHT NOT HAVE COME UP WITH A NEW CONSTITUTION, but the infelicitously named Convention for a Democratic South Africa has at least made a major contribution to the world's political vocabulary. We have invented an entirely new concept: the breaklock. This is when a breakthrough and a deadlock occur simultaneously and repeatedly. Codesa is permanently on the brink of a breaklock.

You know what I'm talking about. You read the papers. Monday: Gloom hangs over Codesa. Tuesday: Breakthrough in working group three. Wednesday: Impasse in negotiations. Thursday: Light at end of talks tunnel. Friday: Who the hell knows?

I don't mean to be cynical about Codesa. As I never tire of arguing, it is a miraculous turnabout of South African events, a development every bit as historic for us as the meeting of the founding fathers was for the nascent United States. But by golly, it can be frustrating.

Earlier this week, attending the usual vigil at the World Trade Centre, I chanced upon ANC negotiator Albie

183

Sachs. 'How's it going, Albie?' I asked. He thought for a moment, and then replied: 'So slowly we haven't even reached a deadlock yet.' Now that's the kind of language we professional Codesa-watchers understand, being as we are at the end of our collective tethers. It's a constant battle to remind oneself that this Mad Hatter's tea party is as important as Life Itself. This week there was a barely resistible urge among those of us outside the committee rooms to simply barge in and impose solutions: 'You – Delport. You want decisions by a 75 percent majority?

'You – Ramaphosa. You want two-thirds?

'Right. Seventy percent it is, and you can all go home now.'

Alas, it is not so simple.

We have to jump through these interminable hoops because of the simple fact that these people represent deeply divergent interests. My plea to the public is for patience in the matter of Codesa. It may be a fairly unsightly repository of a new nation's hopes and dreams, but then we're no oil painting ourselves. It's all we've got, and it's quite astounding that it's got so far. The fact is we need Codesa more than Codesa needs us. If it fails, South Africa fails, in the eyes – and banking vaults – of the world. Sure one gets irritated by the seemingly never-ending rollercoaster ride for which we are paying. Sure one wants to scream when one hears of some fresh impasse in Sub-Committee One of Working Group Two regarding Paragraph Three of the Pretoria Minute.

But always remember that breaklocks are better than deadthroughs. Much more positive emphasis, you know.

SATURDAY STAR, 16 MAY 1992

THE SOUND OF SHREDDERS
SHREDDING

Only the dimmest South Africans could now doubt that pro-found change was unstoppable. Many beneficiaries of the apartheid system began to raid the larder before it was too late.

IF YOU STAND ON A STREET CORNER IN PRETORIA LATE AT night, I am sure you can hear the sound of shredders shredding. Of assets being stripped. Of pockets being stuffed.

I have become convinced, without the benefit or burden of proof, that a gigantic fraud is being perpetrated on us, the taxpayers. It is happening right now, on an ordinary Saturday morning in the twilight days of the old South Africa. In recent weeks the journalistic rumour mills have been grinding away at bales of conjecture, bags of whispers, and it's got to me. I believe there are two types of South Africans today: those who are In On The Deal, and those who aren't.

Consider our situation objectively. We have still in power – untrammelled power – a milch cow government and its millions of suckling babes. All are aware that the supply of cream will be cut off in the not-too-distant future. Their choice is to stock up for all the winters of the rest of their lives, or do without. In the past week alone I have been told, inter alia, the following stories (names and places omitted to protect the innocent, should there be any).

1. Pension funds administered by a government not a million miles from here are being topped up with vast quantities – truckloads – of crisp, fresh rands. Beneficiaries are being allowed to buy backdated policies, ensuring handsome payouts on (early) retirement – certainly more handsome than the individuals' stations in life would suggest. The taxpayer will foot this bill.

2. Long-term employment contracts are suddenly being signed in government-funded institutions (broadcasting corporations included?). These will ensure that individuals, whose services might – in a future age of unsheltered employment – be found not to be entirely essential, will receive bloated retrenchment payouts, courtesy of the taxpayer.

3. Megabucks parastatals ('strategic' industries?) are suddenly going 'private' and entering the market with new logos, big assets and big plans. It is not clear to whom these assets – paid for, it goes without saying, by the taxpayer – now belong. We are talking billions here.

Many, many similar tales are being whispered. Small wonder that the In On The Deals seem unperturbed by the prospect of the new South Africa. It is probably too late to stop the bulk of the larder-raiding. On a recent visit to Germany, I was chilled to discover how effectively the former East German nomenklatura had laundered their records and their people's money in the brief interlude between the time they saw the writing on the Wall, and when it came crashing down. It was a matter of months. Our transition has been going for two years already, and shows every sign of still having plenty of time to run. German Democratic Republic party grandees managed, under intense pressures of politics and time, to contrive for themselves managing directorships of companies created out of erstwhile corrupt co-operatives. Here, nest eggs can be arranged expertly and at leisure.

Just think about it. If officials of the Department

of Development Aid were up to thieving, shamelessly thieving, millions while the going was still good, then what do you imagine they would do when it was clear that the game was up? The snouts-in-troughs analogy has never been more apposite.

If there is an unanswerable, apolitical argument in favour of the immediate installation of a multiparty caretaker government in this country, it is surely that we must do all we can to try to ensure that when the larder door is finally opened, there is more inside than a row of beans. There is a real danger that it will be bare. This is a nauseating prospect for ordinary whites who don't have access to the national autobank, but it must be all but unbearable for blacks who have never had their fair share from the State's coffers.

It is a lot to ask, but what the nation needs now, desperately, is an honest man or woman. Someone who knows what is happening, and is prepared to say so. History would treat them kindly.

SATURDAY STAR, 23 MAY 1992

AVERTING OUR EYES, HOLDING OUR NOSES

A spate of corruption scandals rocked the country. The public reaction was strangely muted - as if South Africans were shell-shocked by the daily onrush of dramatic developments.

———————

HAVING JETTISONED OUR SENSE OF MORALITY SOME TIME ago, we are succumbing to straightforward madness. A considerable proportion of the government's energies – and our resources – is being expended on matters which any rational outside observer would regard as clear manifestations of national insanity. This is happening with hardly a hint of protest or even curiosity from the nation.

There is, as we speak, a protracted dispute about 'retrenchment packages' for employees of the Civil Co-operation Bureau. The people who were paid by the State to perform some of the filthiest acts in our history are now complaining that their handshakes are not sufficiently golden. These gentlemen allege, in hurt tones, that the government is mounting a smear campaign against its brainchildren. The government, in response, refers the matter to Mr Justice Piet van der Walt. Gene Louw, our newest Minister of Defence, says with no obvious sense of irony that the judge will 'assist in the *termination* of all

188

relevant matters'. The relevant matter, surely, is that jail terms should be under discussion, not sinecures.

Remember the sequence of events. The existence of the B was revealed by journalists, at considerable risk to themselves. The government, after not a little encouragement, agreed to establish a commission of inquiry. The commission called for the relevant B documents and witnesses. The documents were gone and the witnesses refused to testify. The then-minister of defence, uncharacteristically, said he was quite powerless to do anything about that. The commission freely conceded that it had been unable to fulfil its tasks. End of story.

Now we have to listen to an argument over how much money we must pay the people who gave the finger to the commission and went entirely unpunished. Perhaps I am missing something here – though I can't imagine what – or we are swallowing an absolute outrage. It has been openly stated that General Eddie Webb ordered the destruction of the B's files. Where is General Webb now? Where is 'managing director' Joe Verster? Haggling over their settlements for services rendered, no doubt.

The madness is by no means restricted to the B saga. We learn this week that a former director-general of the disgraceful Department of Development Aid – a man mentioned in the Pickard report – has just retired as a director of the Development Trust Corporation, with full pension benefits. Land Affairs Minister Jacob de Villiers bids Gilles van de Wall farewell with thanks for his 'committed and dedicated service'. Again: am I missing something here? The Development Aid scandal was at least one that did not manage to get entirely away.

What has become of the public's right to see culprits punished? It is a right we surrendered long ago by allowing absolute power to corrupt absolutely and cow us. There are innumerable other examples. The new headquarters for the National Intelligence Service is costing R145-million, instead of the budgeted R45-million. Who is it for? Why is it not stopped? Instead of asking, we sit in mesmerized apathy, listening to ministers' high-minded mouthings about why a member of parliament should not be allowed to use parliamentary privilege to air allegations about 'dirty tricks'. Something was certainly done about Jan van Eck. He was chucked out of parliament. Pity about the B – but then perhaps the B men have a hold on the government which the hapless Van Eck does not enjoy.

There is a stink in the air; the stink of amorality. The silence of the victims merely heightens the likelihood of it becoming endemic, as much a part of the South African way of life as *braaivleis*, rugby, *pap* and *fahfee*. Because the nation allows this government to behave like this, the next is more likely to indulge in variations on the theme. It is a nauseating prospect.

We need a caretaker government. Not necessarily the government's 'transitional structures' or the ANC's 'interim council', both of which are designed to deliver maximum advantage to the respective parties, but a multiparty caretaker government in which everybody will at least be watching everybody else for signs of cheating.

Meanwhile, the rot is setting, rock hard, while we, the people, do nothing but avert our eyes and hold our noses.

SATURDAY STAR, 6 JUNE 1992

THE SMALL MAN PAYS

The loosening of the vice-grip of apartheid's laws unleashed social change at every level of society. Property rights were soon placed at the cutting edge of the new South Africa.

———————

PITY THE SMALL MAN AND WOMAN AS WE BEGIN TO PAY THE price for the decades-late arrival of the new South Africa: they are being told to dig deepest. I want to talk, in this week of big tragedies, about small people locked into a small one that threatens to engulf them.

There is a man called B who lives in a house north of Johannesburg. He is a good and much-loved man who treats people right and works to the limits of endurance to provide for his family. With the help of the bank, he bought his house more than a decade ago and with his wife and three children turned barren land into a lovely oasis. It also represents this family's wealth in the world. B is not a particularly political person, but he is one of those white South Africans who have taken an interest in the unfolding political drama and have reached their own conclusions. Long, long ago B recognized that apartheid was wrong, and could not be sustained. He and his wife voted 'yes' in the reform referendum with relish and high hopes.

He has now been told of the Transvaal Provincial

Administration's decision to locate a squatter camp within a kilometre of his house. He has been told that the value of the house will fall by as much as 80 percent. This means that having paid off a bond on the property faithfully for more than 10 years, he suddenly finds himself owing more to the bank than the land and house are now worth. He is quite desperate, for this constitutes financial ruin after a lifetime committed to building up security for his family.

B, let there be no mistake, is not a racist. He welcomes black South Africans buying and building homes in his area. But the poor, powerless people who are to be dumped next door are able to do neither. They are to construct any shelter they can on a piece of ground 20m by 10m. They are to use whatever roads as can be scraped on to the *veld* in time, they are given vague promises of 'chemical toilets' and even vaguer ones of electricity, eventually. The lack of infrastructure makes it certain that Nietgedacht will – whatever the efforts of its inhabitants – become a vast, growing slum.

Now B is told in pious terms by 'experts' who live in the comfort of city suburbia that he must simply accept the situation as a new reality of South African life. Those who have never faced the prospect he faces call him a 'nimby' ('not in my backyard'), content in the knowledge that their backyards are safe. He is accused of worrying only about his 'view'. Well, he has some questions to ask.

Why must he pay alone – and pay such a devastating price – for apartheid's crimes, when its architects continue to live, literally, off the fat of the land? Why is he told that he must propose an alternative site for the poor squatters, when he obviously has no power to do so? Why, if there is not proper infrastructure in either place, are the squatters to be moved from Zevenfontein to Nietgedacht? Could it be because there are powerful interests in the former area, while in the latter there are only ordinary people who have no financial muscle to flex? To what lengths should he go to try to protect all that he and his family have? These are real and painful questions for B, and he is getting no answers. Meanwhile, the minutes tick by and resettlement and ruin draw closer.

South Africa's problems are vast and the sufferings of its people immense. The horror of Boipatong showed that again this week. But why is it that the small people must always bear the brunt of tragedy and injustice? B faces disaster because of the Group Areas Act, the scandalous theft and wastage of the Department of Development Aid, the billions poured into nonsensical homelands when housing for black people was needed in the cities years ago, and so on. He had nothing to do with all of this. And the guilty ones still drive Mercedes-Benzes and retire behind their electronic gates on Waterkloof Ridge.

This disaster should not be allowed to befall a good man like B, and the many other honest, hard-working people in his community. If it is indeed too late to stop the ill-considered resettlement of the Zevenfontein community, then all those whose life investments are threatened with decimation must be fully compensated. Rezoning, if it will help them, must also be implemented. The uncaring, inept bureaucracy must be forced by the public will into responding to the plight of the ordinary people who are being punished for a situation not of their making. They cannot simply be ridden over roughshod because they do not have the financial strength to bend the TPA to their will. It is an injustice which serves only to compound that already suffered by the homeless.

B, by the way, is my brother.

SATURDAY STAR, 20 JUNE 1992

193

RAMBO TURNS INTO PC PLOD

The South African Police, famed and feared for their ruthless efficiency in containing the anti-apartheid forces over the years, now appeared unable to track down township killers.

_____

IN THE 1980S, IF IT WAS SO MUCH AS SUSPECTED THAT A 'terrorist' base had been identified, the full might of the South African military machine would be unleashed against it. Often, such targets were suburban houses in far-flung foreign cities. They were bombed and blitzed with complete ruthlessness and relative precision.

Acting upon necessarily untested information, commandos stormed buildings from Gaborone to Mbabane, Maputo to Harare. The circumstantial evidence against the occupants was considered to be so grave – they were believed to be somehow connected with the killing of South African civilians – that they were fair game. They were killed even before questioning, if necessary.

Within the country, it was not necessary to use aircraft, but the tactics were no less effective: dawn raids, detention and brilliant detective work saw to it that the attrition rate for ANC guerrillas was remarkably high.

But now, in the 1990s, something has changed in the modus operandi of these security forces that were once held in awe and fear around the world. There is overwhelming circumstantial evidence that certain clearly identifiable hostels in townships here at home are being used as bases for terrorism – terrorism in its proper sense of violence and coercion against civilians. In terms of body counts, this terrorism is of a scale never before experienced in this country. Again and again, hostel dwellers are linked directly by eyewitnesses to massacres of mind-numbing proportions. The Independent Board of Inquiry estimates that between July 1990 (when the township carnage began in earnest in the Transvaal) and April this year, a minimum of 261 attacks on township dwellers was launched from some 15 hostels. At least 10 of these attacks, claiming 50 lives, came from Boipatong's KwaMadala hostel. This was before the latest and ghastliest bloodbath.

Again and again, huge arms caches are found inside. Media reports alone show that in the same 22-month period, the following weapons were confiscated from hostels: 58 AK-47s, nine revolvers, 18 pistols, 361 rounds of ammunition, and 'truckloads' of knives, spears and the like. But in the case of the hostels, the response of the security forces is strictly-by-the-book, gentlemanly, even diffident. Police spokesmen explain that their men are 'holding discussions' with the occupants of the latest hostel named as a fortress and billet for bloodshed. There is 'some resistance' from the inmates, they say by way of explanation for their extraordinarily sensitive behaviour. They go out of their way to return weapons which they say they have ascertained were not used to commit crimes. It is as if Rambo has suddenly turned into PC Plod.

Savage murderers must be quite pleasantly surprised to discover that they can, en masse, hack, gouge and shoot to death dozens of civilians and expect to get away with it. If they enjoyed the experience, they will probably be keen to repeat it and – given that the chances of punishment seem demonstrably to be so low – will encourage others to join in the fun. Out there, there must by now be hundreds of veterans of such brave campaigns – enough to form a society and swop reminiscences of massacre techniques.

Now there is tremendous surprise and anguish in the land at the fact that negotiations at Codesa have temporarily broken down. The reaction is hopelessly naive. What is being sought at Codesa is a peaceful negotiated settlement – an alternative to bloodshed. Instead, since negotiations started, there is less peace and more bloodshed. The government insists on retaining exclusive control of the security forces, and therefore retains the responsibility for maintaining the safety of all South African citizens. It is failing utterly to do so. It has not even kept its months-old promise to seal off the hostels.

Now, you try telling the bereaved of Boipatong why Codesa is such a jolly fine idea. They'll want to see some murderers caught and convicted first.

SATURDAY STAR, 27 JUNE 1992

THE SCARS OF BOIPATONG

A horrendous massacre in the township of Boipatong briefly revived the outright racial animosity of the 1980s. Residents blamed Inkatha hostel-dwellers - and the white government.

THE POSTERS SAID IT ALL: A PICTURE OF PRESIDENT DE Klerk, his eyes coloured in bright red like a devil's, and the words 'How many more deaths? De Klerk GET OUT'. One teenage boy, in a frenzy, stamped the picture into the dust and then spat on it.

Being in Boipatong yesterday was like being back in the South Africa of PW Botha. Tens of thousands of poor, angry black township dwellers gathered to share their grief and to focus their hatred on the leader of the white minority regime. The Boipatong massacre had recreated, with a vengeance, the deadly racial polarization which the onset of the new South Africa promised to break down. Its cost threatens to go beyond, even, the terrible deaths of the victims.

Boipatong stadium was worlds away from the rarefied, genteel negotiating chambers of Codesa. Here, gathered in fury and defiance, were 'the people' the politicians talk so blithely about. Activists, certainly, and the ubiquitous, vicious young comrades with ersatz AK-47s made out of

197

motor car parts. But also kindly old matriarchs struggling to fend off the sun, young priests, teachers, toddlers – all horrified by what had befallen their township, and all convinced beyond any argument that it was somehow the work of 'the regime'. So deeply politicized were the speeches that the Reverend Frank Chikane was moved to remark that 'we must not allow ourselves to become more important than the people we have come here for (the bereaved relatives of the massacre victims).'

As the sun broke through the winter clouds and beat down, the dust rose to meet it and the wind whipped sharply around the tumble-down stadium in its steel-grey, harsh industrial surrounds. Again and again, speakers conjured up the horrific image of a nine-month-old child being driven through with a spear. This drew renewed gasps of horror; and the bare mention of KwaMadala hostel elicited a low, ominous growl from the crowd. And, every time, the pain was linked to the 'white regime'. It was a startling indication of just how deep is the feeling of alienation about the new society.

It took Anglican Archbishop Desmond Tutu, in a speech which was a curious combination of rancour and conciliation, to leaven the atmosphere just before the end of the protracted memorial service. He mourned the tragedy and castigated the government, but he also got the crowd to laugh, via self-deprecatory jokes, and he offered some hope for life beyond the massacre and its consequences. He took the menace out of the situation. As the crowds snaked slowly toward the burial ground at Sharpeville, there was a final incongruous, discomforting sight. A row of limousines nosed nervously and aimlessly through barricades in the poor, narrow dirt streets of Boipatong. They carried worried-looking diplomats: worried, no doubt, about finding the safety of the main road, but worried too about the state of the nation they had had so much hope for, so recently. Boipatong is leaving scars on all who touch it.

THE STAR, 30 JUNE 1992

198

OUR NOBLE COMPROMISE

Fears grew about the fragility of the future, but so did the realisation that what was being negotiated was a compromise quite unique in African and, indeed, world politics.

PEOPLE ARE TALKING ABOUT LEAVING AGAIN. THIS TIME around there are many middle-class blacks among them. The hope that blossomed in 1990 has wilted. The developing trust in each other's intentions is gone. Those who came back from London, Sydney, Houston, Toronto now ask themselves quietly and disbelievingly whether they have made a terrible mistake.

Not even an international soccer tour – involving the one sport which could truly capture the hearts of all South Africans – has made any impact on our free-fall into depression and acrimony. Instead, it has itself become a symbol of our mean-minded crisis of confidence. Vicious exchanges about black plastic armbands serve the same purpose.

In the townships, people are sick of the system and sick of the struggle. They will stick with the struggle if they have to. In the suburbs, the builders are at it again; adding metres of concrete to walls which were first raised in the 1980s. Even when the walls are painted over, you can see where the lines of fear join. It is like reading the inside of a tree trunk: it tells our history. People are hoarding what little money they have, at a loss to know what a 'safe investment' is in the new South Africa. Estate agents plumb the depths in trying to reinvigorate a teetering property market: 'Look Ma, No Squatters!' They might as well say 'no dogs'.

How did we get here? It all seems so very, very stupid. A negotiated settlement is still the most likely political outcome in South Africa. We are not yet on the brink of the Yugoslavia option. What has happened is that we have retreated headlong, in a wake created by the politicians, to the attitudes and circumstances of South Africa pre-1990. On the surface, the exchange of accusatory memoranda between President de Klerk and Mr Mandela differs from what went before only insofar as Mr Mandela is out of prison and Mr PW Botha is out of action.

It is below the surface that we must look in order to reach a reasoned assessment of our situation, rather than surrendering to blind panic. From where I sit, I proceed on the assumption that the everyday truth lies at a point somewhere between what the ANC is saying and what the government is saying. That point shifts from day to day, and the challenge is to keep up with it. There are two fundamental, interrelated causes of the current crisis. They are the violence, and the erosion of belief, on both sides, in the sincerity of the other. To deal with the second first: the ANC emerged from Codesa 2 in shock, suddenly convinced that the government was not after all committed to a truly democratic outcome in negotiations, but rather to a gerrymandered constitution which allowed it to retain power beyond any electoral support it could hope for. The ANC believed it had come close to being suckered, and the suspension of talks coupled with mass action is the result. It now believes it will have to force, rather than talk, Pretoria into an acceptable deal. From the government's side, it believes that the ANC is reverting to fighting for a classical all-or-nothing transfer of power *à la* the decolonizing Africa, with no reference to South Africa's peculiarities.

The magnetic force that will bring both back to the table is the certainty that neither has the power to secure its ideal solution, however much it would like to. But this force can be unleashed only when a degree of trust has been re-established. This is not trust in the sense of fondness for one another, or friendship. It is trust based on the knowledge that both sides' options are limited, and directly reliant upon one another. This brings us to the violence.

It, unlike arguments over special majorities, senates and regional legislatures, is non-negotiable. While the killing continues, there will be no negotiations. Here, at this particular point on the truth-continuum, the primary onus falls on the government. President de Klerk does not have the power to put a stop to all the violence, just like that. No one does, either jointly or severally: South Africa is too far gone right now. What he does have the power to do, however, is to take the unambiguous practical steps which many of us in the media, and more recently the Goldstone Commission, have been begging for since mid-1990. These steps, including the banning of the carrying of weapons in public, resolving the hostel tragedy and punishing State miscreants, will certainly save some lives immediately, and have a very good chance of beginning to rebuild shattered trust. They are a key to reconvening Codesa.

The uniqueness of our situation is that an agreement is possible – even probable – whereby one leader, Mr de Klerk, gives more than he is forced to give, while another, Mr Mandela, takes less than he is able to take. That is a shining, noble, and deeply hopeful prospect. We the people cannot allow it to be thrown away.

SATURDAY STAR, 11 JULY 1992

VISION AT SOCCER CITY

In the tension-filled days after the Boipatong massacre the politicians stopped talking to each other, but ordinary South Africans illuminated the path to ultimate reconciliation.

NOW HOLD ON A MINUT: IS THIS THE SAME STRIFE-TORN, crisis-ridden, race-poisoned South Africa we're all so depressed about? There in the stands, dancing and screeching and hugging each other in paroxysms of patriotism were staidly dressed whites, trendy township teenagers, and a cross-section of just about every other race and class categorisation you can think of.

The occasion was the marvellous final football clash between South Africa and Cameroon, and the climactic moment came when a bubbling Bennet Masinga did the necessary with an inspirational pass from his captain, Neil Tovey. It was 2-2 at the FNB Stadium – appropriately situated midway between Johannesburg and Soweto – and the new South Africa, forced into hiding by the current political crisis, was making a wonderful and welcome reappearance.

For two glorious hours on Saturday, 55,000 South Africans saw a future, and saw it working. 'Isn't it nice to see this multi-racialism,' a fan remarked matter-of-factly in a strong Zulu accent. In the crowd, like islets in a sea of Sowetans, white fathers sat with their pimply, gangly sons, and traded assessments and cold drinks with all in the vicinity. It was for South Africa an extraordinarily natural, peaceable and – above all – hugely enjoyable affair.

Up went the cry whenever Tovey touched the ball: 'Codesa!' (It was pointed out that the nickname referred to Codesa 1, not Codesa 2, and was therefore highly complimentary.) 'The Doctor!' roared the crowd as Doctor Khumalo stretched an opponent like a rubber band. White fans wearing South Africa's World Cup cricket shirts raised an enormous ANC flag – with a springbok in the middle.

Numbers of people remarked on the tragedy of the fact that the rest of the country was not sharing in, or being touched by, the optimism and happiness of the moment. The television blackout was a sorry reminder that all was not well beyond the stadium fences. But nothing, not missed scoring opportunities or blatant fouls, not irritating announcers or the smog on the horizon, could detract from the experience of those new South Africans lucky enough to be there.

THE STAR, 13 JULY 1992

THE GENERAL WON'T COME TO THE 'PHONE

The arrest of South African agents in London provided sensational new evidence of state-sponsored 'dirty tricks'. At home, the untouchability of the generals was questioned.

IT IS APRIL IN LONDON AND THE FAX LINE OUT OF 10 Downing Street is humming: destination De Klerk. British Prime Minister John Major is initiating a flurry of messages to his South African counterpart. The subject: two South African Defence Force members, caught by British Intelligence far from home, on a mission likely to be detrimental to the health of former police captain Dirk Coetzee. The question to President de Klerk: what is going on, and what are you going to do about it? Major, by reliable accounts, is angry. De Klerk is concerned. An accommodation is reached, and the agents return to South Africa. But that is not, by a long way, the end of the story.

The latest twist in the tawdry tale of Dirk Coetzee points to something much more important than the man himself. It provides irrefutable evidence that, at the very least, some elements of the security forces are operating beyond the control of the government. The evidence refers to here and now, and cannot be attributed to the old days of

204

apartheid. De Klerk has conceded as much. It makes little principled difference to anyone (other than Coetzee, of course) whether the SADF agents were planning to kill him, torture him, or monitor him. They were in London clandestinely, under some order from somewhere in the State, and financed by some State coffer. The excuse that they might have been investigating ANC-IRA links is simply pathetic: if that had been the purpose they would have enjoyed the full co-operation of British Intelligence, rather than being caught out in such embarrassing circumstances. This brings us back to the faxes.

Major has no interest in damaging De Klerk. On the contrary, the British make no bones of the fact that they would like to see a new South Africa in which an array of parties is operating, and De Klerk's National Party is high on the list. They would like to see the ANC make significant compromises on the matter of minority protection. The reason that the London incident was not completely hushed up and forgotten is startling. The British are becoming convinced that there is indeed 'third force' activity in South Africa. Moreover, they think it threatens the negotiating process, and even De Klerk himself.

It was argued last week that far from controlling illegal security force activity, De Klerk finds himself unable to do much about it. He cannot purge the rogues once and for all because he cannot risk alienating the security forces as a whole. He cannot cut off the rogues' resources because they have made themselves largely self-financing. It is a terrifying scenario: the maverick elements can simply make up their own minds about what needs to be done and when – witness the London shambles.

Powerful voices in the British Foreign Office establishment have recently been floating the idea of a general amnesty in South Africa. This emanates directly from their conviction that the third force – or forces – can be stopped only if they are offered a way out. Assuring them that they will not be punished for past crimes, the argument runs, is a relatively small price to pay for preventing them from sowing mayhem and subverting the negotiation of the settlement they so fear. Major's faxes, although they are unlikely ever to be made public, are understood to fit in with this thinking. What Downing Street wants is for De Klerk to seize this opportunity – the suspects and evidence have been handed to him on a plate – to identify and isolate those who are playing dirty games beyond his reach. The British are helping the State President to help himself. Will he do so? The initial signs are not encouraging.

We are told that 'departmental investigations are continuing' and that at some stage 'a decision will be taken as to whether a further public statement is deemed desirable.' In plain words: the defence force will investigate whether members of the defence force did anything wrong. More specifically, Military Intelligence will investigate the activities of Captain Pamela du Randt, former personal assistant of . . . the head of Military Intelligence. On the basis of such an investigation – which might just as well take place in MI's staff canteen – the president will be advised by MI on whether to go public on MI. I think I can guess what they will recommend.

The difference in this case is the international dimension. If the British are as worried as they say they are, they will push for full, timely disclosure of the information. And perhaps the stature of Major will see to it that Military Intelligence chief General Christoffel 'Joffel' van der Westhuizen, who has not been answering his 'phone since his name was linked to the 'Goniwe signal' earlier this year, might finally be persuaded to make himself available for interview.

SATURDAY STAR, 18 JULY 1992

206

ERASING THE NATIONAL MEMORY

The democracy talks were sufficiently far advanced for South Africans to begin to gaze into the future. A profound question presented itself: would there be Nuremburg-style trials?

———————

SOME TIME AGO I REPORTED THAT POWERFUL VOICES IN THE British government were floating the idea of a general amnesty in South Africa. Now the talk is taking place much closer to home: our own government has warmed to the idea quite markedly, and discussions are being held with the ANC. The issue of general amnesty is not a constitutional technicality or negotiating nicety. It has to do with the soul of our nation, of remembrance of things passed, of forgetting for the sake of the future.

At its simplest, a general amnesty would mean erasing the national memory. Political offenders on all sides would be absolved: there would be no prosecutions for crimes committed in the past. But it is important to understand the context in which interested international parties are promoting the notion. In the corridors of Western power – and this is in sharp contrast to the sitting rooms of white South African suburbia – it is accepted as a fact that power-ful elements within our security forces are complicit in the violence. Terrifyingly, it is believed they are operating outside the government's aegis; that President de Klerk cannot purge them without risking an uncontrollable backlash. These are experienced, highly trained, resourceful, determined and ruthless elements who fear retribution if De Klerk is forced to negotiate a settlement which cedes considerable power to the ANC.

The only way to stop them from continuing to act beyond De Klerk's control, so the reasoning goes, is to offer them an escape route from their past and their present. The *quid pro quo* for the ANC would be the release of the more than 400 people the organization regards as political prisoners. The idea has much merit – anything that might stop the spiral of violence must be considered – but it is such a big idea, and one whose consequences we will live with for so long, that it cannot be entertained lightly.

The means to justify the end of reining in the maverick killers would have several major implications. It would virtually ensure that the huge book of unsolved political murders remains shut. South Africans would never know who killed whom, whether the State was directly involved or not, and what form the intervention by security force mavericks was taking. It is one thing to free convicted prisoners under an amnesty – one knows of their misdeeds and can therefore offer forgiveness – but entirely another to tell murderers who have never been brought to book that they are assured of getting away with their crimes. There is good reason, also, to be suspicious about the government's motivation in going along with an amnesty. The investigation into the Goniwe murders is throwing up new evidence, the SADF's involvement in a covert mission in London this year still has to be explained – and as a negotiated settlement draws closer, rats are increasingly deserting the sinking dirty tricks ship. On balance – or rather imbalance – it appears that the State would do much better out of a general amnesty than would its opponents.

Nevertheless, this is not the central issue. The aim is to do away with a key cause of the bloodshed in which our

208

country is drowning, and if that aim could be achieved, it hardly matters which party gets the better deal. But the question must be asked: would a general amnesty necessarily persuade the 'third forces' to put away their guns and become decent citizens? Some, perhaps. Others, horrifying as the idea might be, could well decide that they like what they're doing and believe it to be the right thing. An amnesty will not in itself shut them down. Many are self-financing – a legacy of the necessary deceits of the *B et al* – and they appear to have support in at least some high echelons.

A general amnesty is potentially a noble instrument of forgiveness and reconciliation. But it should be considered only when the State has done all it can to bring criminals within its own ranks to justice. We must have finality from De Klerk on the authenticity or otherwise of the Goniwe 'death signal'. We must see the results of the internal investigation into the SADF agents caught in London. We must know whether the rot goes right up into the General Staff. There is a risk in De Klerk confronting the monster his party has created, but the risk of not confronting it is infinitely greater.

People who murdered in the name of apartheid might qualify for amnesty along with those who murdered in the name of the liberation struggle. But we must first know who they are and what they did – and be assured that they will never do it again. Forgetting comes after forgiveness, not the other way around.

SATURDAY STAR, 8 AUGUST 1992

THE SCREECHING GHOSTS THAT NIGHTLY WAKE US

The reopening of the inquest into the brutal killing in the 1980s of activist Matthew Goniwe threw the amnesty debate into even sharper relief, and revealed the complexity of the issue.

———————

WE CAN ONLY HOPE THAT THE NET WILL EVENTUALLY be drawn tighter around whoever it was who butchered Matthew Goniwe and his three colleagues on that eastern Cape night in 1985. In a country known for its inability to solve political murders – who killed Robert Smit, Rick Turner and so many others? – it would be naive to expect that just because remarkable evidence has been turned up, the Goniwe case will be closed successfully. But there is reason to be hopeful, not least because more and more people who inhabited the dark security force-linked underworld in and around Port Elizabeth are getting scared, and starting to talk.

They certainly believe that the investigation will not fizzle out like so many others before it, and have a shrewd suspicion that if a culprit is to be named, it is likely to be someone from their grubby ranks rather than the elevated echelons. The Goniwe investigation has come to mean something beyond the painful, desperate desire of the activist's relatives and friends to know the truth. It is a symbolic case against which current proposals for a general amnesty should be tested.

The purpose of identifying those responsible for these – and all other – unconscionable acts of barbarity is not retribution. Putting the murderers in jail will not bring Matthew Goniwe back to life, and will not contribute to the spirit of reconciliation without which the new South Africa cannot be born. The purpose is disclosure, and the laying to rest of the screeching ghosts that nightly wake South Africa from its fitful sleep. Without exorcism, the wailing will never stop.

There is a workable and, on balance, a just way to apply an amnesty and at last wipe the bloody slate cleaner. It could be agreed by all sides that an amnesty for political crimes will come into effect on, say, September 1. Between now and then anyone who has been involved in such crimes would have to come forward (to a specially-appointed commission, perhaps) and fully disclose his deeds. This information would be made public, but the individuals would be indemnified from prosecution for any acts committed before the cut-off date. The only condition would be that if it subsequently emerged the disclosure was incomplete or incorrect in any way, the indemnity would be revoked.

To use the Goniwe case as an example, if the culprits came forward they would be identified and the sordid mystery unravelled immediately and without further cost – but they would not be charged. If they did not come forward within the specified period, the investigation would run its course and the full weight of the law would be brought to bear. In passing eventual sentence, it would be considered an aggravating factor that the killers had spurned the opportunity to come clean. The choice facing the guilty would be stark: confess, repent, and start life anew, or be hunted down. All the political criminals hiding in the darker reaches of our country would have to decide, once and for all.

The practical political benefits of such a scheme are obvious. We have scattered across South Africa today a terrifying number of people who have taken part in murders and never been caught. Obviously, having once killed, the chances are that they will kill again, whether for political or financial gain, or plain habit. They have broken society's taboos, they live in the shadow of discovery, and they are lost to the new South Africa. The amnesty I describe offers them a chance, perhaps the only chance, of finding a way back into civil society. Once having been indemnified, their future behaviour would be severely constrained. The glare of public knowledge would, hopefully, immobilize their baser instincts. If they chose the option of rehabilitation, they would spend the rest of their lives trying to prove themselves worthy citizens. How much better a prospect that is for all of us than having them in society's sewers, wreaking havoc.

I would not dare to presume to speak for Matthew Goniwe's widow; I do not know whether she could accept that her husband's murderers should escape physical punishment. But our history is so bloodstained and so tortured that I cannot imagine another way of washing our hands and cleansing our hearts, so that we might start again.

SATURDAY STAR, 15 AUGUST 1992

INSIDE THE PROTECTED
CITADEL

An emotionally-laden rugby test match against the All Blacks unleashed deeply-held grudges over the sports boycott and sanctions. White rugby fans opted for unrepentant defiance.

HISTORIC AS THE EVENT WAS, RARELY CAN A SPORTING contest have been so politically charged. Never have I felt more intensely the schizophrenia of being a white South African.

South Africa was playing New Zealand at Johannesburg's Ellis Park stadium and I wanted, with all the patriotic enthusiasm that only an international sporting showdown can unleash, our 15 rugby players to win, and win gloriously. But I did not want to be party to turning that into a mean-spirited victory over fellow South Africans who are not white. I wanted the historic Test to be a symbol of the benefits for all which South Africa's turn towards justice can bring. It should have been a moment of renewal; a moment, to use the beautiful Afrikaans word, of *versoening*. There were, I know, many others who felt the same at Ellis Park on Saturday, but we had no means of stopping, or even distancing ourselves from, what was obviously going to happen.

The signs were unmistakeable early on in and around the stadium. Thousands of fans (encouraged, incidentally, by the Afrikaans press) were determined to make a political point by flying the old South Africa's flag, and for those who had not brought their own there were hundreds on sale outside. This in itself was perhaps understandable: insensitive, yes, in our time of transition, but not surprising. The defiance soon assumed a sad and ugly quality, however. A small group of liquored-up fans at one of the entrances waved their flags and held a Springbok mascot. Like some grotesque barbershop quartet they sang '*F.. die ANC, f.. die ANC*'. In the stands, notes were passed around urging people to sing *Die Stem*, come what may. As the South Africans and New Zealanders lined up I waited with a sick feeling for the expected announcement of a minute's silence for the victims of Boipatong, as this would surely be the catalyst.

When the announcement came it was not even for Boipatong, after all. The crowd was asked only to observe 'a few moments' silence for peace' in our country. But this was the signal: back immediately came Die Stem, and the raised finger to the devil outside, the ANC. There followed the unexpected formal playing of the anthems. Some people, still upright for the moment's silence which never happened, shifted uncomfortably, uncertainly. A lone black ice-cream seller stared down at his wares, avoiding the faces of all those around him standing ramrod straight. From that moment inside the concrete bowl, it seemed like a besieged tribe had gathered to take strength in their numbers and to send, from the protected citadel, a message of defiance to their perceived persecutors. It felt like being in a bull-ring, and it was uncertain whose blood was more passionately desired: that of the foe on the field, or of the millions outside who knew nothing of the ancient ritual but were believed to be threatening it.

The match itself was riveting. The bad taste came back only after the final whistle. I talked and argued late into the night with friends and colleagues about the experience.

Some said I was naive to have expected anything else, and I accept that. But it does not detract from the hollow feeling that comes with realizing that so many whites are not changing in their hearts; not embracing the new path; not agreeing that change must at the very least involve sensitivity towards those the old system excluded and wounded. More cynically: not even realizing that without the blessing of Nelson Mandela, the All Blacks would never have considered coming to South Africa.

It was pointed out to me that it was not all 70,000 people who issued the shortsighted challenge, that no one could know how many had revelled in the emotional return to the rugby world without seeing it as a victory over the ANC. I accept that too, but still the silent majority – if indeed there was one – was totally outvoted in the eyes of this country and the world. And powerful shapers of white opinion have felt no need to be coy about the political meaning of Saturday's display. Yesterday the newspaper Rapport published these extraordinary words on its front page:

'There are many kinds of tears. Today South Africa is probably shedding a few tears over the defeat. But yesterday before the Test, there were sobs of another kind. Softer tears. Of pride. And an iron will which said: Here is my song, here is my flag. Here I stand and I sing it today. It was the third time it was sung . . . A quarter of an hour before the last two verses echoed around Ellis Park. And again, just before the New Zealand anthem was played, when the man behind the microphone asked for a minute's silence. That was a political request; he received a political answer. South Africa is back . . . It cost blood and tears to get back, and many tears have been shed. Many kinds of tears. But next week, if we beat the Wallabies, then we laugh again. After all, there is only one truly happy laugh. And that is the last laugh.'

You can be proud without being punitive. You can have the decency to observe a moment's silence for peace – peace does not belong to any political party. Yes, ordinary whites are sick and tired of being messed around by the politicians, and having their rugby taken away from them. But what do they imagine that their black countrymen feel – they who have been denied basic rights, not just sports tours? Something good can still be retrieved from these tours by rugby, if only it will now look hard at itself, and think of others at the same time.

THE STAR, 17 AUGUST 1992

WE ARE ALL SORE NOW

The vicious battles over the flag, anthem, and Springbok sporting symbol began to extract a terrible toll. Eventually all sides appeared to recognize that the cost was too high.

———————

THE SHOUTING HAS NOT YET STARTED AT NEWLANDS, WHERE the second South Africa/New Zealand test will be played today. But the nation has shouted itself hoarse in the coarse course of this week. It is somehow typical and therefore appropriate that it took rugby to fully bare South Africa's divided souls, not more abstract things like constitutions and voting rights. They have not been happy, these post-Ellis Park days. All the rancour and fear we ordinarily express, privately and separately in our remaining group areas among people whom we know feel the same as us, burst like a boil and we are all sore now, rubbed raw.

Is it possible that this whole shabby saga has been good for us, cathartic, good for the future? Even without knowing how the next test – sporting and political – will pass off, I think it is probable. In the course of negotiations since February 2 1990 – negotiations which have so far failed to deliver a tangible new system for people to adjust to – tremendous resentments have built up among all South Africans. Much of this resentment has

217

been driven by fear, and there is no fear more tart than that of the unknown. It is as well that all this has come out into the open: it would have erupted one day, and is now being dealt with because it has to be.

There have been hard lessons for white South Africans and black South Africans in the bitter fight over iconography. Whites have been shown that you cannot agree to change and expect to stay exactly the same. If there is a fundamental truth about the 'new South Africa' it is that what black people think and feel matters, whereas in terms of crude power it did not in the past. And blacks have indicated that they will exercise power, if needs be, to demonstrate this point. For their part, blacks have learnt that if you are seen to be taking something away from people unjustifiably, they will resist you. Both sides, whether or not this was their intention, have been given a lesson in tolerance. The outcome of the Ellis Park furore has been to force an open, public agreement among politicians that individuals have the right to sing what they want to sing and wave the flag of their choice – provided this is not an intentionally provocative and hurtful act, and provided they concede the same liberty to others.

Freedom cuts all ways, and if you abuse it when it suits your purposes, it will surely return to bite you when it does not. There can be few more important precedents to establish in this time of transition. I took the view immediately after the events at Ellis Park that an opportunity for reconciliation, for *versoening*, had been tragically and selfishly wasted. This was, to say the least, a view which excited anger and opposition. One reader wrote to compare my stance to Neville Chamberlain's appeasement of the Third Reich. Needless to say I do not accept that Mr Mandela can be compared to Hitler, Mr Tshwete to Goebbels, or the ANC to the Nazi party, but I do not particularly object to the charge of appeasement. Stripped of its historical connotations it is not a bad notion at all. To appease is to calm by making concessions, satisfying demands. If everybody can be convinced of the need to appease everybody else, there is great hope for us. In this even-handed sense it would mean that no-one gets exactly what he wants, but all will get something. That is, in its way, a definition of a negotiated settlement.

President de Klerk has said himself that new representative symbols will have to be found when the time comes; this is surely self-evident to all but those who believe that there can be a return to full-blown apartheid. The war over the flag should stop now. It is hurting us all too much, storing up too much anger for the future. If it does not stop, the most appropriate new banner will be black and white, with a dunce's cap in the middle.

SATURDAY STAR, 22 AUGUST 1992

THE SERBS OF AFRICA

Debate raged over whether a 'third force' was waging a dirty tricks war against the ANC, and whether it was centrally organized or made up of maverick security force elements.

SOMEONE REMARKED THIS WEEK: 'YOU'VE GOT THE THIRD force on the brain. Why don't you go on to something else?' Many people seem to feel this way, so the question is worth answering. In recent weeks newspapers have been digging like mad, trying to get nearer to the truth of 'third force' activities in South Africa. This has been done in the strong belief that if we do not achieve clarity on the issue, the much-prized negotiations process will be bedevilled, indefinitely.

The reasoning is simple: if, as the avalanche of allegations suggests, there is today in our country a shadowy network of security force-linked individuals stoking violence and intervening in the political process according to its own uncontrolled agenda, we as a nation are being held hostage. 'Dirty tricks' – that curiously benign phrase which encompasses acts of murder – can shatter the stability of entire communities. Without stability there is no trust; without trust there is no negotiated settlement. Trust Feed is a case in point: it will take years, perhaps decades, to remove the poison that one night of police-inspired carnage pumped into the veins of the community. Killings lead to killings lead to killings. Readers have now heard detailed allegations of gun running, of cynical manipulation in volatile communities, of hit squads. We would like powers greater than ourselves to establish whether these allegations are true, and the authorities to act accordingly and urgently.

If we can be convinced that the issue has been probed to the full, and the allegations shown to be unfounded, well and good. But this has not yet happened, and that is why we will not leave the issue alone. The third force is not one story among many others of equal weight; it is not a royal scandal which titillates but means little. It is eating away daily at the already-frayed fabric of our society. White South Africans, in particular, have been conditioned by decades of mutant democracy. We have developed a remarkable capacity for credulity, not really wanting to know discomforting things and therefore banishing them from our minds.

The authorities have not helped themselves in the matter of third force allegations. If the mountain of circumstantial evidence is just that – circumstantial – it would have been easy enough to cast doubt on its meaning, at the very least. One example among many: Military Intelligence chief General 'Joffel' van der Westhuizen's name appears on an alleged 'death warrant' signal. If the signal is a fake, one would expect the implicated man to say so – a plain and simple 'It's not true'. But he has chosen to maintain an inaccessible silence. Further, one would expect the State President – the general's commander-in-chief – to ask him. The general surely cannot decline to take Mr de Klerk's calls, as he has done so contemptuously with our journalists.

Instead, we have had silence, and the general's name continues to pop up in suspicious circumstances. He remains head of MI, wielding the vast power that goes with that position, and when two of his agents are caught in

221

London up to no good, his department is asked to investigate itself. It does so and finds one of its members guilty. Of what? Of 'acting according to his own agenda'. Forgive me for sounding conspiratorial, but 'acting according to its own agenda' is precisely what the third force is accused of. We, the people, are not allowed to know what that agenda was – and, sadly, many in this country seem not to be too interested in knowing.

No wonder some foreigners think of white South Africans as the Serbs of Africa. To want to get to the bottom of the third force is not to exonerate the State's opponents: their crimes – in camps in Africa, in horrific political violence – must be exposed with vigour. But we are hearing a cacophony of claims about an evil force operating right here and now, disempowering the politicians and ruining our prospects of peace. Surely we must make its investigation a priority, and surely we should not stop until the job is done.

Minister of Law and Order Hernus Kriel has done something big with the police, even if it is belated, unilateral and limited. He has had the guts to call a problem by its name, and he has made a start. Now for the third force; now for similar courage from President de Klerk on the matter of the military. He says he is concerned about allegations of security force misdeeds. The time has come for us to ask the president (as the Bishop of Bradford did of King Edward VIII, who had expressed an 'awareness' of social problems) that he 'give more positive signs of that awareness'.

SATURDAY STAR, 29 AUGUST 1992

222

THE BIG LEVER IN WASHINGTON

The costs to the middle classes of fundamental change in South Africa were self-evident. But few whites seemed aware of the enormous benefits international reacceptance could bring.

———————

IMAGINE IF OUR POOR BRUISED AND EXHAUSTED COUNTRY woke up suddenly one morning, looked out of the window and saw this sight. Houses, lots of them, being built for the homeless. Health care being provided to the sick who before just had to die slowly. Massive resources poured into education for barely educated children. Training on offer for the barely trained and the wholly untrained. Imagine if on that bright morning bigwigs from the World Bank were walking around busily, calculating the amounts they were about to release to help us dig ourselves out of our deep trough of deprivation. If a top-level trade and investment mission from rich countries like the United States and its allies had just landed at Jan Smuts; if the doors of the International Monetary Fund had swung open to us again; if investors were queuing up to be part of the unexpected miracle that was the new South Africa – the country that defied all the dictates of irrational human history and sorted itself out, a prototype for a new order that worked.

We should not be imagining such unlikely delights. We should be demanding their delivery. The measures described above are not the bathtub musings of an incurable South African optimist. They are considered promises from someone much, much more important: Admiral Brent Scowcroft, national security adviser to George Bush. In a letter from the White House so positive and optimistic that it would bring a tear to the eye of the most depressed South African, Scowcroft has written to Congressman Howard Wolpe setting out the United States's plans to intervene decisively to shore up and nurture fledgling democracy in South Africa. He ends off with a ringing declaration of faith in the future of our far-off country. This is not, to put it mildly, the dominant approach in current state-of-the-nation dinner table conversations around South Africa circa 1992.

What's the catch? There is one, of course. But it's of our own making: Scowcroft makes it abundantly clear that none of the revitalising goodies the US has in mind will be delivered unless and until one thing happens – an interim government is installed. He is sitting in his office in Washington with his hand on a big lever – but he will not pull it until we have done the blindingly obvious, and got our political act together to the limited extent of having in place a transitional structure representative of all South Africans, not just some of specific colours.

One of the most disheartening aspects of our faltering transition is that South Africans are still locked in the world of short-term victories and defeats, wholly unable to look beyond the particular fight of the day. Whites in particular see interim government as a threat to be staved off: the beginning of the end, the thin edge of the wedge. In fact, interim government is the only rational way forward, and it is a *sine qua non* for progress. The inexorable logic of the reform process is that black South Africans must be empowered; interim government is the essential first step. We are stopping Brent Scowcroft and others from pulling their aid levers because we have failed to pressure our politicians into overriding their selfish concerns and doing what needs to be done, now.

Only a fool or a romantic would suggest that international help, like manna from heaven, will sort out for us this mess we have spent centuries making. And, as far as whites are concerned, only the most wilfully credulous will believe Pik Botha when he hints that change can mean staying the same ('I am not saying the National Party can win the election, we will win it.'). Change is going to be painful for pampered whites, but the Scowcroft letter shows it can bring practical – let alone moral – relief if we work with rather than against it. We need all the foreign goodwill we can get, and we need it desperately.

In the course of this week, like so many other weeks in our recent past, the politicians have been dancing around each other but refusing to touch in public. The lesser-known truth is that, Codesa or no Codesa, negotiations are proceeding at a very encouraging pace. I just hope Admiral Scowcroft's attention span will outlast our public pettifoggery.

SATURDAY STAR, 5 SEPTEMBER 1992

BETWEEN ARMAGEDDON AND DAMASCUS

It began to be suggested that South Africa could be sliding gradually into civil war. This merely underscored the miraculous progress already achieved in avoiding anarchy.

AT DUSK THE FAMILIAR BEN SCHOEMAN HIGHWAY WAS busy, as always. Rows of cars, tightly packed, edged along on either side of the motorway. Lights were coming on at filling stations and in houses dotted around the once-bare countryside which is now inexorably joining Johannesburg and Pretoria. Life was going on in ordered normality; the faces in the other cars were serious and distant, thinking about the day's work, hurrying home to families, listening to the radio absent-mindedly.

My friend was unusually silent and gloomy, staring at the traffic. Eventually he spoke his mind. He had a strong sense of 'incipient chaos', he said. Of how the social orderliness symbolized by the thousands of commuters willingly obeying the same rules could suddenly disappear. He made me think of highways in cities like Luanda and Dubrovnik, Beirut and Sarajevo, where the order of decades – even centuries – dissolved in a cordite puff, and never returned. The citizens of those benighted towns didn't expect it either. They are not so different from many of us, those middle-class commuters who found themselves catapulted by political catastrophe into an unthought-of life wherein the search for water and warmth became their highest priority. They found that the 'state of nature' is not something that passed with the previous, primitive centuries; it lies in wait for any humans who are foolish enough.

Since the miraculous turn of events in February 1990, I have argued as an article of faith that we South Africans are not so stupid as to toss away the political life-jacket that appeared in our hands so unexpectedly. Having stopped short on the road to Armageddon, we would turn towards Damascus instead. Well, the events in Bisho sorely test that faith.

We polyglot South Africans have no reason to regard ourselves as more civilized, and by implication more rational, than the people of what was once Yugoslavia. In Yugoslavia, too, a negotiated settlement was on the cards, and difficulties in the process were put no higher than that: hiccups, stumbling blocks, obstacles to peace, all surmountable. But in an apocalyptic instant – it is for future historians to identify the precise moment of dissolution – the country put a foot over the abyss, and tumbled in. The carnage of Bosnia-Herzegovina is the result, and the world seems powerless to pull it back to the place it was so very recently. The people look back at the frustrating period of negotiations as a paradise lost.

Bisho on Monday gave us a taste, a small taste, of Bosnia. For an excruciatingly long time – four days, to be exact – political leaders stared into the black hole, unwilling to step back for fear of accusations of cowardice, and angry enough to consider jumping in. Blame was apportioned without nuance: it was either all their fault, or all yours. For the first time since 1990, both sides broke a taboo and expressed doubt that a negotiated settlement was possible after all. In their different dialects, both sides breathed words of war.

227

It would not take a lot to start a war here; a real one, not one confined to isolated and poor pockets inhabited by black people who paid the most for the construction of apartheid and are now paying the most for its dismantling. I don't think we realize just how close we came this week to unleashing that nightmare. The government could have said: 'To hell with the ANC, we will impose a new system without them,' and the ANC could have said: 'To hell with the government, we march on Ulundi.' Hello Bosnia with African roadsigns.

By yesterday the politicians had drawn back. We should be thankful, but watchful. The ground around the edge of the abyss is dry and brittle. It held our weight this time, but there was the sound of crumbling. It would be wise not to test the strength of that edge again.

SATURDAY STAR, 12 SEPTEMBER 1992

AFTER MASS ACTION,
SATISFACTION

*In the aftermath of a catastrophic massacre of ANC demon-
strators in the Ciskei homeland, South Africa had to decide
what the limits of acceptable peaceful protest were.*

THE WEEK HAS ENDED OPTIMISTICALLY, JUST LIKE IT BEGAN.
That's quite something to be able to say about South Africa
in these times, and it is well worth repeating: a *whole week*
in which hope outweighed dread. It is an indication of the
depth we had sunk to that we are, correctly, feeling buoyant simply because the politicians are putting out signals
of reason and responsibility. They've not acted upon them
yet, of course, but the national psyche is being soothed.

There is now a chance that the De Klerk-Mandela
summit on violence could take place within a matter of
days. If it does not, we should all insist on knowing why
not. Things are now somehow different in the aftermath
of Bisho; that shame might be encouraging us to demand
higher standards from those who presume to speak in our
names. But Bisho has created one unrealistic expectation
among those outside the ANC, and it should be clarified before it leads to inevitable disappointment and another fit of
depression. The fateful march did not mark the end of mass

action, despite the calling off of the Mmabatho protest.

The ANC was fiercely attacked, and quite rightly so, for going beyond the bounds of peaceful demonstration and entering the realms of outright insurrection in Ciskei. The comparisons with the students of Tiananmen Square or the crowds which toppled the Romanian regime simply do not apply: neither group had entered into an agreed process of negotiations with its enemies, as the ANC has done. Nelson Mandela has indicated that the message has penetrated. We should expect him to make sure that the fatal line is never crossed again; the ANC has now seen in close-up the consequences of such recklessness, and it knows that tin-pot tyrants will react with deadly fusillades.

But this does not, and cannot, mean that the democratic right to peaceful protest has now been surrendered in this country. It is a pity that protest is still a part of our lives, but that is because we are still far from being a democratic society – and those who haven't democratic rights think that's an even greater pity. Therefore they will insist on using the only means available to them, in the absence of the vote, to apply pressure on recalcitrants who refuse to allow free political activity. Those of us who have no need to resort to demonstrations now would be foolish indeed to withdraw that right from others – it would justify similarly illiberal attitudes in some future society where power-balances had shifted. The establishment of free political activity in every area of the country is a *sine qua non* for democracy. There can be no free and fair elections if political 'no-go' areas such as Brigadier Gqozo's Ciskei continue to exist.

From the ANC's point of view, this means that when someone like Chief Buthelezi threatens 'civil war' if his opponents so much as dare to protest in his fiefdom, that is total confirmation of the need to protest. As a matter of principle, the ANC must have the right to organize its supporters in a peaceful, orderly and non-provocative demonstration anywhere it likes, and against whoever it likes. But in exercising this right, the ANC assumes some important obligations as well. First and foremost, it has a solemn, principled duty to extend such freedom, in daily practice, to everyone else. This means that a peaceful march on ANC headquarters in Johannesburg, by whoever feels like it, is acceptable. It means that if Inkatha or the National Party want to set up a branch in Transkei, or Sebokeng, or wherever, the ANC must make sure that its members do not interfere with their opponents' rights. I have said that the nature of protest must be carefully controlled: if you go to someone's stronghold with the stated purpose of 'overthrowing' him, you have perverted the principle. The ANC has to draw the line, and stay behind it.

There are other obligations, dictated by the peculiarities of our situation in this country rather than overarching principle. Mr Mandela has accepted that the economy is in a parlous state, and has undertaken to protect it as far as possible from further damage. This view must impact on all decisions regarding mass action: organizers must at every turn ask themselves whether it is absolutely necessary, and how the desired ends can be achieved while causing the least damage to the economy, and avoiding potential outbreaks of violence. All negotiating avenues must of course be utilized before turning to the streets outside.

Mr Mandela said this week that all mass action could fall away when agreement is achieved on interim government. That is a bright prospect. He also criticized Mr de Klerk for having agreed at Codesa to ensure political freedom throughout South Africa, and failing to deliver. This is manifestly true. We should not expect a sudden end to mass action until these obstacles have been overcome, and we might look to a political summit, soon, to do precisely that.

SATURDAY STAR, 19 SEPTEMBER 1992

THE LAST OLIVE BRANCH

Negotiations had reached a nadir, and for the first time leaders expressed doubt that a settlement was possible. Nelson Mandela concluded he and FW de Klerk had to save the situation.

———————————

NELSON MANDELA EMERGED FROM HIS GARDEN, SET BEHIND high walls in what was once an all-white Johannesburg suburb. Looking unrealistically relaxed for a septuagenarian with a murderous workload, the myth now made man held out a long, smooth, prison-preserved hand. His face shone in the warm late afternoon Sunday sunlight of the Highveld.

It was a gentle moment in a hard country; an unusual moment. Looking at one of the two men who shoulder much of the burden for saving South Africa from disaster, it was impossible not to feel a surge of irrational optimism. Optimism that in spite of Boipatong, Bisho, train massacres, the Natal killing fields, a broken-down economy and broken-off negotiations, the miracle of the 'new South Africa' could still happen. Mandela, who is not always so benign and has been known to turn fiercely on his critics, wanted to communicate precisely this feeling. In the frightening aftermath of the Bisho massacre, when

232

South Africans realized for the first time that Yugoslavia-style civil war was not an impossibility in their country, the ANC leader was about to hold out an olive branch to the Pretoria government. It was up to him and President FW de Klerk to stop the slide into anarchy, he said, and, for that, compromise on both sides was essential. He accepted De Klerk's invitation to an urgent summit on violence, and said his organisation wanted to return to the negotiating table.

In a long discussion, Mandela showed his soft side, the side that endears him so deeply to those close to him. At one point, he spoke personally about President de Klerk, almost to himself: 'I phoned him two days ago,' Mandela said quietly, 'and I must say he sounded a bit down. He is a very brave chap, you know, very bright and confident, and it was worrying to hear him sounding so down.' This conversation with Mandela took place a week ago. When it was publicized, the government reacted to the conciliatory tone positively – if cautiously – and the national mood changed at a stroke from one of deep despondency to hopefulness. Government ministers let it be known privately that they had been told to clear their diaries for the summit meeting, soon, and ANC negotiators said they sensed a breakthrough. South Africans were shown just how much their destiny depends on psychology.

Five days after Mandela's intervention, however, things were going awry again. The summit was still on, but it would certainly not take place as quickly as had been hoped. It is important to understand how we South Africans arrived at this point, in order to predict whether we can find a way beyond it.

The formal side of South Africa's transition from apartheid to democracy began to break down in May this year, at the second plenary session of the Convention for a Democratic South Africa (Codesa). Among the particular reasons for this was a disagreement between Mr de Klerk's negotiators, who were insisting on a 75 percent majority for approval of a new constitution, and those of the ANC who

233

had offered 70 per cent. There were several other detailed points of difference, but a more profound, and psychological, development was taking place. The process had got beyond the point of rhetoric and ringing declarations about justice and democracy; it was now time to talk about power and the politicians were manifestly unprepared for this. It is this scar that has yet to heal, and which still threatens to destroy the negotiations process and the country.

After Codesa 2, attitudes hardened considerably on both sides of the government/ANC divide, and soon developed into vicious caricatures reminiscent of the PW Botha era. The ANC, for its part, concluded that the white government had been trying to trick it all along – that in spite of De Klerk's blandishments, the National Party had no intention of giving up power. The Boipatong massacre in June solidified this view, and very soon De Klerk was being referred to, like Botha before him, as a murderer. Where there had been at least ambivalence and at most grudging respect for De Klerk from black leaders, there was now a sense of betrayal, of the confirmation of worst fears. In this atmosphere, ANC leaders embarked on their campaign of aggressive 'mass action': the common wisdom was that the government could not be talked into a settlement, but had to be forced.

On its side, the government turned to its supporters and said: 'You see, they are political terrorists after all. They are controlled by communists and they want nothing short of seizure of power.' A two-way process of demonization got under way, and swiftly undid the tenuous progress that had been made in the past 18 months towards grudging reconciliation. Both sides still accepted the fact of the other's existence, but instead of seeking common ground and taking their followers along with them, they let it be known that a settlement would have to be fought out. Once again, they were enemies more than negotiating partners.

The current state of mind of ordinary South Africans, post Bisho, could not be further removed from the generosity of spirit that briefly asserted itself in the aftermath of

De Klerk's 1990 speech and the release of Mandela. In the ranks of the black majority, there is talk of returning to armed struggle, even though it failed before. In the white suburbs, the middle classes, egged on by the bellicose utterances of political warhorses such as Foreign Minister Pik Botha, now say they have had enough of the ANC – as if it is in their power to wish the organization away. A bitter joke is doing the dinner party rounds: did you hear that the ANC has released a new calendar? January, February, March, March, March, March . . .

These attitudes are revealing of the still-racial nature of South Africa's political divide, and in bad times they are fallen back on eagerly by the politicians. If there is to be a settlement which has any chance of sticking, something has to give in the two-tone world of South African prejudice. The biggest danger, in today's atmosphere, lies in the possibility that attitudes will be allowed to harden to the extent that leaders will find it difficult to sell compromises to their embittered followers when the time comes to do so. South Africa is in an interregnum of sorts: the old system no longer has the power to suppress its opponents, and its opponents do not have the power to overthrow the old system. The only hope for a peaceful solution lies in the hands of De Klerk and Mandela. De Klerk has to be prepared to give more than he is forced to give, and Mandela has to be prepared to take less than he is able to take.

The Bisho massacre frightened both leaders to the extent that, having stared into the abyss of civil war, they drew back. The coming days will tell if they have the courage to stay there. Whites, in particular, seem not to be ready for the practical consequences of change; the majority appear to believe that they can stay exactly the same in the new South Africa. The mean-spirited battle over the singing of the white anthem and the waving of the white flag at recent rugby matches bears sad testimony to this, and the longer that the inevitability of non racial interim government is held off, the more recalcitrant whites will become. This is why it is so critical that De Klerk exercises leadership now. It will soon be two years since he launched his reform programme. In that time, formal power balances have changed not a jot: the government still controls the budget, the security forces, the State and practically everything else that matters in civil society. For this reason alone, it is clear that the impetus for a breakthrough towards a settlement will have to come from his side.

There is growing agreement among South Africa's intellectuals that we might be running short of windows of opportunity, and that to fritter them away for short-term party-political gain is irresponsible in the extreme. In holding out his olive branch to De Klerk, Mandela was simultaneously sending a message to the revolutionary firebrands within his organisation. These are people who taunt him with the lack of results produced by months of negotiation with the 'regime'. If Mandela cannot point to practical benefits flowing from conciliation this time, his leadership will face a sore test. He will have to choose between sticking to the path of rapprochement – rewards or no rewards – and bowing to the harsh logic of the militants who want to march on the homeland stronghold of Zulu Chief Mangosuthu Buthelezi at Ulundi, whatever the cost.

Mandela's resolution of his own dilemma will affect all South Africans. If he is given the slightest chance by the government, it seems he will put his political credibility on the line and go for the summit, perhaps within weeks. But he knows, as does De Klerk, that this will be no ordinary summit. This one simply cannot afford to fail, as ANC secretary general Cyril Ramaphosa has said: there will have been too many false breakthroughs already. In this critical week in South Africa, Mandela is digging deep into the political capital he built up over three decades. The smile on the face of the old man in his garden hides a deep fear for the future if this latest initiative doesn't work. Now we wait to see whether De Klerk will smile back.

NEW STATESMAN AND SOCIETY, 25 SEPTEMBER 1992

THE SAVIMBI SYNDROME

Jonas Savimbi's decision not to accept the election results in nearby Angola provided a frightening vision of what could happen in South Africa if the first poll was mismanaged.

WHAT IS HAPPENING TO THE NORTH OF US IN ANGOLA should be sending shivers down the collective South African spine. If we're clever we will learn from our continental compatriots' mistakes: if we're not it's odds-on that we'll repeat them in the near future.

In its own way, Angola has been going through a process of political transition not dissimilar to ours. The peculiarly South African 'apartheid factor' was not the central issue, of course, but Angola also had to move from domination and endemic instability to openness and democracy. The inevitable, essential climax of the transition there was – as it will be here – an election. Angola got through its equivalent of Codesa, its ceasefires, its accords and minutes and records of understanding relatively smoothly, and surprisingly quickly. The process faltered sporadically, but the end result was an agreement on when to hold an election and how it should be held. The election came to pass.

The world should have known the outcome some time ago. Jonas Savimbi and Holden Roberto should by now have been in a government of national unity with Jose Eduardo dos Santos in Luanda. Instead, Savimbi's Unita generals have pulled out of the fledgling 'unified security forces', MPLA officials have been forced to leave several Unita-dominated towns, and the Commandante himself has departed Luanda for Huambo in his old southerly stamping ground. All the painstaking, exasperating, courageous negotiating work of the past months threatens to unravel like a ball of wool. If it does, the knots will be tighter than ever before. What went wrong?

A few simple issues stare out from what is an inordinately complicated situation. The most glaring is that we Africans, in general, talk a lot about democracy but don't really know – or pretend when it suits us not to know – what obligations the term carries. We are full of praise for its benefits, contemptuous of its duties. There was deep concern in Angola before the elections, emanating from both the MPLA and Unita, that in a country so ravaged and battle-scarred, a free and fair poll would be a tall order. Unita feared that the incumbent government would use its position to influence the outcome. The MPLA feared that Unita's powerful benefactors, the United States and South Africa, would work quietly to swing things the other way. Part of the solution – that is, a solution in so far as it was possible to reach the point of actually holding the election – was to utilise the good offices of the international community, in the form of the United Nations, to verify the process and the result. This had worked admirably in Namibia.

Warning signs flashed in the early stages of the lead-in to polling. It was noted worriedly that a country with a population 10 times the size of Namibia's was to be given one-tenth of the number of UN monitors that were dispatched to Windhoek. Nonetheless all the political actors agreed that the elections could go ahead. At that point responsibility for the verdict on whether the election was free and fair was handed over to the international monitors. The unspoken, but sacrosanct, principle was that if they said the result reflected the will of the people, then it did: 'May the best party win'. The international observers duly said the poll was a sufficiently accurate indication of Angolans' political affiliations. All signs pointed to a victory for Dos Santos, but also to enough support for Savimbi to make him an extremely powerful leader of the opposition. But then the Commandante cried 'foul'.

This is a terribly dangerous example for South Africa. If we, having gone to the polls, do not accept the result . . . well, the hackneyed phrase will apply that Angola's problems are a picnic by comparison. ANC supporters believe they will win 60 per cent or more of the vote. Pik Botha and Dawie de Villiers are convinced a Nationalist-led alliance will get a majority. Chief Buthelezi insists that opinion polls grossly underestimate Inkatha's support. Somebody's got to be wrong. But will they accept that when they discover it?

Savimbi agreed to abide by the rules of the game, and he is going back on his promise. His position is as immoral as that of the Algerian government, which simply annulled an election result which was running against it. In our even more difficult case, we simply have to ensure that this cannot happen. Saturation monitoring is part of the pre-emptive solution, but so is the extraction of written, solemn, public promises from each of the leaders before our election that they will accept the result with good grace. We need to decide early on who will be the judge of freeness and fairness. Democracy means, among other things, that you recognize that you might lose, this time round.

SATURDAY STAR, 10 OCTOBER 1992

THE GOOD SHIP TRICAMERA,
SAILING ON

Parliament might have lost much of its power, but none of its members had lost their voices. The intriguing duality of South African politics was on display for all to see.

WE HAVE ALL BEEN BACK IN THE TRICAMERAL PARLIAMENT this week, not entirely sure why, but always amused to watch the weird old institution showing signs of life when rigor mortis should have had its way long ago. The short special session has not failed to produce its quota of *bons mots*. There was never-say-die Allan Hendrickse musing: 'Life can only be understood backwards'. He was clearly thinking back to the time when he had about twice the number of Labour Party MPs that he does now. There was an argument of sorts over whether the special session was costing the taxpayer R2-million or R10-million. This particular inconclusive altercation cost the taxpayer several thousand, at least.

The Conservatives, unhappy about their whipped-cur image since the referendum, came up with a new insult for FW. 'Ian Smith', they bellowed when the president rose to speak. 'Ian Smith. Ian Smith.' Some Nationalists made a point of looking up at the public gallery to see whether the old Rhodesian warhorse was paying a courtesy visit. A woman with a reedy voice stood up in the gallery and prayed loudly. Parliament should repent, she said, before being escorted back into the real world outside. Parliament remained unmoved, and unrepentant. Its members were by now used to thousands of ANC supporters baying for their blood from beneath Louis Botha's statue, so a single evangelist in the house was not a problem. Presently, after a few rowdy exchanges, the Speaker made a ruling. It was OK for CP members to interject, he said, 'but they should not make their interjections as a choir'. The CP hecklers ensured that their contributions were not in tune.

Watching all of this one thought, unavoidably, of Admiral James Stockdale, Ross Perot's hard-of-hearing running mate and surely the world's most disarmingly honest politician right now. His phrase, coined in this week's television debate with Quayle and Gore, resonated in distant Cape Town: 'Who am I? Why am I here?' The only one who really knew who he was and why he was here was President de Klerk. This was as it should be, as the whole thing was his idea in the first place. FW had no doubt whatsoever that he was the leader of the forces of light, and that his task was to dump on the forces of darkness. He did so magisterially. One was tempted to ask why it was necessary to have parliament recalled in order for everyone to attack the ANC, but it was too late for that.

There is an intriguing duality to the politics of South Africa today: normality and madness are present in almost equal measure. The continued functioning of the tricameral parliament shows off both elements to great advantage: you can't ignore it, but then again it's difficult to take it completely seriously. As this week's session drew to a close I thought of what Luigi Lucatelli said all those years ago when politics got too much for him. 'Farewell, good sirs, I am leaving for the future. I will wait for humanity at the crossroads, 300 years hence.' See you there, South Africa.

SATURDAY STAR, 17 OCTOBER 1992

THE PROCEDURAL PUPPY-DOG

Unperturbed by its defeat in parliament, the government bull-dozed a controversial law through the President's Council, one of the most discredited institutions of the old system.

———————

THERE ARE TIMES FOR CHOOSING ONE'S WORDS CAREFULLY, and times to say to hell with that. This time calls for the latter. To hell with the President's Council.

This shabby, gerrymandered institution – a lingering legacy of the arrogance of the PW Botha era – has been used to foist upon South Africa a law that only Nationalists and AWB members want. The Democratic Party's David Gant, not an intemperate man, describes the saga as 'procedural rape'. Tony Leon calls the Bill 'a charter for crooks, criminals and assassins.' Consider the undemocratic lengths to which President de Klerk has been prepared to go to get this grubby law on to the statutes. A parliamentary committee and then the tricameral parliament itself – hardly made up of South Africa's most radical politicians – could not stomach the Further Indemnity Bill. They threw it out. De Klerk picked it up again – with evident distaste, but that does not excuse his actions – and passed it to his pro-cedural puppy-dog: the aptly-named President's Council, with its fully warrantied NP majority. Then, just to make things even more transparent, the PC's debates (the outcome of which we all knew anyway) were truncated because the government wanted a decision right away. Having gone so far, Pretoria seemed to decide, it wasn't even necessary to keep up pretences. Wouldn't you love to know the real reason for the government's desperation to enact an amnesty via the back door? It must be a humdinger.

But leave aside for the moment the PC's shameful role in railroading this legislation through. Look at the institution itself. Before this final glare of publicity, this belated moment of perverse relevance, the council continued to tick over in sumptuous obscurity. According to the government's figures, the PC costs about R10-million a year. What has it been doing? Well, up to this point in the De Klerk presidency, it has kept its head down and tinkered with a few 'research projects', of which no-one took too much notice. I have no axe to grind with individual members, but it is not unreasonable to argue that the council was in large part a jobs-for-pals exercise; a kind of five-star retirement village for loyal servants, a suites-only Lost City on the Cape peninsula.

It served at the pleasure of the state president, investigated things he wanted investigated and, because of its composition, commonly told him things he wanted to hear. In spite of having members of the parliamentary opposition in its ranks, it functioned as little more than a (very expensive) private research institute, publicly funded. The PC's Nationalist controllers were not unaware of this image. In a briefing earlier this month at the President's Council complex on Stalplein – easily the most luxurious of government buildings – journalists were told: 'Ladies and gentlemen, this is not a political document, nor are its contents part of a political viewpoint . . . ' The report being presented was a study of electoral systems, requested by the state president. As it happens, the study was interesting, but the point is that it was deeply political, and to pretend otherwise was to insult the public's intelligence. If the NP wants to have a think-tank, that is fine by me – but they must pay for it with their money, not yours and mine.

The PC's own propaganda pamphlet is revealing in the self-justificatory lengths it goes to: 'The image of the President's Council as a creator of a climate conducive to reform must be emphasized. Media commentary and public opinion largely confirm its reform contribution . . . As the first President's Council pursued consensus decision-making, this means that consensus politics in South Africa was largely initiated by the President's Council.' Oh really? This model of consensual politics yesterday reported, unblushingly, that 'the majority of its members agreed that the (Further Indemnity) Bill met its objectives' and therefore recommended that it be forwarded to the state president for his assent. Only that 'majority' and its governmental masters agree. This is a curious interpretation of consensus.

It is scandalous enough that we, the taxpayers, have allowed the President's Council to plod on profligately, without protest. We are now paying an even higher price for our apathy, watching helpless as what was at best an expensive irritant transforms itself into the instrument by which to flout every surviving democratic tenet. It is high time that the PC is dissolved and the millions are put where they are really needed. But the government is doing no such thing. We will have to content ourselves with calling on those members of the PC nominated by opposition parties to resign in disgust. They can no longer lend their names, even obliquely, to the travesty.

SATURDAY STAR, 31 OCTOBER 1992

MORE OF THE SAME
IS NOT ENOUGH

The outrageous levels of violence in South Africa were no longer news - and nor were successive security force attempts to restore law and order. The public was losing faith.

THE SIGHT OF TROOPS POURING INTO NATAL BY THE planeload should be encouraging but it is not. The country should be saying thank heavens as it watches the soldiers disembark and snake off into the hills of death but it does not. Instead the country says so what, because it has seen this all before.

People know that Operation Iron Fist did not close any of our open wounds. Why should they believe Operation Peace will be any different? And so there is dull fatalism. Is it not extraordinary that in the wake of the announcement of the latest security intervention in Natal, no-one – not politicians, not the media, not the public – has enthusiastically expressed the hope that this time the violence might really be stopped? The assumption, unspoken, is simply that this will not happen. We have to look at ourselves, at how conditioned we have become to accepting the unacceptable.

In important areas of South Africa the violence and

crime now qualifies for the description 'endemic'. When the Minister of Law and Order talks about the government still being in control, he means still in control of the security forces. Equally demonstrably, it will not be brought under control by the mere fact of sending in more soldiers and more police. Voices from all parts of South Africa and many parts of the larger world out there have called on Nelson Mandela and Mangosuthu Buthelezi to meet, as a precursor to a sustained political effort to bring peace to Natal. These calls are right, and history will judge the politicians harshly for turning up their noses at each other while people die horribly and in their hundreds. But even if this meeting were to take place today, would the killing stop? It would not. It has to be stopped by practical as well as symbolic measures, and this is where the folly of yet another 'Operation Peace' comes in.

It is time for us to take a leap into the future. The alternative is to let the present strangle us. Anyone with eyes to see knows that part of the problem – an irreparable part, not one that can be fiddled with – is that the security forces do not enjoy the confidence of the vast majority of South Africans with whom they have to interact. The reasons for this are irrelevant. It is a fact. We therefore find ourselves trapped like hamsters on a spinning wheel: we are told that only when there is an interim government can we have a restructured, representative army and police force, but we cannot reach interim government while there is violence. The present army and police cannot stop the violence because they are not of the communities, or trusted by them. So the wheel spins: violence increases and a negotiated settlement draws farther away.

In a 70-page memorandum to the United Nations in July, Lawyers for Human Rights director Brian Currin suggested a way out of the impasse. It has not, to my knowledge, been taken seriously by anyone of consequence. Briefly put, the proposal provides for the immediate formation of a South African 'peace force', made up of members of all significant parties in various areas, and

246

accountable to the National Peace Accord. Currin writes that the 'peace force will both figuratively and literally be a visible and bold symbol of the multi-lateral (negotiations) process.' He visualizes agreement between all the parties involved on the way in which the peace force should be structured, and the drafting of a clear and achievable mandate. Confidence-building symbolism would be critical: the peace force would have a special uniform, it would fly a special flag over its special bases, and its activities would be monitored by international organisations. Further its members, beady eyes on each other constantly, would effectively monitor themselves. The force would undertake everything from crowd control, to paramedical assistance, to socio-economic development. If it worked it could serve as a visionary example of what the installation of interim government might do for South Africa's sagging spirit; it could well be the future in embryo.

If you say this sounds like a tall order, you are right: there would be vexed questions of financing and ultimate control, and of interaction with the crime-prevention functions of the existing forces. But the idea has the potential to break the deadlock. Simply doing more of what has been done before does not.

SATURDAY STAR, 7 NOVEMBER 1992

SCANDAL FATIGUE

Allegations of corruption and dirty tricks came thick and fast - so thick and so fast that a sensation-weary public could hardly keep up. The government rode out the troubles.

A SCANDAL WHICH IN ANY NORMAL COUNTRY WOULD TOPPLE a government broke in South Africa this week. In point of fact, there were four of them. By next week they will be all but forgotten. Our scandal fatigue is now chronic, our sense of morality moribund, and our power to voice outrage about corrupt practices in future governments tragically undermined.

This week's roll of dishonour, in descending order of demerit, is as follows: Project Echoes, Parsons, De Meyer and Van den Heever. In Project Echoes, the SA Defence Force blithely admits to a plot to dig up dirt on the ANC and feed it to journalists, thus strengthening the position of the National Party in negotiations – all at the expense of the unconsulted taxpayers, many of whom happen to support the ANC. The Parsons report shows, inter alia, that seconded white security force officers connived with a KwaNdebele mafia, causing the deaths of many people in the process. The De Meyer report shows that seconded white bureaucrats connived with a greedy Lebowa elite to thieve millions for themselves. The Van den Heever report shows that a SA government department charged with black education stumbled and stole its way through millions, too.

All these revelations of contemptible, criminal behaviour elicit little more than a weary sigh from a profoundly disillusioned public. Why? Because we've had them before, and we've not seen anything like appropriate punishment being meted out. We expect the same to happen this time and, in fact, we fully expect further nauseating revelations in the months to come. We may not say it out loud, but we realize that in the matter of corruption, we are no better than the worst of the crooked countries north of our borders. With one difference: we alone have perfected the concept of the non racial corruption co-operative.

In its implications for the immediate future, Project Echoes speaks dark volumes. Let us get the facts straight: The Star secured top-secret military documents which indicate that in the first half of this year – that is, fully two years after President de Klerk declared a fair political fight in South Africa – the 'neutral' SADF hatched and funded a secret project to undermine the National Party's main negotiating partner. This was authorized by the Chief of the Army, with the concurrence of the chief of Military Intelligence, and probably with the knowledge of the minister – at the very moment that these people were smilingly engaged in a variety of negotiations with the ANC. It is a bad-faith scandal in the Inkathagate mould, but we cannot even be sure that this time a minister will be sent into the forests as ersatz punishment. I argued at that time that we had surrendered all claims to moral consistency. The government never once apologized for Inkathagate, and we were too weak-minded and lazy to make it do so.

The most frightening aspect of Project Echoes – besides the public apathy about it – is that the SADF does not appear to realize that it might have done anything wrong. 'Oh no,' say high-ranking State-employed witnesses, 'you don't understand. We weren't on a secret mission in London to kill Dirk Coetzee – we were only there to find embarrassing information about the ANC, plant it on selected journalists for publication, and thus discredit the organization in the eyes of the world.' What reaction did they expect? 'Oh, that's all right then, we thought you might have been doing something actually dishonourable'? And the arrogance of the SADF's apologists in pooh-poohing allegations of gross foul play is breathtaking. Yesterday Beeld, in a thunderingly self-righteous leader, took The Star to task for daring to call Project Echoes a 'dirty tricks operation'. It was the SADF's duty ('as the official protector of the land') to investigate external threats. Oh yes? And to secretly manipulate public opinion for blatantly party-political purposes? With our money? Beeld is right in saying that in terms of the constitution, the SADF remains our official security force. But it would do well to remember that it remains that on sufferance: the majority of people in this country do not want this constitution and they do not want the SADF as currently constituted. While the SADF waits to be transformed into a respectable and representative institution, it should keep its arrogant nose out of negotiations.

Will President de Klerk fire senior people for Project Echoes? Recent history suggests not. What a paltry, minor indiscretion does Richard Nixon's bugging of Watergate seem by comparison to our levels of cheating. It is difficult to imagine what magnitude of scandal it would require for South Africa's public servants to accept public responsibility. Ah, you say, but this is not the United States and after all we are a hardier people. I say we shame ourselves.

SATURDAY STAR, 14 NOVEMBER 1992

250

A HERO IN THE LAND
OF VILLAINS

One of the country's most respected judges, Richard Goldstone, used his statutory commission to raid a base for 'third force' operations - presaging a purge of the security forces.

BY NEARLY ALL ACCOUNTS, INCLUDING THE ANC's, Lieutenant-General Pierre Steyn is an honest man. The former Mirage pilot and air force wunderkind is a decent sort whose own code of ethics would not easily allow him to take part in a cover-up. That's what the people who know him are saying.

I do not know General Steyn, and so what I have to say is not a personal attack, but a political one. In response to the profoundly damaging revelation of a Military Intelligence task force whose purpose in life was to dig up dirt on the ANC's military wing, the government has done what the government always does. It has appointed a representative of the accused to investigate the accused. Time, and much more, has been bought. General Steyn and his SA Police colleague General Conradie are to report to President de Klerk on the doings of the State's security services. We are not told when this investigation should be completed – and even when it is, the president will decide what parts of the

251

findings, if any, are suitable for public consumption. We have been often in this place before, and I don't like it.

The hundreds of files discovered at a secret MI hideout in Houghton are now safely in the possession of the generals. I predict that we will see only a fraction of their contents, if we're lucky. But perhaps the most worrying element of the latest dirty tricks scandal is the fury it has elicited from the answerable-to-no-one security forces. Mr Justice Goldstone, the messenger, has been attacked in order to distract attention from his message. Listening to SADF and SAP spokesmen – and their apologists – one is forced to ask: just who is on trial here? Instead of expressing shock at his revelations (and gratitude to the judge for bringing them to public notice), the army and police vent spleen against Goldstone for not knowing his place.

The simple fact is that without Goldstone, South Africans would never have known about the grubby plan to hire a convicted double-killer and CCB agent to discredit the government's chief political rival. Just as, without the courage and tenacity of the *Vrye Weekblad*, we would never have known about the CCB. It would still be fully functional; General Eddie Webb and Colonel Joe Verster would still be hatching plots in sumptuous offices, and Staal Burger would still be the head of 'region 6'. It says a great deal that the government has never brought itself to say thank you to those who have identified this poison in the system. A clean government might have been expected to say: 'We are shocked. Could this really be happening in our departments? We will root it out immediately.' Instead we get cold rage and defensiveness. We are told that if we – newspapers, judges, human rights groups and others with limited powers – can do all the detective work, the police work, write up the charges and make them stick, then, if the government cannot find a hole in our arguments, it might perhaps consider 'appropriate action'. Like early retirement for an offender, with a fat pension package.

It is difficult to resist the conclusion that, in the Goldstone Commission, the government has created a monster.

Used to appointing commissions of inquiry which interpret their briefs so narrowly that legalism overrides the quest for truth, and which take so long in their investigations that the public loses interest, Pretoria now has to come to terms with Mr Justice Goldstone. This is no tame judge and no political lackey. If he can withstand the profoundly unfair barrage of criticism being levelled at him – and his record suggests he can – then the government will come to realize that, having invoked his commission, they cannot simply do away with it when it no longer suits them. Judge Goldstone is perhaps the most important lifeline to credibility the government has. Like it or not, it is going to have to give him at least some of the additional powers he has requested, or face losing him altogether. And Pretoria has made life more difficult for itself by greeting his earlier findings, which were properly harsh on the ANC and Inkatha, with almost indecent relish. It cannot easily turn around now and tell him where to get off. In short, it cannot have it both ways.

I fear we have lost the battle of the MI files. We will not again be presented with the bald illuminating truth of dirty secret documents, because the internal investigation will not act in the way that Goldstone did. But the war for the truth has been stepped up by this week's events, and no amount of blustering and spitting from those with something to hide can change that. In a land of villains, Judge Goldstone is a South African hero. No matter what the generals say.

SATURDAY STAR, 21 NOVEMBER 1992

THE BLACK MAN WITH THE GUN
AND THE GRIN

A terror attack on whites at a golf club in Kingwilliamstown raised the spectre of uncontrollable racial violence - reminding South Africans that its absence was surprising.

———————

THERE HE STOOD, LARGE AS DEATH: WHITE SOUTH AFRICA'S worst nightmare. A black man with a gun, pointing it at people for no fathomable reason other than the pallid colour of their skins. And worse . . . he grinned before he opened fire, before the grenade he rolled among the innocents ripped their limbs from their bodies.

It has long been a curiosity to the outside world that in the whole history of apartheid, the number of straightforwardly racial black-on-white 'revenge' killings has made up but a fraction of the vast national death toll. Whites here have thought about it too, but the fear has been too deep to be spoken aloud. No longer, after King William's Town. Now white people, ordinary decent white people, are frightened as never before. Brutal robbery, and the rape and murder that so often accompany it, is one terrible, reprehensible, but perversely comprehensible thing. The golf club killings are somehow different. They are a vision of outright madness.

How have we reacted? In a way, in my view, that feeds the madness rather than fights it. We have had an orgy of recriminations, of 'my-loss-matters-more-than-yours' idiocy. Whites have howled in proper, but uneven, outrage. Blacks have screamed in anger at the fact that the white outrage was absent at Folweni, Esikhawini and a hundred more place names now known for their massacres above all else. Both responses are understandable, of course, but lamentable at a moment in our history when we must all help each other or surely perish.

It is true, what the foreigners say about us: we South Africans have been stained by the seas of blood in which we swim. Whites especially are callous about atrocities in the townships, where most of the victims of our political folly still live. But can it help anyone to take pleasure from the whites' pain when it arrives? I believe we have to understand and overcome one gigantic obstacle that stands in the way of all of us discovering our common humanity. King William's Town was middle-middle-class South African suburbia benignly at play. Whites know people like the golf club victims, are people like them; people who have never seen a Boipatong or Crossroads, and who simply cannot fix a picture in their minds when they hear a report of a massacre at a shebeen or a night vigil. Now, with a small leap of understanding, they can and must. And on both sides of the still-intact racial divide, we can share compassion and anger and above all the will to make the killing stop – whether in King William's Town or Khayelitsha. It is possible for a society, united to one end, to change itself.

It is not true, as some media reports have it, that the golf club attack was the 'first of its kind'. There was the random, mad black-on-white stabbing spree on Durban's beachfront. Further back, there was Poqo and the Bashee River. But if they did not focus the national mind, then perhaps King William's Town can. Black deaths, white deaths, all deaths are South African deaths, and for each we will pay an equal price. Our country is in many ways unique. In the matter of fratricidal killing this is not so. In this week of black and white horrors I happened to read an account by a man who had just returned to his native Northern Ireland. He wrote: '(My nation's soul) is a soul that never quickens except to the dead, harsh rhetoric of its demagogues. It is a soul that is content to be soothed by the dull pieties of its priests and pastors. The horrors that occur almost on a daily basis are now taken for granted. A killing condemned is a killing forgotten . . .

'One of the most striking features of Northern Ireland is the gulf between middle- and working-class people. The killing is almost entirely confined to the poorer quarters. As far as most middle-class Ulster people are concerned, it might as well be happening in Bosnia as Belfast. The real problem is smugness. It is all-pervasive, and prevents people from confronting the consequences of their own hatreds and bigotries – some 3,000 corpses and still rising.'

How painfully easy it would be to substitute 'South Africa' for 'Northern Ireland', and just multiply the death toll. We can learn from the level of self-knowledge that the Irishman has achieved.

I was also struck this week, reading the journal of William Ten Rhyne of the Dutch East India Company, written in 1673 when he first came into contact with our land and its nascent citizens. Of us Ten Rhyne wrote: 'Nothing is more barbarous than this country, where the rugged climate and rocky mountains seem to have produced men of their own kind.'

Can we prove him wrong?

SATURDAY STAR, 5 DECEMBER 1992

THE CRUSTACEAN MENTALITY

The year ended badly, with negotiations still foundering and confidence on the wane. It was already clear that only a new government could effectively tackle the violence and crime.

THE MOOD OF THIS HOLIDAY PERIOD IS VERY DIFFERENT from what has gone before for the sun-lovers on the southern tip. I hope it will not be the same this time next year. This year we are staying at home while foreigners are staying away. We are frightened; ours has become a truly frightening homeland in the past 12 months. We are also poorer and expecting to become more so, and there is a wholly non racial sense of uncertainty and fearfulness about what the new year will bring. Everywhere the crustacean mentality is on display: tuck into your hard shell, make yourself small and inconspicuous, scuttle rather than swagger, protect what you have and take no chances. I suppose this indicates that we are still a logical people. Caution is a rational response to what has transpired in our country since Codesa 1. But it cannot last forever, or we will shrivel into near-nothingness.

What has to change between this Christmas and the next, if we are to regain our natural boisterousness? A great deal, of course, in practically every corner of society.

Some specific statistics are worth looking at. It has been reported widely in London (and this is why so many potential tourists from the UK would rather risk IRA bombs on Regent Street than dying on an idyllic Indian Ocean beach) that South Africa's numbers just don't add up as a tourist destination for foreigners. For the moment. This has nothing to do with exchange rates – even after the devaluation of sterling, the pound is a mammoth to the rand's mouse – but simply with security. It is a plain fact, albeit galling, that the murder of two British tourists in Natal will cause widespread holiday cancellations whereas a massacre in the Midlands will not. I do not believe that this has as much to do with the race of the victims as it does with nationality. Foreigners see our fratricidal violence (be it in Boipatong or Ventersdorp) as our business, an internal affair. When a tourist from their own country falls victim, however, all sorts of alarm bells ring.

And so to the statistics. Officialdom tells us that 33 times more people are murdered every year in South Africa than in Britain, which has a population twice the size of ours. In 1990 the British police reported 669 cases of homicide, including murder, manslaughter, and infanticide. Last month the South African police reported that this year's murder rate was running at an average of about 60 a day – hardly good reading in a travel brochure.

We are still, in the British Foreign Office's formal estimation, not a high-risk destination. Thus the situation is worsening, but not yet out of control. It could of course become so, very quickly, if we toss away 1993 politically, as we did 1992. Crime and general social atrophy, we have learnt, will increase as long as we remain stuck in the interregnum, the nether world between apartheid and the new South Africa. It is a depressingly safe bet to say that if we reach the festive season next year without an operational and racially representative interim government, we will all be hiding deeper within our protective shells.

Next year must be the year of interim government. And an interim government must make a priority of re-establishing respect for law and order in South Africa. The constitution-making it must facilitate is of course crucial, but it will remain merely a piece of paper if the spiral towards anarchy is not arrested. The interim government will be fraught with its own special problems; no-one expects it to be a panacea for all our ills. But it will mark the first time in our history that we have all begun to govern ourselves together, and to share power and responsibility. It is our best, our only, shot. Bring it on.

SATURDAY STAR, 19 DECEMBER 1992

AN UNSOLICITED SMILE
IN THE STREET

*Suddenly the mood began to change with the arrival of 1993.
This was the year in which the first fruits of negotiations would
arrive, and the waiting would begin to end.*

A STRANGE MOOD IS ABROAD IN THIS COUNTRY. THE SIGNALS
are mixed, but there are enough of them to make one sit
up and take notice. The thick, introspective, awful fog of
gloom which settled on most ordinary South Africans last
year is lifting slightly. There are unsolicited smiles in the
street again, noticeable now because they have been absent
for so long.

A cynic might say – and be right in saying – that the
reason people are feeling a little better about life in 1993 is
because 1992 is over; a year which will take its place alongside the Rinderpest in South Africa's historical hit-parade
of unspeakable interludes. But there is more to it than
that. I detect the resurgence of this country's (non racial)
bluff, frontier spirit. People are tired of crouching behind
walls and waiting for the sound of the cataclysm; they are
thinking about looking over the parapet and maybe – what
the hell – trying to make a go of things again.

Perhaps the holiday sun was too warm and the sky too

cloudless, and perhaps I am seeing things where they are not. But if I am right, then we are witnessing a little miracle, and it must not be squandered. There have, since February 1990, been several half-moments of optimism which cried out to be seized, and each time, the politicians saw them only once they had passed. We are lucky to have been given another chance.

In terms of negotiations, the biggest problem in South Africa today is not substance but psychology. We already know in broad brushstrokes what the preliminary 'deal' will be, and we can describe more or less what an interim government will look like and how it will function. That much was achieved long ago, in the run-up to the disastrous second plenary session of Codesa. What was lacking then, and might be appearing now, was the will on the part of the political leaders to place the national interest over their own, and to do what has to be done.

If, as it does seem, the desperate urgency of achieving tangible progress towards non-racial government has finally sunk in, we have a fighting chance. But somehow the leaders have to be persuaded that it is not enough simply to realize there might be nothing left to fight over if things carry on as they have. They must act on this realisation. This brief period of proto-optimism, if that is what it is, should be treated by the politicians as a sensitive plant, the likes of which might not be seen again in a hurry. What is needed now, from at the very least President de Klerk and Mr Mandela, is a concerted, co-ordinated effort to enthuse South Africans about the prospect of interim government. It is no good to talk about progress to other insiders, with a nod and a wink, while the masses outside the negotiating halls (or, these days, negotiating *bomas*) live on in fear and ignorance.

Many people are fearful of interim government because they do not see it for what it is: the first proof of real progress towards a workable non-racial system. It can provide proof to blacks that the changes will indeed affect their lives, and proof to whites that the changes will not

261

destroy theirs. De Klerk and Mandela should be spreading this message intentionally and tirelessly, creating a sense of expectation and excitement. I would like to see them sharing a platform, and saying: We are political enemies, and we shall be fighting one another in an election, but we are also South Africans who agree on the basic democratic shape of the future. They should be urging ordinary South Africans to come along with them on the greatest political adventure in our history.

If we are not already in an election year, we are very close to it. We have a tremendous amount of work to do before polling day dawns – not just in the logistical areas of voter education and the like, gargantuan as those tasks are, but in teaching each other that democracy means participating in the full knowledge that one might lose this time around. The lead must be taken by the leaders. What statesmanship we have had so far – De Klerk's courageous leap into the future, Mandela's exemplary lack of bitterness – has been occasional and unco-ordinated, and overshadowed by the sorry catalogue of attendant disasters. The time has come to come together.

It may never again be so propitious.

SATURDAY STAR, 9 JANUARY 1993

BUSHVELD BONHOMIE, BUCOLIC BILATERALS

Yet another new term entered South Africa's cluttered political lexicon. Bosberade, or bush meetings, became the events at which the most important decisions were taken.

———————

LIKE IT OR NOT, WE'VE PLACED ALL OUR EGGS IN ONE *bosberaad*. Well, more than one, but you know what I mean. At a selected *boma* near you, South Africa's politicians are contemplating the coals and trying to find one another by the roseate glow of the flickering flames. One hopes there are ample supplies of Klipdrift. Because the outcome of all this bushveld bonhomie is a matter of life and death for every one of us.

Last year when the negotiating process ran into trouble (which was approximately weekly), the preferred solution was the working group. Sad to relate, this did not do the trick. Codesa 2 collapsed in an undignified heap, and everyone fell over everyone else in the rush to pull out of negotiations first. As the year drew to a close it looked hopeless. Until someone thought of . . . the *bosberaad*.

What is the difference between a *bosberaad* and a working group? you might ask. Well, the wonderful African surrounds, for one thing, but also something else. The working group sessions of 1992 were characterized by an hour or two of absolute secrecy, followed by a veritable flood of 'leaks' from the various participants as each tried to put his or her particular gloss on the compromises they had just made. The result, inevitably, was that once everyone's version of events made it into the media, whatever agreements that had been reached were swiftly reneged upon.

The point about a *bosberaad* is that it does not take place in the World Trade Centre, there are no journalists hanging around at coffee breaks, and the only telecommunications available are used to inform the nearest human beings about the latest peregrinations of the indigenous wildlife. In short, a *bosberaad* is practically leak-proof – at least until the protagonists make it back to the metropolis. And that gives agreements a better chance of sticking. I have no doubt that this simple distinction has contributed to the fact that the handful of *bosberade* which have taken place have achieved more – in terms of making real negotiations possible once again – than a year's worth of working groups. Therefore, we should be deeply grateful to the prescient Nationalist who came up with this unique political device in the first place.

And yet . . . It is true that our straits are so dire that practically anything is permissible if it will help to get us out of them. But the *bosberaad* style of politics is setting a very unhealthy precedent; comfortable for the politicians, deceptively dangerous for the rest of us. Hindsight tells us that one of the many flaws of Codesa Mark I was the fact that the process became somehow dislocated from the people. While the rest of South Africa went about its heterogeneous business, the professional negotiators were surging ahead privately like long-lost cousins, understanding each other better and making allowances for one another's foibles. The ordinary folk had no detailed idea of the process that was taking place: witness the chasm between the ANC's top leadership and its run-of-the-mill militants when they got together at a post-Codesa policy conference.

264

The multiparty negotiating forum should become a travelling roadshow, holding plenary sessions in town halls from Potchefstroom to Piketberg, so that 'the people' might come to identify with it and claim it as their own. It is not too late to do this, so long as the *bosberaad* habit has not become an addiction. Full speed ahead to each and every bucolic bilateral that is scheduled between now and the end of next month, by which time everybody should be ready to reconvene Codesa in some form or another. But then we must thank the *bosberaad* for its assistance and bid it farewell. Codesa 3 – or call it what you will – cannot take place in a shroud of secrecy, or it will fail to take the people along with it.

The single most liberal proposal yet made in the course of negotiations has come from Joe Slovo, chairman of the Communist Party. He it was who suggested that Codesa's deliberations be fully opened to public scrutiny, so that those outside the smoke-filled rooms could judge for themselves the quality of the decisions being taken in their names. It is a proposal he should make again; and it should receive support from every politician who uses the word democracy without crossing his fingers behind his back. We need this period of excessive discretion in order to re-establish the minimum amount of trust and reason required to restart talks, and stave off a stupid, second-rate war. But we must never forget that it is a means which, if taken to its extreme, will nullify the end.

SATURDAY STAR, 16 JANUARY 1993

ANOTHER LAST WHITE
PARLIAMENT

Parliament assembled yet again, but even the MPs realized the
limited role of the institution. Little of importance could be done
without the say-so of the surrogate parliament up north.

FOR THE THIRD YEAR RUNNING, I FIND MYSELF ATTENDING
the opening week of what we annually describe as the 'last
white parliament'. It really is going to be embarrassing if
we're all back again next year, doing the same thing. But,
with the uncertainty of experience, it looks as if finally this
is going to be a decisive negotiating year.

There are rough patches ahead (in fact we should be
hitting one just as you read this), but nevertheless when
parliament reconvenes it will no longer be the expression
of white control over our country. It will be something
different. Already, this opening of parliament has been
different to what went before. One got the distinct impression, listening to the large troupe of performing ministers
and deputy ministers, that they were choosing their words
carefully. Also, something very familiar was missing from
most of the briefings: the ritual savagings of the ANC. Like
De Klerk's opening speech itself, the outpourings of the
ministers were oddly consensual – as if the speakers were

aware that they were talking on behalf of a group wider than just the government. Indeed, it seemed obvious that ministers such as Louis Pienaar were painfully conscious of the fact that they could not make unilateral pronouncements, no matter how much they might want to.

Major speeches, including those of De Klerk, Roelf Meyer and Derek Keys, sounded more like report-backs of what had occurred outside parliament than serious attempts to convince the assembled MPs to support a particular line of action. The old system has not been buried, but it has been partially paralysed. All eyes are now focusing beyond this parliament and on the logical outcome of the reform process, elections. The ANC was too busy to protest at the opening of parliament this year, because it was preparing for elections. Pienaar's Home Affairs ministry is working round the clock . . . registering people so they can vote in elections.

We need these elections, of course, and desperately so. They will be final confirmation to ourselves and the world that we have come up with a rational alternative to racial armageddon. But I wonder if we have any idea of the scale of the exercise we are letting ourselves in for, when we speak blithely of erecting 7,500 polling booths around the country for a ballot towards the end of this year, or early next. Minister Pienaar's labours notwithstanding, I don't believe we are doing nearly enough to prepare the country for its great democratic catharsis.

Time is desperately short, and we need to start now. Not just with the logistics, as daunting as they are, but with drumming into each other's heads democracy's maxims. I sometimes wonder, even, whether it wouldn't be a good idea for the multiparty negotiating forum to commit itself soon to a firm date for elections, but to make that date considerably later than those already proposed – say mid-1995. In this way everybody would have certainty about the ultimate outcome of the process, but we would have much more time to prepare.

Whatever the date settled upon, the Savimbi syndrome

remains a frightening prospect. In fact we cannot countenance it. We have to get in place a series of mechanisms which will rule it out. An independent electoral commission, a rule book for elections, an effective monitoring package, agreed and credible security measures, and so much more. It will take time to do this properly.

The politicians have, in many ways, already started their election campaigns. That's okay, but first we need to start a campaign to make elections possible at all.

SATURDAY STAR, 6 FEBRUARY 1993

BURGLAR-BARRED, BENIGHTED, BELOVED LAND

Coming home to South Africa from abroad reminded one of the palpable tension and fear in the country's cities. But also of the excitement, expectation, and plain old patriotism.

I CAME HOME THIS WEEK AFTER A MONTH ON THE OTHER SIDE of the world, in a country that held an election campaign during which the most violent incident was the throwing of an egg at the leader of the opposition. The egg missed, but still was front-page news. Everyone howled about 'political intolerance' and Australians tut-tutted about what their country was coming to. I wished we had a flying egg problem in South Africa, rather than a flying grenade problem. I wondered how I would feel coming home, this time. I had not heard a car alarm go off in four weeks, not perused a nightly death toll, not passed a single Immediate Armed Response van, not glanced with sheepish suspicion at the late-night diners occupying the table alongside mine in a restaurant. I had not, needless to say, read any newspaper reports in the mornings about a family in a car being strafed with automatic rifle fire for no reason that anyone in his right mind can fathom.

And yet I was not prepared for the surge of affection I felt for our benighted, burglar-barred homeland on arrival. Jan Smuts is still a funny-looking place compared to the great gateways of the Americas (and the antipodes), but I like it. It is much less ominous these days, too. In former years, returning residents used to be given the third-degree treatment (as if merely by having ventured into the *buiteland* we would be assumed to have committed some offence), but now one sweeps through proprietorially, as one should in the country of one's birth. We no longer have to fill in complicated and accusatory arrivals forms – since when? – and customs officers smile without damaging their career prospects. There seems to have been a loosening-up about the place (perhaps it is just lassitude), and it suits us better than the old gulag atmosphere. The uncertainty of being between old and new systems has its benefits.

It also has its costs, and sometimes these are more evident from the outside than from within. The fact is that the world out there – or those dwindling parts of it which are still intensely interested in us – is mightily confused about that our fate will be. They have got their heads around the fact that apartheid is gone, sort of, but they cannot understand why we have not yet come up with something to replace it. They don't know whether to relate to us as participants in a racial miracle, or wretched souls doomed to disaster. If anyone needs reminding that we are far away from having sorted out our future, that reminder comes from every foreigner you meet. We have joined that select band of beleaguered nationalities that automatically unleashes a set of unpleasant assumptions in others. It is bad enough that at home, when you announce your intention to visit Australia, most people immediately ask whether you will be seeking work in Sydney, or in Perth. It is worse when Australians ask the same question, and greet the answer that you have no intention of leaving home with a look of faintly amused, avuncular scepticism. They still think those of us who can leave, will leave. They think this because we have not shown them the system under which we intend to stay.

I went to the World Trade Centre at Kempton Park, now taken out of mothballs, to find out whether our negotiators are any closer to devising that system. They are. After the horrendous wastage of 1992, when the world really did begin to despair of us, we are again under sail towards our only national salvation: transitional structures, elections, interim rule and democracy. Then, with the political Pandora's Box out of the way, perhaps we can start to live like normal people. We can do it, as difficult as it might seem now. And I very much hope that if I ever do visit Australia again, at least some of the good burghers of Sydney and Perth will be asking me about the chances of emigrating *to* South Africa.

SATURDAY STAR, 20 MARCH 1993

ENOUGH SAD SUBURBS IN FOREIGN CITIES

No-one talked about it, but everyone knew it was happening. Thousands of whites were quietly emigrating, so full of fear for the future that they could not stay to face it.

THEY ARE EERIE, THE FAR-FLUNG, *LAAGER*-LIKE settlements of the modern-day South African *trekboer*. You find them all over the world now. It is 1993, the eve of our date with destiny, but many of our people have already gone away forever. Most major English-speaking cities have their 'South African quarter' these days, and they look like permanent places.

Drive into the suburbs of London or Houston or Toronto or Sydney which have been colonized by thousands of recent emigrants from the southern tip of Africa, and you cannot fail to feel unsettled. We are accustomed to the exotic 'Little Italys', 'Chinatowns' and 'Latin Quarters' of foreign capitals, but haven't realized that we have become a distinctive part of this cosmopolitan community of the displaced. The local taxi drivers, if they haven't yet picked up on your accent, will remark matter-of-factly as they drive through an area: 'That's where the South Africans live'.

For the most part, the South African 'ghettoes' are not

ghettoes at all, save for their ethnic claustrophobia. They are usually leafy and opulent. The road signs might be different – as is the vegetation, and the look of the sky – but they could otherwise be mistaken for Sandton or Constantia. The air is filled with the flat vowels and get-your-own-way injunctions of South Africa's white, English-speaking, middle-to-upper-middle classes. Often there is a Nando's Chickenland and a shop on the corner that sells *boerewors* and biltong, even to those who didn't frequent such establishments before they left home.

Why am I talking about the emigre suburbs we have spawned? Not because they are an entirely new phenomenon; nomadism is a defining characteristic of our century. Not because I have the right to sit in judgment over those who exercised their individual rights and left. (I don't believe any of the leavers have gone without twinges of regret, and I think very few of them will truly assimilate into their new societies. They will content themselves with the hope that their children might.) Rather, because they fill me with sadness and I wonder whether we recognize the meaning of these places, and the messages they send in a gradually dwindling stream of cards and calls to those who stayed at home.

These South African quarters are a symbol of South Africa's collective failure to believe in itself. Most of the leavers have left because of this. With them have gone container loads of university degrees, professional skills and productivity, accompanied by supertankers-full of money, exported who-knows-how. Our yet-to-be-born new society is gravely impoverished by their departure, and we do not yet know how many more will go. We are sitting on our hands, doing nothing, waiting to be told the answer.

It is more and more obvious that more and more South Africans feel, to use the latest ugly but accurate jargon, 'disempowered'. They think that whatever they do they cannot influence their own destinies; it is in the hands of others and they are not sure if they trust them. Research shows – and perhaps this will come as a surprise to white suburbanites – that this feeling of powerlessness courses just as strongly through the veins of the townships. We are like a nation of domestic pets, hoping against hope that someone else will look after us. If we, in all our different shapes and sizes, cannot convince ourselves that we can do something to make the new South Africa a place we want to live in, there will be many more faraway surrogate suburbs – just poorer ones. There will also be at home sprawling urban dormitories filled with resentful and fearful South Africans who wish above all that they could have got away. We will have talked ourselves into failure.

This week one segment of our society served notice that this fate is not good enough. The Consultative Business Movement published a book – 'Managing Change: A Guide to the Role of Business in Transition' – which tells its readers how they can grab hold of, and influence, the direction of the future. I attended the launch of the book in Johannesburg and saw the doubts on the faces, the disbelief born of disillusion, but also the dawning that if we don't grasp individual responsibility, we cede it to others. 'Managing Change' is a handbook for businessmen, but also a blueprint for civil society. Everybody should read it.

It might mean fewer South African suburbs in Sydney.

SATURDAY STAR, 27 MARCH 1993

OUR HOUR OF GREAT CRISIS

Chris Hani, arguably the most popular leader in South Africa after Nelson Mandela, was assassinated outside his home. The country teetered on the brink of disaster.

THERE ARE SOME PEOPLE IN THIS COUNTRY WHO ARE STUPID enough and vicious enough to think that Chris Hani 'had it coming to him'. They should now, in this hour of great crisis, confront their own idiocy.

Chris Hani's death will not further the atavistic white Right's hopeless cause. Quite the reverse: it will make a fair settlement among all the races of South Africa much more difficult to achieve – and at the very moment that the outlines of such a settlement were beginning to shimmer on the horizon.

When, three years ago, President de Klerk and Mr Mandela set us on this difficult course to an entirely new society, everything changed overnight. Each credible political leader, of whatever ideological hue – including erstwhile tyrants and terrorists – became an essential cog in the engine of change. From that day on, to lose any cog was to hear the motor sputter; to lose a vital one was to risk seeing it die forever.

Chris Hani was a vital cog. Our newspaper took the

Umkhonto we Sizwe chief and Communist Party leader to task whenever we believed his demagogic outbursts were inflaming already raw passions. We took him at his word and praised him when he criticized human rights abuses in ANC camps, called the township self-defence units to order and challenged Apla. But we never, never failed to take him seriously. He was a man with immense support, and he was consequently a great potential force for good – or evil. When Chris Hani spoke, the militant youths of the townships listened with an attentiveness that few other leaders could command. The assassin's bullets were therefore the instrument of unimaginable ignorance, as well as cruelty.

Political leaders have thus far reacted remarkably to the sickening news of the Boksburg assassination. Fury, pain and shock have been expressed, as they should, but all sides have grasped the wider implications and called for the acceleration, not the dissolution, of the negotiating process. We must do all we can to ensure that this understanding filters down to the ordinary people of South Africa.

It must be understood that 'white South Africa' did not kill Chris Hani, any more than 'black South Africa' killed Clare Silberbauer. Sick elements from either side did, and the rest of us, the vast majority who want peace, must band together to isolate and frustrate their designs. The politicians have made their start, at the top. Ordinary citizens can respond in their own way, showing in how we talk to one another that we understand each other's pain, and that we will not tolerate these atrocious killings from whatever ethnic group they might spring.

When Chris Hani said, as he often did, that 'the struggle continues', most whites winced and snarled. They thought of the man in the battle fatigues in an African guerrilla camp, plotting the downfall of the Pretoria government. Yes, he talked of guns and liberty, but in fact, and especially in the last days of his shamefully proscribed life, he was speaking primarily about a 'struggle' with which every decent South African can identify: the struggle for peace.

He was not a saint, and there is no need to canonize him or whitewash his memory, either way. He was neither the vengeful demon nor the all-wise deliverer of our country's schismatic folklore. He was a complicated, unfolding, mighty South African character who was playing, and deserved to play, a big part in creating a new country out of the old. South Africa needed Chris Hani. His implacable political enemies, of whom there were many, have seen this truth clearly. The memory of this talented, committed countryman will be properly served if whoever eventually replaces him can pick up the gauntlet he threw down; the gauntlet of waging peace, a task so very much more difficult than that of prosecuting war.

Rest in peace, Chris Hani, and peace be with us who remain.

THE STAR, 12 APRIL 1993

WHEN WORDS CAN KILL,
SHUT UP

The levels of warlike rhetoric were raised as never before. Politicians claimed they did not intend to incite their followers - but many took their words literally.

THERE ARE MANY PROMINENT PEOPLE IN THIS COUNTRY who should not be sleeping easily this weekend; their consciences should be gnawing at them. They should be thinking about some of the words they have used, and the effects those words might have had – might still have. Kipling called words 'the most powerful drug used by mankind', but here we toss them around like harmless playthings.

Before the assassin made up his mind to take Chris Hani's life, Hernus Kriel, from the platform of parliament, described Umkhonto we Sizwe as 'a bunch of criminals'. A powerful newspaper told its readers Hani was mustering a terrifying, vengeful 'Black People's Army'. Before lawless youths went on their stabbing and stealing spree on Wednesday, ANC Youth League leader Peter Mokaba told a gathering of youngsters: 'The young lions must not only bark and roar, but you must bite'. And before this whole sorry saga started, we had Eugene Terreblanche exhorting his followers to revolution, Inkatha members being encouraged to 'bugger up' the ANC, PAC leaders endorsing the slogan 'one settler, one bullet'. The list goes on.

Every one of these people will today swear they didn't mean what you thought they meant. These were euphemisms, metaphors, allegories, parables . . . they didn't really mean it *literally*. Well. It is too late to tell that to the people who listened to, and believed, those words. They missed the subtleties. Not nearly enough people in our country can read. Pitifully few will have been familiar with John Locke's wise observation that 'we should have had a great many fewer disputes in the world if words were taken for what they are, the signs of our ideas only, and not for things themselves'. The National Peace Accord, piously signed by so many of these figures, specifically outlaws inflammatory statements. It has been ignored; and no-one has been locked up for ignoring it. Once people discovered they could get away with mocking their undertakings, they did so with impunity. Chilling statements are commonplace in South Africa today. It is fair to ask whether we are not now reaping their mean harvest.

In Boksburg on Wednesday, an SACP speaker bluntly told the crowd that Kriel had issued 'an order from parliament for the assassination of MK leaders'. Kriel will of course say he did not mean that at all; and in turn the SACP speaker will insist he was not blaming Kriel specifically for Hani's death. However, there is no guarantee that the original audience to either statemant will be there to hear the disclaimers. The words come around and around again, leaving a vicious tangled trail behind them.

Loose, irresponsible words played their part in killing Chris Hani, just as they played their part in stoking the hatreds of Natal's warriors and the roadside assassins. We have become so accustomed to intemperate talk that I wonder whether we are still able to listen to quieter, less passionate reason. I will forever feel dulled and sickened by the terrible waste of Chris Hani's life. There is never any pleasure – or use – to be derived from saying 'I told you so'.

But I (there were others) did try to warn against the image that was built up of the man in white South Africans' eyes. We demonize each other so unthinkingly, so dangerously.

I got to know him in the course of my work, and I worried about the obvious chasm between his public persona and the human side of this exceptional South African. Hani was a politician, and he rightly came under attack for his views, often. But white South Africa knew nothing of the person away from the podium. He was intellectually razor-sharp, witty, warm, interested, principled, 'normal'. Once, while watching a soccer match, he asked me with laughter in his eyes: 'Why is it that most of our goalkeepers in this country are white?' I replied: 'Because we whites are more conservative, and that is a conservative position.' He roared in amusement, and said that made perfect sense.

But much more importantly, he convinced me early on that he was truly committed to a peaceful, negotiated settlement, fair to everyone in our country. This talk of his latter-day conversion to peace does not tell the whole story. Two years ago it was clear that he was on board the negotiations bus being driven by Mr Mandela. The danger was quite evident then that Mr Hani might become so demonized that when the time came to convince whites he was 'okay' after all, their fears would be too deeply etched to be removed.

SATURDAY STAR, 17 APRIL 1993

YOU KILLED A NEW SOUTH AFRICAN

So many people were dying violently that newspapers could not even report every death. More and more of the victims were random innocents, like Ali Weakley.

———————

A LOT OF PEOPLE DIED HORRIBLY IN SOUTH AFRICA IN THE past fortnight, as people have been dying here for a long time now. Even the best-intentioned among us begin to lose track of the numbers, names, places, details. Who, beyond the bruised community itself, can tell you the names of the Sebokeng dead, what sort of people they were, whether they had families, what made them laugh? I cannot. When someone like Chris Hani dies, someone known to so many, that event reaches into every corner of the country, as it should. But other deaths seem to pass us by.

One of those who died in the awful aftermath of the Hani assassination was not a major political figure, but I and others knew him and I would like to mark his passing. He was a big man, in body and heart, and in a country less used to senseless murder, this stupid, sickening killing would have touched more people than those who wept at his funeral in Grahamstown.

Ali Weakley and his brother Glen were shot to pieces, with automatic rifles, as they returned in their bakkie from a day's fishing near Mpandi in the Transkei on the eve of Chris Hani's funeral. There was no attempt to rob them. The gunmen who shot from the bushes disappeared into the soft-looking valley. No-one has any idea of who they were, or why they did this terrible thing. What we do know is that somehow, Ali and his brother were random victims of the crime committed in Dawn Park, Boksburg, such a long way away to the north. The dreadful dominoes started falling soon after Hani fell bleeding on his driveway; Ali was one of them.

What a victim for fate to have chosen. What monstrous irony, what obscenity. Ali was a 'new South African' long before most whites began even to think about the morality of the system under which they prospered and others groaned. At Rhodes University in the 1970s he was a rare specimen: rugby captain and instinctive, from-the-gut liberal. Ali had an annual intervarsity match against the University of Port Elizabeth called off, because in those weird days UPE wouldn't allow Chinese students to attend the post-match ball. He persuaded his team to do this because it was right – even though, at that time, they had a good chance of winning. Later, Danie Craven threatened to ban him for life if he played in a non racial match in Port Elizabeth. Ali told him where to get off, played the game, and was rewarded with the attentions of the security police.

There is more to the sad irony: Ali's family, like Chris Hani's, came from Cofimvaba. He learnt to speak Xhosa from his childhood friends, but he was no *bwana* or *baas*. The faces at the funeral showed that. Both he and Chris Hani took their degrees from Rhodes – Hani via Alice, Ali via Grahamstown. Like Hani he loved Transkei and felt he belonged there. Ali was not, I think, one of those white South Africans who feared the future so much that he felt powerless, inclined to flee. He was not a politician, but he got involved where he could. His friend Ian Macdonald, professor of philosophy at Rhodes, who delivered a moving eulogy at the funeral, recalled that long ago Ali would roll up his sleeves and do electioneering donkey work for PFP or Democratic Party candidates. More recently, he involved himself in Grahamstown's local peace committee and its efforts to deal with the crisis of local government in Rini. On the day he was buried, he was supposed to be involved in a mediation meeting. Ali felt that if you expressed political views, you had to act on them: you had to 'put your money where your mouth was', he said.

Now he is dead, in his 44th year, and everyone he touched is shattered and bewildered. The pointlessness and unfairness of his end is a terrible burden to bear for that large circle of intimates, confidants and admirers he has left behind in the eastern Cape. It is made worse because they do not know what drove the men with the guns to fire on the fishermen.

There is some opaque measure of comfort to be derived from the fact that it seems, from the outside at least, that Chris Hani's murder might be 'solved' – solved in the sense that the bereaved will know who did it and why. Ali's people deserve to know, too.

There is nothing that can be done to the gunmen which would undo their act. But there is something that can be said to them: shame on you, you killed a new South African. Shame on you, shame on all of us. I hope Ali can go fishing in peace, wherever he is now.

SATURDAY STAR, 24 APRIL 1993

WONDERLAND AT THE WORLD TRADE CENTRE

Although they continued to move forward, the negotiations began to assume an Alice in Wonderland quality. It became difficult to differentiate between the sense and the nonsense.

———————

And as they went, Tigger told Roo (who wanted to know) all about the things that Tiggers could do.

'Can they fly?' asked Roo.

'Yes,' said Tigger, 'they're very good flyers, Tiggers are. Strorny good flyers.'

'Oo!' said Roo. 'Can they fly as well as Owl?'

'Yes,' said Tigger. 'Only they don't want to.'

'Why don't they want to?'

'Well, they just don't like it, somehow.'

Roo couldn't understand this, because he thought it would be lovely to be able to fly, but Tigger said it was difficult to explain to anybody who wasn't a Tigger himself.

'Well,' said Roo, 'can they jump as far as Kangas?'

'Yes,' said Tigger. 'When they want to.'

'I love jumping,' said Roo. 'Let's see who can jump farthest, you or me.'

'I can,' said Tigger. 'But we musn't stop now, or we shall be late.'

    'Late for what?'

    'For whatever we want to be in time for,' said Tigger, hurrying on.

Forgive the indulgence. It's just that sometimes, in trying to fathom what is going on at the World Trade Centre, one has to recognize the limitations of the scholarly texts on negotiations and power-broking, and reach for something altogether more human. AA Milne shows us that Tiggers can't do a number of things they say they can do – things they spend a lot of time saying they can do. In spending this time discussing what they can do, but actually can't or won't do, they don't do very much at all, save to give the impression of hurrying along to do them. Tiggers don't climb trees. Codesa (I have decided to keep calling it that on principle, until they come up with another name) doesn't climb trees either. It just doesn't want to, somehow. When will it want to?

The Pooh Bear/Alice in Wonderland quality of current negotiations is inescapable. Go out to Kempton Park and you will see for yourself. It was Lewis Carroll who said: 'When I use a word, it means just what I choose it to mean – neither more nor less.' He held this to be a very functional and useful approach. He has avid fans in the negotiating forum.

As things now stand, we are in a forward-moving phase in the talks, having just come out of a stint in reverse gear. The fundamental difference between the two, it seems, is that whereas before we were being told that everything was not fine, we are now being informed that everything is fine. It is fine because everyone says it is fine. Lots of things don't look so fine from close up, but that is not the point right now. It will be, later.

There has been agreement that a) Elections should take place within 12 months and b) The naming of the precise date should take place within four weeks. At face value, that tells me that we will go to the polls by May 1994, and we will know the D-date by the end of this month.

These are important things to know, as this column has argued ad nauseam that naming the day is vital (even if that day is far off) because South Africans need the security of knowing the destination so they can plan what they will do when it is reached. But do the words that were spoken at the World Trade Centre mean the same thing to everyone who spoke them?

First, it must be noted that two parties – the Conservatives and the Ciskei government – refused to speak the words at all. But others were Carrollesque: a senior Inkatha Freedom Party official voted for the resolution, but subsequently said he thought it was useless. He had only been following instructions, he said. The ANC's Cyril Ramaphosa, by blinding contrast, said the words meant just what they said, and constituted a breakthrough. The government plumped for a sort-of in-between position, saying it could be a breakthrough, but people shouldn't get too excited.

Then it indulged in quadruplespeak of its own. The government and Afrikaner Volksunie came out of a conclave, friends again. They had agreed that the matter of 'self-determination' could be dealt with within the negotiations process. Now, as I understood things, everybody – including the ANC – had been saying that all along. So what had changed, where was the breakthrough? Aha: the AVU's Andries Beyers understood self-determination to mean government support for a *volkstaat*, while the government just meant that the AVU was welcome to discuss Afrikaner self-determination.

Both could tell their constituencies that great progress had been made. A confusing and complicated, but functional code. The Tiggers said they could fly and jump, only they didn't want to, somehow. Perhaps there's no other way forward in Wonderland.

SATURDAY STAR, 15 MAY 1993

NOBODY'S SETTLER

Pan Africanist Congress militants dismissed white South Africans as mere 'settlers'. The vast majority of whites did not agree - this was their home and they were staying.

————————

THERE WILL COME A MORNING, AND IT IS NOT THAT FAR OFF, when we South Africans who happen to be white will wake up and reach for those little alphabetical indexes that sit next to our telephones at home. We will go through them, crossing out all the familiar numbers of friends who have left.

If they were very close friends, we might insert their new and unfamiliar country and city codes. But with many we will know in our hearts that contact will eventually break down. We might not even bother to write out the foreign addresses. We will feel sad, of course, but we will also have a new sense of certainty.

The metaphorical day I am speaking of – it is happening already, has been happening for some time – will come when the new South Africa is well and truly with us, when the interregnum is over, and when we can look around at each other in the near certain knowledge that we are the ones who are staying.

There will have been, I expect, one or more further spasms of departure, disgorging many more thousands of

287

talented and decent white South Africans. These will be the people who are agonizing over their decisions right now; it is unlikely that anything negotiations produce in the coming months will be sufficiently dramatic to still their fears.

But the sense of certainty will come from the knowledge that the vast bulk of those names still in the telephone books, untouched, on that morning, are not going anywhere. We will be the new white South Africans, freed of the debilitating consideration of flight, ready to fight and work to make this extraordinary country the happy home it should be. Many, admittedly, will have stayed because they could not find a way to leave, but for many others it will have been a conscious decision; one to be proud of in its own small way.

I look forward – with no malice intended towards those who are still to go – to the morning when we can finally stop this incessant talk of 'leavers' and 'stayers', and get on with throwing our talents and energies into building a better new country out of the old. We will also, for the first time, be ready to shed our guilt: we will be citizens like all others, with no more and no fewer rights, to be judged on our own worth as human beings, not on the basis of pigmental privilege.

The emigration/immigration graph covering the past seventeen years (South Africa's human balance sheet, with all its debits and credits) mirrors the path of a fairground rollercoaster. It plummets into negatives in 1977 and 1978, after the Soweto uprising, soars into positives in the early 1980s, plunges again at the times of the States of Emergency, equivocates and stutters at the end of the decade, rallies in 1990 (8,000 more arrivals than departures), and then begins to tail off. In 1992 a fraction over 4,000 people were in the credit column. When the figures are out for 1993, we'll be lucky if there's one immigrant on the plus side of the equation. But again: we will know who we are.

We will be mostly native-born South Africans (most of the current leavers are expatriates) and we will be nobody's settlers. This will not be Portuguese Africa, with the populations of entire cities sailing in sad flotillas over the horizon, en route back to mother Europe. This will not be Rhodesia, its white population halving in an instant. We will be many, and we will be forever, one shade in the people's rainbow that makes up Africa's most unusual country.

I can't wait for that day. I am a South African, have never been anything else, and do not aspire to be anything else. This is my home and my history, my skylines and landscapes, my people. I am not afraid of my compatriots being afforded, finally, the basic rights I have always enjoyed; I would be afraid if that were not to happen. It is odd and saddening that white South Africans, this polyglot product of mixed antecedents and influences, should now be defined more by their shared fear than anything else. Each of us, with all of our ethnic nuances, spring from brave, pioneering forebears. We need to rediscover that frontier spirit. For the new frontier.

SATURDAY STAR, 22 MAY 1993

AN ICEBERG CALLED
FEDERALISM

Even implacable opponents of negotiations now accepted that they could not reverse the process of change. Rhetoric gave way to debate on substantive issues – like federalism.

———————

CONSTRUCTIVE FILIBUSTERING. NOW THERE'S A POLITICAL non sequitur to conjure with. It comes in a long line of them, all made in South Africa. From the country that brought you the expansion of pass law restrictions and called it the abolition of pass laws; that ethnically cleansed its universities and called that an extension of education; that condemned blacks to second class citizenship and called that separate development . . . the new South Africa is preserving its traditions.

The phrase constructive filibustering appeared in a document presented to the World Trade Centre negotiations at Kempton Park this week. It came from one of the moving (some would say unmoving) forces of the Concerned South Africans Group, the KwaZulu government. The document's import, reduced to essentials, was to serve notice that while the KwaZulu delegation will remain at the talks (give or take a walkout or two), it will do so with the specific intention of seeing to it that the talks proceed painfully slowly if at all. Unless, that is, its opponents agree to its demands pre-emptively.

The document was filled with threats, putting one in mind of a boy in a school playground who agrees to take part in a game as long as the others agree at the outset that he will be allowed to win. It was a frustrating week at the World Trade Centre.

Two questions, among others, need to be considered in order to understand what is happening now between Cosag and the remaining majority of parties to the transition talks. The first is: have the Pretoria Government and the ANC, along with their respective sympathizers, secretly ruled out a federal-style option for the future South African state? The second is: are the Cosag parties so scared of the verdict the electorate might pass on them that they will stop at nothing to stall the transition?

The issue of federalism – or devolution of power, or regionalism, or any number of variations on a principled theme – is like an iceberg towards which the negotiations ship has been steaming unsteadily ever since it left port. This week the ship struck the tip. Political radar screens have indicated the impending collision from the outset, but there was no certainty about when it would take place. Now that it has, some initial judgments can be made.

The Cosag argument is, circuitously, that constitutional principles (including the matter of federalism) cannot be negotiated until they are agreed upon. The other parties reply that the reason one negotiates is to achieve agreement: if you make the decisions first, what is there left to talk about? But Cosag is adopting this radical line because it does not trust the intentions of its negotiating opponents; it believes a pact has been struck and that when the negotiations are concluded, the will of the bigger of parties will prevail.

But in fact there is nothing in the growing stacks of talks documentation that rules out federalism in some form. The National Party, as is well known, wants the powers of the future central government to be severely constrained. The ANC, for its part, has softened markedly in the past three years on power devolution. The details are up for negotiation. In this sense, Cosag might be punching a phantom. But in doing so, it is postponing the main bout, at the risk of having all the paying spectators leave in disgust.

It is not for us to pronounce on whether Cosag's fears are genuinely felt, or being used as an excuse for the filibustering. But it is important to note a growing perception among the group's political opponents that what is really motivating the negativism is Cosag's fear that when elections come, the group's constituent elements will fare poorly. This is a serious problem, because it is not one on which the other parties can compromise and placate - they cannot declare the voters' loyalties for them.

The problem is serious because, if it is the case, then the Inkatha/KwaZulu thinking is not going to change, whatever happens at the talks. They will go all out for a 'one stage' transition because that would mean the unelected Negotiating Council, on which they wield considerable influence, would fashion the new country. The 'two stage' model has it that once the electorate has its say, relative support bases will be clear, and parties will exercise influence according to their proven share of the popular mandate. Some parties – and this includes parties outside the Cosag fold – will be blown away, politically speaking, and others will have their status reduced. Politicians do not, as a rule, easily contemplate these sorts of prospects.

And so there are powerful undercurrents beneath the surface problems at the talks. It is not always easy to divine them, but we need to make the effort if the opaque onrush of daily events is to make any sense at all.

SATURDAY STAR, 19 JUNE 1993

A NEW JOB FOR
AN EX-PRESIDENT

*The transition was so far advanced that parties began to discuss
the nuts and bolts of the future. One pertinent question to arise
was what job FW de Klerk could expect.*

LEAVE ASIDE FOR THE MOMENT WHAT IS, OR ISN'T,
happening in public at the World Trade Centre. Our
country's reformist revolution is reaching an advanced
stage. In recent days a very practical, down to earth, and
inestimably significant question has begun to be asked:
exactly what position will FW de Klerk occupy in South
Africa's new government?

The question is made even more fascinating because of
who is asking it, and who is expected to answer. The
interlocutor is the Pretoria Government; the response is
required from the ANC. Direct feelers are being put out
to Nelson Mandela's organisation, because the National
Party wants clarity now on how it can reassure its followers that it will play a significant, guaranteed role in
the new dispensation. Emissaries have asked the question, and now they are waiting.

The underlying assumption now common in South
Africa is that Mandela will be president after the first

elections. But even accepting this, the situation is not as clear cut as it might seem. There are attendant questions. What will the powers of the president be? Will he be bound by consensual Cabinet decisions? And, most topically, will there be a post for a vice-president?

To the cynical observer, the debate over De Klerk's role in an interim government might appear akin to shifting deck chairs on the Titanic. With violence and the economy concentrating the public mind, that is not surprising, but the issue has implications far beyond the mere individual status of prominent politicians. It goes to the essence of the type of power-sharing – call it what you will – compromise that will emerge from negotiations.

De Klerk has indicated that he sees himself in a role elevated above that of an ordinary Cabinet Minister. The role of the state president during the five year transition period would be limited, being bound on fundamental decisions by agreement with the 'inner Cabinet', which would operate by consensus. The ANC's rejection of this construction has been unequivocal, but that does not mean that the issues raised are not real, and enduring. Joe Slovo said the ANC-led alliance was not moving away from its position that minority parties should be given 'a major and meaningful' place in the executive of a new dispensation. The semantic gulf seems wide, but that might be secondary.

The ANC's 'President Mandela/Vice-President De Klerk' ticket has much to recommend it, obviously enough in terms of racial reconciliation, but also from the point of view of sending a message about stability to the international community. We are fast approaching the time when the details of what constitutes a 'significant role' will have to be decided. FW de Klerk has placed the first of his cards on the table.

THE STAR, 22 JUNE 1993 (WITH CHRIS WHITFIELD)

THE KHAKI-BOYS OF
KEMPTON PARK

The right wing seemed to grow more desperate as the election which would forever change South Africa approached. Thugs invaded and occupied the negotiating chambers.

———————

YOU'VE GOT TO KEEP ON YOUR TOES IN THE NEW SOUTH Africa. An hour ago, at the time of writing, this column had begun by expressing cautious optimism that the negotiating act was sufficiently together for FW de Klerk and Nelson Mandela to be able to submit a convincing progress report to President Bill Clinton in Washington next week. Then right wingers drove an armoured vehicle through the glass frontage of the World Trade Centre and occupied the Negotiating Council chamber. Bill Clinton will see this on his television screen. FW and Nelson have some more explaining to do.

What happened yesterday in Kempton Park does not look good, from whichever angle you choose to view it. Armoured cars ramming their way into buildings conjure up images of eastern Europe, and real revolution. Moreover, the apparent inability, or unwillingness, of the security forces to disarm and eject the wild demonstrators adds vivid colour to the picture.

Joe Slovo's question – what would have happened if the invaders were blacks? – answers itself, and concern about the neutrality of the security forces resurfaces. Investor confidence, that increasingly rare specimen, retreats deeper into the woods. Oh dear, we have come up with another home-made disaster. But how high up should we place this one on our political Richter Scale. Well, let's calm down first.

The invasion of the World Trade Centre was an incredible lapse of security, but no-one, mercifully, was killed. The subsequent inaction of the security forces at the scene was baffling, and worrying, but it is too early to talk about open defection to the right wing. The negotiating halls have been messed up, and a precious day of negotiations has been wasted, but the World Trade Centre will live to talk another day. And, more important than all of this, the fanatical white right has shown its true, lawless face to the country and the world.

De Klerk and Mandela, if they play their cards correctly and simultaneously, should be able to use the Kempton Park fiasco to underline to Clinton the urgent need for unprecedented international support for the peace process. It should be presented not as a sign of the failure of the constitutional talks, but proof that they are getting somewhere – to the extent that the minority diehards feel the need to resort to brutish showmanship.

The negotiators' case will be greatly strengthened if the neanderthal perpetrators and participants are quickly rounded up and arrested on public violence charges. We do not want to hear from the police, this time round, that they are having trouble identifying the suspects. They can start with Messrs Terreblanche, Hartzenberg, Langley and Viljoen, and they can rely on the eyewitness accounts of dozens of terrified (black) negotiators, as well as a larger-than-usual contingent of journalists. An offensively confident Terreblanche said, on telling his thugs to leave the chamber, that he had been given the assurance none would be arrested as long as they 'behaved in an orderly manner'. Orderliness-after-the-fact is not, to say the least, any defence in this case.

No, the important meeting with Clinton has not been scuppered by yesterday's antics. It is another sign of the rapidly shifting power balances in our country that the right wing does not enjoy the power to do this, break windows and yell about 'kaffirs' as it might. The outstanding problem for De Klerk and Mandela in convincing the world that we are worth worrying about has its home in Ulundi, not Ventersdorp.

Away from the chants of the khaki-clad bully-boys, a much more important initiative is under way. The Government and the ANC are trying to persuade Chief Buthelezi of two things: that it is in the national interest for the stages of transition to be formalised, and that they have no intention of unfairly sidelining Inkatha in a future dispensation. These efforts are of real significance; they represent the substance, not the showbiz, of our political pilgrim's progress. If Buthelezi can be persuaded, he will deserve credit for recognizing that it is more important to convince the world of our ability to reach a rational accommodation than it is to worry about the fact that his political rivals are drawing the accolades and the television spotlights.

As is so often the case, what really matters in our country is not necessarily the most dramatic event of the day. Perhaps the right wing's foolishness will galvanise Buthelezi, convincing him that his interests really lie with the negotiators, not the brownshirts. If so, the price of the panes of glass will be a reasonable one to have paid.

SATURDAY STAR, 26 JUNE 1993

WHERE PIMPS ARE VIRGINS

All sides blamed each other for the failure to bring the violence under control. It was clear to all with eyes to see that few parties were entirely innocent.

THE WORDS GO ROUND AND ROUND LIKE FLIES TRAPPED IN a small room. There is much sound and little sense; no purpose, no outcome. Another massacre: another orgy of indignant recriminations, another cycle of hand-wringing and finger-pointing. Another week in South Africa.

So who was to blame for July 1993's bout of butchery on the East Rand? Here's Inkatha: 'the ANC started it'. The ANC: 'sinister forces opposed to the election'. And the police: 'the ANC's self defence units'. In other words, 'anyone but us'. The rhubarb factor was even more prevalent than usual this week. The various parties were so predictable in their declamations and disclaimers that they might save themselves some trouble and pre-record them for use next time round. They need only change the place names and dates; the otherwise familiar incantations will serve the purpose just as poorly.

It is difficult to understand how politicians can still, after all this time, shrink from admitting what is self-evident to most South Africans. That is that all the parties involved

298

have long had their hands bloodied, and cannot know from the comfort of their headquarters whether it was their guys or others that started the killing this time. It's much too late for protestations of virginity from anyone. The East Rand is a small-scale war zone and in a war zone, as the people of the former Yugoslavia will tell you, everyone fights dirty.

But we had few such illuminating shafts of integrity this week. Instead we had spokesmen selectively citing court judgments to 'prove' the other side was actually the evil one. In fact, the record shows that in recent years members of the ANC and Inkatha and the security forces have been convicted of horrible crimes. There are plenty of examples, and if one is sufficiently dishonest, one can pick and choose among the cases, ignoring those that queer one's argument. That is why we are none the wiser. Yes, there were peace meetings eventually, and the fighting appears to have stopped. But the interventions were after the fact – and by no means rule out a repetition. We are a brutalised nation incrementally accepting, albeit unconsciously and unhappily, that we are slipping downwards, week by week and notch by notch, into the mire.

So here we are stating the problem again. What are some solutions? Well, it doesn't help to be mesmerised by the detail of the immolation. We have to step back, wipe our faces and try to work out all over again how we got here. It is clear that political leaders have either not taken their public peace commitments seriously, or they are flouting them. Nelson Mandela and Mangosuthu Buthelezi committed themselves to holding joint rallies in strife-torn areas. Both their organisations say urgent plans are afoot, but can give no details. Moreover, a close study of agreements which already exist, such as the National Peace Accord and the Record of Understanding between the ANC and the Government, shows that their implementation leaves much to be desired. The Peace Accord committed signatories and the security forces to doing everything possible to avoid violence – and set out a number of practical measures to this end. These, including a ban on incitement and the setting up of special criminal courts, have been observed only sporadically at best. Similarly, the Record of Understanding's call for the fencing of hostels and a ban on the carrying of dangerous weapons has gone largely unheeded.

It is little wonder that the perception most common among ordinary South Africans today is one of a failure of political will and ability among the country's leaders. The leaders know this: they have been told often enough now. Surely they cannot respond with rhubarb forever.

SATURDAY STAR, 10 JULY 1993

DENYING BLIND REVOLUTION
AND BRUTE REPRESSION

The Transitional Executive Council was about to be brought into being. Despite its unprepossessing name, it would be the first tangible sign that negotiations were succeeding.

———————

NEGOTIATIONS START UP AGAIN AT THE WORLD TRADE Centre next week. If all goes well, this will be the last round. Within weeks a political settlement could be wrapped up, and it will be for the special session of Parliament in September to pass laws that start the final transition from old South Africa to new.

The conference halls at Kempton Park will have served their political purpose, and can revert to hosting exponents of world trade – more of them, hopefully, than in the sanctions-strangled past. The negotiators will have to find premises from which to operate and run the Transitional Executive Council, South Africa's first experiment in truly non-racial government. It may not look and sound like it, but these are heady times.

With the nation's fascination (ranging from rapturous to morbid) centred on next year's election, no-one is making too much fuss about the step in between, the TEC. This seems a pity. Seen in its proper context, and with a bit of talking-up, the moment of the TEC's birth later this year could be turned into a trigger point for a surge of optimism and renewed energy. Such opportunities to enthuse a punch-drunk public do not come by all that often, and should be seized upon. If – and any valid political prognosis in this country should be preceded by that two-letter word – all or most of the parties at the talks behave as sensibly as they should, the TEC can be the first tangible proof that all we have been through in the past three years is both worth it, and leading somewhere.

The TEC has huge symbolic significance, first and foremost. It can be an indication to the voteless majority that change for the better really is coming, and simultaneously an assurance to the previously privileged that change is not going to mean chaos. It is an embodiment of a potentially magnificent compromise.

For the first time in nearly 400 years, a structural start will have been made in distributing power, and responsibility – a task once considered quite impossible. For the first time, also, we would be able to look forward with hope to a system with sufficient legitimacy to stamp out the wild and destructive elements which have flourished in the interregnum.

The symbolism will go way beyond our borders: a message will be sent out that rationality still prevails in South Africa, that the transition has not spun out of control, and that stability is not a chimera. We should all, whatever our skin pigments and living standards, be popping champagne corks on TEC day - the day the dictates of blind revolution and brute repression are denied.

SATURDAY STAR, 17 JULY 1993

302

OUR FATE IN THE HANDS OF MERE MEN

A bitter private exchange between Nelson Mandela and FW de Klerk served as a reminder of how much the future of South Africa depended on individual personalities.

———————

SUCH IS THE COMMONPLACE HUMANITY OF HISTORIC moments in the life of a nation. One man raises his voice against another who, offended, turns his back and walks out of the room. If a way is not found to bring these two towering, simmering personalities back together, and quickly, the country will be in crisis.

When they met a fortnight ago to discuss the state of the nation, Nelson Mandela and FW de Klerk clashed directly and personally as never before. It was a private meeting, and so of course the public was none the wiser. But the details have now been corroborated sufficiently to bear responsible repetition.

The subject was the spasm of violence wrenching the East Rand; the two leaders were accompanied by senior colleagues from their parties. Mandela challenged De Klerk as to why only white policemen were being deployed in the affected townships. De Klerk replied that this question smacked of racism. Mandela, in anger, raised

303

his voice to say De Klerk was in no position to lecture him about racism. De Klerk walked out, followed by most of his entourage. His Minister Kobie Coetsee hung back, praising Mandela's qualities as a leader, but charging him with being unfair to De Klerk. He then left the room. Mandela's lieutenant Cyril Ramaphosa moved between the two camps, and after a time Minister Hernus Kriel came to tell Mandela that De Klerk felt offended. Mandela sent a message asking De Klerk to return. When he did, both leaders dismissed their colleagues, and Mandela apologized for having raised his voice, 'especially in public'. De Klerk accepted the apology, although Mandela specifically did not retract what he had said. The apocalyptic moment had passed.

What if it had not? What if Mandela had got up and left too? What if De Klerk had insisted on a full retraction of the accusation? Never has South Africa's future depended more on the personalities of its political leaders. There are times when the great tides of history simply take their own unstoppable course – when individuals are incidental – and times when politicians have the power to unleash or stem the tides. We are living through a time when men, ordinary frail human beings, hold our destiny in their hands.

Today both Mandela and De Klerk feel angered, hurt and let down by one another. Who is right and who is wrong on which point and to what extent is secondary to the serious effect this has: both sincerely believe that they are correct, and are therefore not just playing politics. Mandela believes beyond argument that De Klerk is behaving disingenuously. He remains convinced that Pretoria could stop the violence if it had the will, and he is infuriated by what he sees as De Klerk's deceitful behaviour over the appointment of the SABC board – he believes the president gave him a firm undertaking that he would be consulted, and that this was reneged upon. The ANC leader feels that he established De Klerk's credibility in the eyes of the world by describing him as a 'man of integrity' in 1990, and that this gesture has been abused and exploited. Therefore all Mandela's dealings with De Klerk are potentially explosive: he is wary, on the lookout for secret agendas and double-dealing. He still accepts as an unarguable reality that De Klerk is an essential element of a workable settlement, but he simply does not trust him.

For his part De Klerk sees Mandela as unreliable and unpredictable, sometimes illogical. He believes that the ANC leader frequently 'reinterprets' agreements in a way which alters their meaning, and he is infuriated by continuing attacks on the National Party as the party of apartheid, which he views as a cheap and often condescending tactic. He further believes Mandela does not exercise sufficient control over the ANC leadership, and that he is prone to embracing bad advice. De Klerk, too, accepts that there can be no settlement without Mandela, but he also does not regard him as a trustworthy partner in the new South Africa project.

Thus the men who might have marched into the future as 'loyal opponents' – to adapt the Westminsterian term – are instead edging their way forward along the same tunnel, surrounded by bodyguards, with their backs to the walls, and eyes peeled. This is not as it was in the heady days of early 1990.

A political settlement, as I have argued repeatedly, is now attainable and even visible in reasonable outline. That is miraculous: the paperwork which many thought was beyond us, is within reach of completion. But its implementation will depend on more that just the skills of the deal-drafters. It will depend in part on whether Mandela and De Klerk, as individual, flawed men, can find a way to see through one another's different-coloured eyes.

SATURDAY STAR, 21 AUGUST 1993

LAUGHTER ON THE STREETS
OF SHAME

The National Peace Committee called for a symbolic five minutes' of silence, to show that most South Africans were opposed to the violence. The response was astonishing.

A FEW MINUTES BEFORE MIDDAY ON THURSDAY, PEOPLE spilt out of their office buildings in Johannesburg and on to the sidewalks. The city changed for that instant. These sidewalks have not been filled with bustling, laughing and relaxed faces for a very long time.

Jo'burgers stood around talking easily, shooting the breeze, instead of walking quickly and defensively to a destination, hugging their possessions to their chests and eyeing every passer-by as a potential attacker. At first, not many of those who broke their working routines seemed to know what to expect. The atmosphere was like that of a school camp: it wasn't the particular occasion that was interesting, rather the fact that it was a break from class. But then some unexpected, magical genie popped out of the bottle here at the foot of Africa. As noon approached the light-hearted cynicism about the peace gesture – for it was no more than a gesture

– disappeared with sudden force. The traffic stopped, the talking stopped. The city went silent.

Hands clasped other hands, blue ribbons fluttered from lapels and car aerials, and we the people of South Africa looked at one another with the wide, inquiring eyes of children. The thick cataracts of fear and hatred melted away. Stomachs knotted, throats tightened, tears started in the corners of tired eyes. Something very big was happening.

The moments in history that matter are often identified only much later. It is possible that we shared such a moment on Thursday. There have been peace campaigns before in South Africa, there have been ribbons and white doves, but they did not let loose this startling emotional charge. They did not bring out on to the streets that once-mythical majority we call 'peace-loving South Africans'. This is the first time that we really can talk of the possibility of a popular groundswell, the tangible expression of the will of a people who want to change the way they are living.

No-one can say why this peace call struck this chord. Perhaps it is that some critical point has been reached in the equation of a nation's endurance. Perhaps it is that we had not realized what damage the strain of dealing with our fears alone, in our homes in suburb or township, has done to us. Thursday's response, in the city centre streets of Johannesburg, was not political and it was not intellectual. It just happened: there was a huge, gasping flood of relief and emotion as people realized that thousands of others, from all walks of life, were going through the same pain.

When the five minutes of silence had passed, the crowds burst into laughter and applause, and dour Sauer Street held an impromptu mardi gras. Drivers hooted, passengers hung out of windows, and in the melee there was an idealised glimpse of what the new South Africa might be, if only . . .

We the people are a polyglot bunch. There were workers

in overalls, men in suits, children, matriarchs, Johannesburgers all. Well-heeled occupants of German limousines leant over to shake hands with scooter drivers, delivery trucks pulled up alongside a gold Rolls-Royce as the two-fingered peace sign flashed from car to car. Yellow police vans had ribbons tied to them, and the policemen smiled. Suspicions, and guards, were momentarily dropped.

We have never really done this before – demonstrated all together for the same thing. It was a moment of illumination. It said our pious words and rhetoric could be true: most of us do want peace, wherever we come from and whoever we are. We have had enough of torment and, although our tears alone cannot stop the killers with the guns, we confirmed to ourselves and the world that we are many and they are few. It is not we, the multicoloured masses, that make South Africa the world's most violent country – it is others, and we have had enough of them. We felt the power of numbers surge like an electrical current around a city block. We want not to be frightened any more. We want not to be paralysed, reduced to responding to things out of our control and stifling our energies and creativity. We are ready to start building a new country if we are allowed to do so.

I haven't heard South Africans laugh like that for a very long time. It was just a moment, but a delicious and different one. We didn't want to leave to go back to being alone with our fears; we were walking on air.

Now of course we can't tumble out on to the streets every day, and if we tried to pull off the same exhilarating trick again too soon, it would probably fail. Of course we must not expect that there will be no more bloody horrors. But we did something ourselves, and together, for the first time. Somehow, the impossible happened: South Africa's daily death toll plummeted through an effort of collective will. We have helped open a window to a future we can all live with. We have to keep it open now.

SATURDAY STAR, 4 SEPTEMBER 1993

THE CHIEF IN HIS TENT

With the political deal now tantalisingly close to completion, one spectre gave cause for alarm. Chief Buthelezi, isolated and angry, refused to have anything to do with the settlement.

CHIEF MANGOSUTHU BUTHELEZI HAS NEVER SET FOOT IN the World Trade Centre, where South Africa's settlement is being negotiated. This extraordinary fact has been somehow forgotten in the political hubbub. His pointed absence through the long months of talks underscores the depth of alienation that now exists between the Inkatha leader and the new political centre which is driving the transition to its next phase.

Buthelezi has been brooding in his tent in faraway Ulundi, and his mood has steadily worsened. It is as if the Government and the ANC on the one hand, and the IFP on the other, are inhabiting different worlds with wholly unrelated expectations of what is to happen in our country in the coming months.

The official IFP/KwaZulu government position, notwithstanding the struggles going on in the IFP's top echelons at this moment, is that they will have nothing to do with the Transitional Executive Council or the election. The irascible chief is firm on this score, and his bellicose lieutenants are openly aggressive. The tension has been ratcheted up considerably this month by the comprehensive failure of KwaZulu's court challenge to negotiations and the fact that Buthelezi has returned from abroad having completed what was, politically speaking, possibly the most difficult journey of his life. Buthelezi is an isolated, angry, unrepentant and potentially desperate man: this is an explosive emotional cocktail, which should give no cause for pleasure even among his implacable enemies. It should give cause for great concern among all who recognize that we have to get this transition of ours right, first time.

Buthelezi's objections to what has taken place at the World Trade Centre are complex and arguable, but it is clear – as his dogged absence illustrates – that the IFP/KwaZulu axis has been uncompromising at the talks. It is difficult to disagree with parties complaining that the IFP has not embraced the 'give' aspect of the give-and-take equation that defines negotiations. But that is merely to describe the problem, not to promote ways of solving it.

In trying to find ways to draw Buthelezi back into the process without an unacceptable loss of face on any side, it is essential to try to understand his state of mind, on the assumption that although the transition could conceivably go ahead without Ulundi's support, its prospects would be immeasurably improved if the IFP and KwaZulu were on board. All indications about Buthelezi's mood are worrying: they suggest his feeling beleaguered to an unprecedented degree, simultaneously defiant, and possibly out of touch with the realities of South African power balances. His impatience and occasional vindictiveness in dealing with questioners in recent months is one such signal, but it goes much further than that.

Before his latest journey to visit world leaders, Buthelezi had an extremely tense meeting with British Prime Minister John Major. So fraught did the atmosphere become that Buthelezi was on the brink of walking out when aides intervened to save the situation. This, of course, was not reflected in any official communiqués. Similarly, the full story of his most recent trip abroad has not yet been told. Sources confirm that Buthelezi's meetings with the Danish and German foreign ministers went badly; that attempts to encourage him to return to talks did not have the desired effect, but rather the opposite. Importantly, Buthelezi's mood is said to have sown confusion in his traditional conservative European support base – with them emerging from encounters unsure of their long-standing positions. It is too early to tell, but it seems unlikely that this unhappy journey will cause the chief to think again and moderate his current positions. If anything, the apparent erosion of sympathy and support could exacerbate the go-it-alone, do-or-die mentality.

It is easy to say that the chief's sense of his own importance is out of kilter with reality, that he – like Nelson Mandela and FW de Klerk for that matter – must recognize that in world terms he is merely one leader of a middle-ranking country, and should be more solicitous in dealings with major powers. But this does not solve the problem. If he believes he is being short-changed, he will act on that basis whether it is true or not.

The crunch could be coming soon regarding the Buthelezi factor. If Inkatha moderates who favour waging battle at the negotiating table prevail, then opportunities open up for further attempts at compromise. But if the give-nothing approach persists, then conflict looms. It is the duty of all negotiating parties to do everything possible to bring Buthelezi back in where he belongs. But for this to succeed he will have to respond in kind.

SATURDAY STAR, 11 SEPTEMBER 1993

NOBELS OBLIGE

The outside world recognized South Africa's remarkable achievement by conferring the Nobel Peace Prize on Mandela and De Klerk. Many embittered South Africans weren't so sure.

MOST OF THIS WEEK IN SOUTH AFRICA WAS TAKEN UP WITH looking back. Back at the terrifying, idiotic death of Chris Hani, back at the vicious and dumb SA Defence Force raid on Umtata. But it ended looking marvellously forward: the Nobel Peace Prize awarded jointly to the two men who, for combined reasons of accident and design, have ended up holding the future of our country in their hands.

Cynics, and we breed a lot of them here, will dismiss the news as practically irrelevant. And they will be right to the extent that an award ceremony in Oslo will not still the gunmen of Thokoza and Edendale; nor will it increase the growth rate, lower the birth rate, or ensure that the drought is broken. But they will be wrong, our cynics, if they see the awarding of this honour to Nelson Mandela and FW de Klerk as being without value. The Nobel Prize, leaving aside the nice medals and healthy cheques attached, is about symbolism and psychology. We need help in both departments, and the selection committee has offered it to us on a large silver plate. All that is now required is some fairly fancy political footwork from the ANC and National Party leaders to ensure we accept the help graciously and constructively, and that we exploit it to the full internationally and back home.

Taking the international dimension first, it is crucial to note that the committee which chose our men over the Salvation Army, Rabin and Arafat and the like, has not done so lightly. Their reputations, and that of the Nobel Prize itself, are at stake. If the recipient country were to slide into chaos and anarchy within months, it would be embarrassing for them as well as life-threatening for us. Therefore, we have been given a most important vote of confidence: it can be utilised widely, among other things, in calming the jitters of potential investors. Secondly, the stage-managed event in Oslo has again pushed us right up the interest-scale in the eyes of the world. We had slipped lamentably in the past year or so, and this extraneous boost is a bonsella. Looked at from the outside in, the joint award is like a huge-budget advertising campaign, devised for us for free.

But we need simultaneously to make sure that the punters at home are happy, or the foreign goodwill might be shortlived. There are some evident dangers, calling for statesmanship to be exercised almost immediately. We must accept that at the outermost political extremities of our country there are people who do not want a negotiated settlement to come about and for whom the Nobel Peace Prize is a slap in the face rather than a kiss on the hand. They might try to throw a bucket of blood over the proceedings; that is a risk we live with.

But among those parties which are out of the talks process but not averse in principle to a negotiated settlement, something can be done. Humans that they are, certain leaders will not be overjoyed by the prospect of saturation television coverage of their smilingly triumphant rivals receiving the obeisances of an adoring world. They will be feeling left out and spiteful. It is up to Mandela and De Klerk, no matter how much this may stick in their

313

respective craws, to go out of their way to stress that the award is for the country as a whole, not for specific political parties. If they can bear to, after the bad blood created by months of walkouts and slanging matches, they should even consider naming names of other leaders – including them in the overall honour which has been bestowed on the country for having stopped short on the road to Armageddon and sought a more circuitous but safer route forward. That's what it's all about, after all: the world had long ago written us off as a certain disaster waiting to happen, and now it is patting us on the head for having flown in the face of irrational human history. We may not have been the prettiest of sights over the past three years, but we are a lot prettier than we were under the tutelage of PW Botha. If managed properly, the Peace Prize can act as a further fillip, injecting energy and optimism back into a transition process in some danger of running out of breath.

In other words what we need, if you'll excuse my French, is some Nobels oblige.

SATURDAY STAR, 16 OCTOBER 1993

A MEMORY OF MOSCOW

The sudden explosion of violence in the faraway Russian par-
liament reminded South Africans that the worst could happen,
if it was allowed to.

IT IS JULY AND WE ARE IN THE DOWNTOWN MOSCOW OFFICE
of Mikhail Fedotov, Minister for Press and Information of
the Russian Federation and close confidant of President Boris Yeltsin. Fedotov, jowled and sharp-eyed, sits
smoking at the end of a long table under a portrait
of Sakharov. He is agitated, telling us about the impending showdown between the ruling Yeltsinites and
the recalcitrant parliamentarians.

His manner suggests utmost seriousness: he goes on
lyrical flights, bangs the table, raises his voice. 'We are
going to declare war on the Supreme Council,' he says, 'we
will fight to the end.' The inexpert South African audience
listens interestedly, but with the detachment of journalists
who spend their lives hearing politicians' war talk, and dis-
carding most of it as hyperbole. 'We will not allow a return
to totalitarianism,' says Fedotov, 'we would rather be killed
first. This battle will reach a peak in September.'

Outside everything seems peaceful and stable, so far as
we can see, and there is no compelling reason to take

words like 'war', 'fight' and 'kill' too literally. We stroll out into Moscow's benign summer sunshine and on to another meeting. 'I wonder if he's serious?' says one of the party after a while. We all wonder, but not for too long.

A few days later, I am in the Russian Parliament building across from the Novo Arbatskaya. It is recess and the politicians are absent, leaving us free to roam the corridors of the 'White House', the imposing Finnish-designed structure built for Brezhnev and referred to disparagingly by Muscovites as 'the commode'. We wander past the Cabinet room, where the praesidium meets, through the great foyers where the hammer and sickle still stands in relief, and linger to look at the magnificent art treasures still adorning the walls: outsized oils depicting Pushkin, Rasputin and dozens of legendary Russian figures.

Come September, two months later, and I am looking at the same building, but this time from far-off Johannesburg, on a television screen. There are shells screaming into the upper floors where we had walked, blackening the White House and destroying, in chutes of dark, violent smoke, much of the contents. People are being killed inside and out, and tracer bullets are flashing across the wide road where we promenaded lazily with Moscow's summertime citizenry.

Where is Mikhail Fedotov now? Is this what he was trying to tell us? Did he really think this would happen? Did he mean it? I try to telephone him but, unsurprisingly, he is unavailable. I remember Boris Yeltsin's first words after his constitutional putsch: 'There will be no bloodshed'.

Do they all mean what they say? When Chief Buthelezi talks about the TEC having to use 'force of arms' in KwaZulu, does he really picture troops pouring across his border, to be met by volleys from trenches? If he doesn't, he shouldn't be saying it. Muscovites will tell you it might just happen.

SATURDAY STAR, 23 OCTOBER 1993

316

THE ELECTION STARTS TODAY

If proof were still needed that apartheid was to be voted out of existence within a matter of months, it came with the launching of the ANC's sophisticated election campaign.

ON THIS VERY MORNING, AT A MOTOR CAR FACTORY IN Uitenhage, Nelson Mandela is firing the first shot in the ANC's campaign to win a landslide victory in the election scheduled to take place fewer than six months from now. It is a big shot he is firing; the precursor to political fusillades which will lead to barrages, to carpet-bombings. South Africans will in time be shaken by the effects of this morning's events, left trembling in glee or trepidation depending on their political preferences.

At first glance, Mandela's heart-to-heart with workers at the Volkswagen factory in the eastern Cape Town might look like a run-of-the-mill political meeting. It is quite the opposite – a watershed moment in our breathlessly-paced recent history. It marks the start of a carefully worked-out and highly ambitious ANC campaign strategy for the remaining months before April 27. It has a specifically African, indeed South African, flavour, but in its scope the plan is as sophisticated as that which swept Bill Clinton to power in the United States.

The campaign can be broadly divided into two consecutive parts: a 'hearing' phase and a 'telling' phase. The Uitenhage meeting is the prototype component of the former. As of today the ANC will hold what it calls 'people's forums' all over our country. Mandela himself, or other members of the ANC's top leadership, will arrive at public gatherings convened by local ANC structures. Those attending will have responded to an open letter – signed by Mandela – inviting them to come and talk to the leaders. Each meeting will have a theme or focus – on workers, women, squatters, farmers, teachers, minorities and the like.

In Uitenhage, Mandela will join other ANC officials on a makeshift podium. In front of him will be the leaders of the ANC's local region. Around them, in a horseshoe formation, will be crowds of motor industry workers. Breaking with political tradition, Mandela will not present a speech at all. He will, in the manner of the Athenians or the ancient kingdoms of Africa, invite the people to tell him what their expectations are from a future government. Then he will enter into a discussion with them, and promise to take their views into account. Aside from their primary purpose of taking the temperature of the voting masses, the meetings are also cleverly designed to achieve maximum symbolic effect. Thus, when it is time to listen to the mineworkers, Mandela will go down a shaft and hear them out where they work; when it is time to meet squatters, the gathering will be held in the teeming informal settlements where they live.

By mid-January, with little more than three months to go before polling day, the ANC will move into phase two of its election campaign: the more familiar and mainstream head-on hustings against its opponents. The battle for the political kingdom of the new South Africa will be in full swing, and the die well and truly cast. It has long been speculated by commentators that the chasm between the ANC's electoral inexperience, and the National Party's record of ruthless efficiency, would be blindingly obvious once the campaigning began. The ANC's start suggests that this assumption should not be made too glibly.

SATURDAY STAR, 6 NOVEMBER 1993

SO HERE'S THE DEAL

Both the government and the ANC told their supporters something different, but it was finally evident that each had made significant compromises to allow for coalition rule.

SO AT LONG LAST IT IS CLEAR: THE 'DEAL' ON EXECUTIVE rule during the transition, hammered out between the National Party and the ANC, depends for its workability not on cast-iron constitutional guarantees, but rather on two political abstracts. They are good will and good sense.

Gone are all those ideas of 'rotating presidents', Cabinet vetoes and the like. The enforced coalition Cabinet which will run South Africa until the end of the century will work only if its participants want it to. There are no fail-safe mechanisms for dispute resolution – there is only the mutual realisation that without good will and good sense the system will seize up and collapse in a heap on its components.

As things stand we will have a president and one or more deputy presidents, heading a multiparty Cabinet comprised proportionally of leaders whose parties garner more than five percent of the vote. In terms of the latest technical committee proposal, the president will be obliged under certain conditions to consult his deputies or the whole Cabinet, but then he will make his own decision. Let us put this even more bluntly, assuming a hypothetical electoral outcome in which the ANC emerges as the majority party and the NP a clear runner-up. A President Mandela, before making a major policy intervention, would have to consult a Deputy President de Klerk. De Klerk could advise Mandela not to go ahead, but the final decision would be the president's. If he did indeed persist, and the issue was considered to be sufficiently serious, De Klerk's option would be to resign. If he did so, that could spell the end of the multiparty Cabinet.

This scenario suggests that the NP has made a major concession: the leader of the majority party will be president, and to a large extent the president will have the final say. Indeed, there has been an important NP concession but those, particularly in the Freedom Alliance, who equate this with a throwing in of the political towel, have missed the highly nuanced bigger picture. The compromise traffic has not flowed in one direction only.

The i's have not yet been dotted, nor the t's crossed, on the final draft of the Interim Constitution. There are still worrying grey areas. Much bargaining has yet to be done, and deadlines will be subject to slippage yet again. But the shape, form and philosophy of the enforced coalition executive under which transitional South Africa will be ruled is now out in the open. Concerning the proposed specific workings of the executive, it is an extraordinary deal, light-years ahead conceptually of what the Cabinet circa Dr Gerrit Viljoen's era and the ANC in its pre-negotiations phase considered as an option.

In 1990 the Government wanted a settlement whereby the ANC shared in the running of the country but was subject to an entrenched and constitutionally unambiguous veto. For its part the ANC wanted a settlement whereby the party that won the elections could do pretty much as it pleased. Both sides have given way; neither has got what it originally wanted. The Government has accepted

321

that crude constitutional brake pedals like alternating presidents are non-starters. The ANC has accepted – via thought processes first articulated in Joe Slovo's 'sunset clause' proposals of last year – that a complete transfer of power is not feasible.

One result is the proposal for a multiparty Cabinet and executive Deputy Presidents. It is on the foundation of this coincidental recognition of realities that sufficient trust has been built to allow compromise. Moreover, that trust has allowed for the compromise to be founded not on heavily footnoted legal documents but rather on abstractions. The two sides still prefer to use different terms to describe the compromise they have reached. There is no reason to expect they will ever agree on the nomenclature; they do not really have to. Thus Minister Dawie de Villiers can refer at the World Trade Centre to the government of national unity as a 'power-sharing formula', and ANC negotiator Valli Moosa can call it 'a means to provide constitutional continuity between the old and the new systems'. They are talking about the same thing, the language is barely distinguishable, and it indicates that the interminable *bosberade* have had their effect. This might not be the most elegant of compromises but it is, considering the various starting points, historic.

Both sides will argue, especially within earshot of their constituents, that the other gave more. Both should be allowed to do so. In fact the Government has given more, but that is merely logical: it, after all, is the party that started with everything, and the point of the process is to change that.

One question will nag. Why is the NP confident that a President Mandela will not simply ride roughshod over his opponents once the ANC has its hands on the steering wheel of State? The answer to that resides on the realpolitik side of the equation; the good sense rather than the good will. For the foreseeable future, the NP will be the party that represents certain very powerful interest groups in our society, not least among them the civil service. The government of national unity needs a functional civil service if it is not to collapse under its own weight; there are very good self-interested reasons for the majority party to keep its minority partners sweet. The minorities are settling for powers of restraint, not compulsion.

So a big chunk of the future depends on our politicians displaying traits that are not characteristically South African. Only a fool can be sure it will work. But it is a mature, sophisticated approach to a hellishly complicated problem; an attempt to develop an entirely new convention in South African politics.

THE STAR, 12 NOVEMBER 1993

AU REVOIR, UGLY DUCKLING

After its marathon run in the forefront of South African politics, the World Trade Centre wrapped up its proceedings at last. There was some nostalgia about its departure.

———————

THE BELL RINGS IN THE CORRIDORS, AS IF FOR DINNER. THE lights go on in the council room and the delegates begin to trickle in, as if returning to class after first break. The summer rain is tapping down gently on the roof.

There's Dawie de Villiers, joking easily with the ANC's Valli Moosa, there's Barney Desai of the PAC chatting to Essop Pahad of the Communist Party. On the other side of the room Amichand Rajbansi is making a point of some sort to Corlea Kruger of the Afrikaner Volksunie and smiling a lot. The seats reserved for the Inkatha Freedom Party, the Conservative Party and sundry others are still empty.

It is Friday afternoon at the World Trade Centre, the scene is comfortably familiar. But it is also one of the last of its kind, reminiscent of a classroom of matriculants who have just realized that they will shortly vacate the known cosiness of the form for the big bad world out there. I am suffering a wave of nostalgia about the imminent return of the World Trade Centre to something like its former state of obscurity. A funny old friend is leaving town.

By next week, we are told, the negotiations-process-without-a-name – most just call it 'Kempton Park' – will be wrapped up. (Yes, we were told that last week too, but the end is now nigh even if it is imprecise.) The odd, warehouse-like collection of buildings alongside the airport will get a few more political leases of life from negotiations spin-offs like the Independent Media Commission, but its real glory days will be over. It will then be the turn of another curious choice as repository of the nation's political hopes: the old Saambou building in Pretoria, which will house the Transitional Executive Council. We sure know how to pick 'em.

The fact is that for all their inelegance, discursiveness, irritation and cant, the Kempton Park days have been very special. Not for the low drama of the right wing invasion, though that incident will long be remembered, but for the quotidian grind – day after day, month after month, year after year of shuffling forward to a political deal that all South Africans can accept. The process developed a life of its own, and deeply affected its participants along the way. With the passage of time, we will come to look back at this period as having been fairly short, fairly fluid and fairly efficient. It will have been quicker than its more famous forebears – like the meetings of the American Founding Fathers or the Middle East peace talks – and it will have the distinction of having brought together some of the most disparate groups imaginable.

It is true that the process will end on an uncertain note, what with the empty chairs and the bilious stares from the outsiders. It is true that if there are cheers and champagne corks out Kempton Park way when the final session ends, they might be a little forced, because there is still a long road to travel. But it is also true that what has happened over all this time at Kempton Park has laid the foundation for the future.

It has also provided more than its share of bizarre amusement. It seems a pity that some of its most accomplished entertainers will be vacating the national stage once the democratic will of the people has been exercised. We should wish the ugly duckling World Trade Centre well in its future. Let it trade on its past, inviting paying guests to spend a night in the Planning Committee Suite, the Bilateral Boudoir, or the Azapo office which has never been occupied. It's been the butt of public bitterness and frustration, but it has played its part.

SATURDAY STAR, 13 NOVEMBER 1993

THE END OF THE BEGINNING

The final hours of constitutional negotiators were briefly interrupted by President de Klerk's surprise appearance in the chamber. He did so just as apartheid was consigned to history.

HISTORIC DAYS ARE SUPPOSED TO BE PREGNANT WITH moments of symbolism, pathos, emotion. Yesterday's final hours of talks at the World Trade Centre lived up to this standard. There was President de Klerk making a surprise guest appearance in the Negotiating Council, slipping into a seat at 4.10pm – precisely the moment at which it was agreed to extend the franchise to all South African citizens.

It was pure chance. The talks agenda is so elastic and the final spurt so frenzied that he could not have planned the coincidence of his entrance. But there he sat, smiling at the multihued multiparty delegates around the horseshoe talks table, as the three-year-old logic of his revolutionary reform initiative was turned into practical fact.

On the other side of the room, ANC secretary general Cyril Ramaphosa rubbed his eyes theatrically in surprise at the NP boss man's appearance, and looked across familiarly at his negotiating partner Roelf Meyer. Outside the chamber, more pathos. Erstwhile egghead of the National

327

Party Dr Gerrit Viljoen had come to look on as the child he helped to father came of age. He smiled avuncularly as he praised his protege, Roelf Meyer. Viljoen, the old campaigner who the process wore out, pronounced the imminent completion of the talks 'a small miracle'.

In the council chamber De Klerk told the negotiators he shared their joy at the achievement, and there was indeed a lot of joy in the corridors of the WTC. It is true that all eyes were heavy-lidded from sleep deprivation and extraordinary caffeine intakes, and true that there remained concern and disappointment about the will-they-won't-they stance of the Freedom Alliance. Everyone knew, too, that the document which emerges today will not be precisely the one they wanted, and that it will still gestate between now and South Africa's real political catharsis, election day. But they felt the frisson of excitement that comes with reaching ends and facing new beginnings.

Ramaphosa had the energy to grin broadly and execute a satisfied skip as he rushed from last-minute bilateral to deadline-dogged debate. He felt mighty good about being alive today, he said. Transkei's chief negotiator Zam Titus was a happy man too. 'This is the day the people of South Africa have been waiting for,' he enthused. 'The time has arrived for us to build from the ruins.' Joe Slovo of the Communist Party said: 'It marks the beginning of the real Great Trek – towards liberation and freedom.'

In the auditorium, construction workers scurried about preparing things for today's plenary session. Fresh paint was slapped on, platforms dragged into place. Their deadline was every bit as urgent as that of the talkers in the council. Tuesday marked a small *fin de siècle* at the World Trade Centre.

THE STAR, 17 NOVEMBER 1993 (WITH ESTHER WAUGH)

THE PLENARY SESSION
OF NO RETURN

Characteristically, the meeting which was to set the seal on South Africa's constitutional deal got under way several hours late, and ran on into the early hours of the morning.

———————

GIVE THE WORLD TRADE CENTRE NEGOTIATORS A GOLD star, or a stiff drink, for stamina. It was more than eight hours after the scheduled starting time when they trudged down the stairs from the Negotiating Council into the cavernous hall for the plenary session of no return. They did so briskly and managed to smile through exhausted eyes.

Eleven o'clock at night is not the ideal time to begin a long, seminal meeting marking the rebirth of a nation. It is especially inopportune when one considers that the participants are all but dead on their feet after murderously long negotiating sessions, and the visiting dignitaries – not to mention party leaders – have been impatiently kicking their heels in the corridors for the better part of the day.

But then South Africa's history has never been predictable or conformist. There was a sneaking sense of appropriateness about the haywire timetables, last minute scrambles, boycotted benches, fatigue-induced giggles and occasional tetchy outbursts. The whole thing was as authentically South African as the range of accents echoing around the chamber.

There was also a sense, heightened by the jangled nerves and the lateness of the hour, of a country shifting on its own axis in front of the watchers' eyes. Stomachs knotted with mixed excitement, tension and uncertainty as the laborious endorsement procedures began. All eyes were on those who had brokered this turn of events, so unexpected and so unlikely, from which there would be no turning back.

The ratification of the painstakingly negotiated – and maddeningly still incomplete – transition package is by no means the last moment of high political drama to come on South Africa's road to something new and entirely different from the country its citizens grew up in. But it was one of the moments that will matter forever.

No-one at the World Trade Centre felt entirely sure about what the future will hold, or whether history will judge the labours that gave rise to this historic compromise well. But the image which persists is profound, of a changing of the guard. President de Klerk came into the chamber early, and sat smiling and gracious as Nelson Mandela made what can only be described as a presidential entrance. It is not that De Klerk is a forgotten man – he is a vital moving part of the new South Africa. But he had finally made room for others to take their rightful places, and things would never be quite the same again.

THE STAR, 18 NOVEMBER 1993

ABOUT CYRIL'S BIRTHDAY PARTY

It was not in the negotiating halls, but at an impromptu party after the historic settlement was signed, that the extraordinary changes that had been wrought were on display.

THERE IS PLENTY TO BE CYNICAL ABOUT IN THIS FRAGILE country of ours. But there are also moments when you should allow the tears of undefined hope that are welling involuntarily in your eyes to flow freely. I cried like a child in the early hours of Thursday morning. There was no need, for dignity's sake, to try to hide it.

Other South Africans, all sorts of them, were crying too, in a subterranean room at the World Trade Centre; crying for a knotted ball of reasons pressing high up in the stomach. Crying for a future that everyone said we couldn't achieve but we might, a past that lurks malevolently in our own shadows, a present that is briefly, gloriously, about all that is best in human beings.

It was after the interminably delayed plenary session at Kempton Park, in which negotiators finally signed the deal that is the scaffolding for our climb from apartheid to democracy. The speeches ended at 3.37am, on a strangely flat, quiet, anticlimactic note. It seemed everyone was too tired to be emotional; the moment lacked the cohesion and the drama it should have commanded. Delegates drifted out eerily, staring far ahead or at their feet. Television crews packed up their equipment and headed home, the story over.

It was not over. It had not begun. There began to gather after 4am in the Trade Centre's canteen an extraordinary group of hollow-eyed, sallow-cheeked people. Politicians, technicians, journalists, administrators, advisers, secretarial staff, waiters, none sure why they were still there but somehow convinced that it could not be allowed to end like this. They were all in their own ways veterans of the process that had just scaled its greatest hurdle, and in crowding together at this pregnant instant they opened an emotional floodgate which had been shut tight for all of three tumultuous years. It was one of the most generous moments I have ever experienced in my country.

A tableau took shape. Roelf Meyer, haggard but strong, was speaking into a microphone, presenting a birthday cake to his friend Cyril Ramaphosa and wishing him well. Ramaphosa was beaming, not in selfish triumph, but with warm-hearted pleasure. The room was full and charged: every single person present was feeling the same thing at the same time. In here, not in there, was a vision of what a new South Africa could be.

Albie Sachs, maimed by our foolish history, embraced one of his former enemies. Leon Wessels stood on my right, chin trembling with emotion in recognition of the magnitude of what he had helped to do, and of the rightness of it. Kader Asmal dried his eyes and spoke softly and beautifully of the nobility, the uniqueness and the rationality of the racial compromise that had been achieved. Then he whirled like a dervish, willing the throng to dance for joy.

One after the other, ANC officials spoke – as if to themselves – not of a victory won over others, but of a pact sealed for the higher good of a polyglot people who must stand together or die. Government figures said the same: it was a fair settlement, a good settlement, a

332

South African settlement. I ordinarily distrust the sincerity of politicians, and I question the durability of such high-mindedness when it is faced with the temptations of power. But on that highveld morning there was no doubt that, for now, they meant what they felt and said. This process has changed people.

There will be the duty and opportunity, soon, for laying into members of the new political elite as they make the mistakes of stupidity and venality that come with governments. But I think there is also a duty to recognize, now, the extraordinary achievement of the likes of Ramaphosa and Meyer. Ramaphosa had to negotiate a settlement fair to his expectant, maltreated followers, without crippling his former enemies. Meyer had the loneliest task of all: he, representing those who had everything, had to give to his former enemies what was rightfully theirs, while guarding jealously a fair future for his own constituency. These things took incredible courage and stamina; the costs show on the faces of the men. We should not be too suspicious and too mean-spirited to salute them for having guided our country this far.

The deal is not perfect, nor is it final. But it is an amazing outcome, given where we started from a few short years ago. We were mightily lucky, those of us who were there in that murky room that morning, because we have a sacred moment to hold on to. It is tragic that the cameras did not record the unplanned catharsis for the rest of the country to share in, because it could not have failed to give courage to all who accept the justice of our non racial future, but are frightened by its brittleness. The new South African birthday party was a glimpse of a terrific force for good which lies latent on our beloved landscape; I know, I was there.

SATURDAY STAR, 20 NOVEMBER 1993

333

LIVING IN FEAR OF YOUNG
MISS MOFOKENG

Now whites had a clear idea of the kind of society they would be asked to live in. But as the crowning of the first-ever black Miss South Africa showed, not all were ready for it.

A 21-YEAR OLD SECOND-YEAR UNIVERSITY STUDENT WAS sitting in the studio of a local radio station in Johannesburg, fielding calls from listeners on a mid-morning talk show. The voice coming through the headphones belonged to a middle-aged white woman. Her accent, not unusual in this part of the country, was both flat and slightly nasal; her tone nasty.

'She's got a fat arse,' said the caller, 'and she should get her teeth fixed.' The remarks were about the studio guest, but directed to the talk show host. The young lady whose physical attributes were being thus analysed said nothing. It was another small, bizarre vignette in the Incredible Journey from the old to the new South Africa.

Palesa Jacqui Mofokeng from Soweto, 'Miss South Africa 1993', is the first full-blooded black African woman ever to take the title. Her predecessors, as we well remember, are a bevy of pure white Pennys, Suzettes, Andreas, Annelines, Sandys, Janines and Dianas. Last year, in a modest fit of gradualism which mirrors neatly the country's process of political reform, Amy Kleinhans got the nod amid muted controversy. Miss Mofokeng, however, has been another story. The reaction to her crowning springs from emotions far more profound than preferences about beauty contests.

Large parts of white South Africa were just not prepared for this. The lady caller was among the most blunt, but she was certainly not alone: the station's switchboard was jammed with denunciators claiming the decision was a political swizz, and that white girls no longer had a fair chance. It takes the oddest things to lift the lid on the bubbling cauldron of white fear in our country. Most whites who are still here know they cannot leave, and although many are plainly terrified about what awaits in the colourblind future, by and large they do not talk about it openly. Now and then, though, something causes the steam to burst out.

That something is hardly ever a matter of State – there is an overwhelming lack of interest in and knowledge about the detailed constitutional blueprint which will lead us to elections – and it arises most unexpectedly. If you think about it for a moment, it's true to say that prior to the panic occasioned by Miss Mofokeng's arrival on the scene, the things which really got ordinary whites going were the undertaking that Die Stem shouldn't be sung at rugby internationals, and suggestions from political leaders that the old orange, white and blue flag might sensibly be put away until they came up with a new one. (Predictably, this prompted rugby fans to sing the anthem and wave the flag as never before.)

But beneath the superficial silliness a very serious issue is at stake. It is called 'affirmative action' in polite company, and 'reverse discrimination' elsewhere. For historical reasons which have been documented to the point of profound boredom, access to the good things in South African life is still skewed horribly in favour of whites. No matter how favourable a political compromise President de Klerk wrings out of Mr Mandela, something is going

335

to have to be done about this – and whites are clever enough to know at which end of the give-and-take equation they're going to find themselves. The unspoken question on whites' minds is: How much will we be expected to give, and will life still be worth living?

Getting steamed up about beauty contests is one way of confronting the real issue without saying so. Everyone knows there will be irresistible pressure to promote black people into positions of authority – and wealth. In an economy which has been in its deepest-ever recession for close on five years, this is not likely to be done simply by creating more opportunities (although that is where our eventual salvation lies), but also – let's be honest – by a radical redistribution of those that are left. (Transnet is an extreme case in point.) Statisticians are useful, for once: they tell us that as things stand, black South Africans occupy *one percent* of top executive posts in business. The temperate National African Federated Chamber of Commerce demands that by the year 2000, 30 percent of all seats on the boards of listed companies be occupied by blacks. Nafcoc also wants blacks to hold 40 percent of equity and 60 percent of posts at all management levels. The arithmetic speaks for itself: things are never going to be the same again.

South Africa's high schools, technikons and universities produced some 600,000 graduates this year. It is estimated that three out of every 100 will secure formal employment. The white youngsters among them don't fancy their chances. Interviewed by The Star in Johannesburg, a number said they were giving up on hopes of careers in law or commerce and were instead acquiring 'emigration skills' through computer and secretarial courses. Black interviewees, instead of marvelling at their fortunate timing, grumbled that they didn't like the idea of getting jobs because of ethnic quotas. Everybody, as has become the custom in South Africa, is complaining.

'Affirmative action' is not the only cause of secret sleepless nights in white suburbia, however. Although fears of wholesale nationalisation by an ANC-dominated government have receded (thanks in large part to the collapse of the Eastern bloc), there is much talk about reparations of other kinds. The ANC has cleverly avoided sticking its neck out with a policy on the issue, instead letting individual members float ideas 'in their personal capacities'. With each flotation, white South Africa's hair stands on end. Earlier this year Mr Tito Mboweni of the ANC's economics department suggested a once-off 'wealth tax', whereby the (overwhelmingly white) middle classes would have all their assets assessed, and then be required to pay a certain percentage into a 'reconstruction fund'. Being as they are among the most over borrowed middle classes in the world, this caused among the putative assessees in the suburbs more than a frisson of concern. More recently Mr Jayendra Naidoo of the Congress of South African Trade Unions told a group of businessmen that it might be an idea to levy a tax on all citizens who have swimming pools. The 'Pool Tax' (which prompted as much spontaneous outrage here as the Poll Tax did in Britain) contributed to another flood of enquiries at foreign embassies, and full houses at the 'seminars' international removal companies now hold routinely for wannabe emigrants. Mr Naidoo issued a statement to say he'd been joking, but this did not entirely still the jitters – especially in view of his additional remark that if whites 'did not like the idea' of having to contribute toward the upliftment of their poorer brethren 'they'd better emigrate'.

In themselves these incidents should not come as a surprise – some form of redistribution, by whatever name you choose to call it, is a logical necessity let alone a moral one – but what is surprising is the reactive rather than proactive approach of the targeted middle classes. It is perfectly understandable that those who stand to lose something should be worried; it is rather more perplexing that they should be doing so little about it, hitting easy and irrelevant targets like Miss Mofokeng when they should be analysing probabilities, proposing solutions and working out 'bottom lines' they would be prepared to live with.

After all, there are voices of practical optimism within the din of disquiet. If the miracle of economic turnaround is performed, say a variety of eminent professors, economists and analysts, then there will be an acute skills shortage and whites will have all the opportunities they could ask for. The trick is keep their chins up sufficiently so as to survive the rollercoaster years of transition, and it is more difficult to pull off because we South African whites have grown up spoilt. It is true now that living standards have been significantly squeezed, and that South African salaries cannot compare with those of the western world, but still the middle classes are accustomed to a considerable measure of comfort. They are, I think, prepared to further reduce that level of comfort for the sake of peace, but they need urgently to know precisely to what extent. South African whites are not 'adapting' as easily as their relatives in independent Namibia, because they don't know what they'll be expected to adapt to: the fear of the unknown lends to the atmosphere its special tartness.

This explains why the benign, charming and blameless Miss Mofokeng should evoke such passions. The white reaction to her crowning is drawn from a much deeper well. Of course she was the wrong target for white fears; that's probably why she was chosen. The country out there is as polyglot as they come, and the crude logic of Mr de Klerk's reforms is that whites are going to have to share out the goodies. Beauty contests, necessarily arbitrary things that they are, fall into this category, but they are the wrong hills to die for. Forward-thinking, open-minded whites should be coming to terms happily with what Miss Mofokeng's elevation represents – and putting their minds instead on the things that will really matter to them in the new South Africa.

PENTHOUSE, DECEMBER 1993

INTO AFRICA, AT LAST

The Transitional Executive Council – the most representative political body ever to meet in South Africa – gathered in Cape Town for its first session. The election began to loom large.

———————

THE NECK OF EXCLUSIVE WHITE RULE WAS GENTLY EASED under the guillotine's blade this Tuesday, December the 7th, at the end of this breathless year near the end of this breathtaking century. There was neither a bang nor a whimper; proof of the success of a process specifically designed to differ from the standard historical scripts – those which teach us that old orders go down screaming defiance, and new orders destroy all that went before. The blade cut, but did not sever.

In the chamber of the President's Council on Stalplein, that architecturally glorious building with the politically inglorious past, a new order gathered in embryo and began to form its own personality. It was astoundingly representative of South Africa's people, by comparison with the past, and although the sad absence of the boycotters reduced some of the Transitional Executive Council's symbolic impact, it could not be nullified. Here was the first practical fruit of the years of talking, with a couple of cherries like IMF loans and lifted oil embargoes placed on top.

The arguments over the TEC's precise powers do not mean much, though they will be loud. It is a transient body which should not, for its own selfish sake, do anything too controversial. Its participants know this. They understand the limits, the sound and the fury notwithstanding. Everyone needs it to work, for collapse would threaten the election – and compared to the election, the TEC is an historical footnote.

So we are on the road to this new South Africa, one way or another. So much is happening that it is impossible to predict the precise nature of the destination with any confidence. In this season of pantomimes it is all too easy to mistake the stage action for reality, and the real thing for fantasy. It is not easy to know for certain which is which; the actors themselves are not sure.

This week fanatical right wingers occupied a fort near the Voortrekker Monument, dug trenches, laid minefields, set up mortars, and vowed to fight and die. Except that the trenches were desultory, the minefields fictitious, the mortars made of wood, and the will to fight evanescent; a boyish braggadocio that evaporated with the first shafts of morning light. It could have been different, of course. Instead of the interestingly named Commandant Ratte fleeing the sinking ship, there could have been a kamikaze bloodbath. It didn't happen that way, but no-one could have told you that at the time.

There are many other crazy imponderables. The TBVC states exist and do not exist. They will be reincorporated without incident, or there will be bloodletting. Winnie Mandela's spectacular rehabilitation means a wild, militant change of course for the ANC. Or it doesn't, rather heralding the pragmatic taming of the firebrand. Chief Buthelezi's talk of civil war is serious and considered, a likelihood rather than a threat. Or it isn't, and will fade from memory once the magnetism, the ineluctability of the march to the new South Africa pulls him in to participation. He is likely to retire hurt from politics, to become a malevolent spectator from the sidelines . . . or he isn't, and actually has no intention of vacating the national stage. The Afrikaner Volksfront is preparing for war . . . or it isn't really. The National Party has conceded so much that it has presaged its own disappearance . . . or it will be a force to be reckoned with for decades to come. And so on and so on. Who can say for sure what are the real dangers ahead and which are mere chimeras?

There is so much to our situation that is unreal, that could be interpreted – equally plausibly – as laughable or deadly. Over there is a man called Mickey Webb, now a well-known Xhosa spokesman, speaking blithely on behalf of what he calls 'his people' in Ciskei. The unelected military dictator of that pathetic statelet has made him 'Minister of Foreign Affairs'. It would be hilarious were it not so cynical. Over here is that well-known neo-Tswana, Rowan Cronje, doing the same in Bophuthatswana. What will they mean in the future? Who knows.

What is clear is that while brakes might still be applied to our transition, it can no longer be stopped. A long-drawn-out moment of truth is approaching, and the harbinger is the sitting of the TEC. It will become clear, in the months and years ahead, whether those of us who consistently argued in favour of this process in spite of its flaws – who had the temerity to call it miraculous in its own way – have been wise or hopelessly naive.

We are still living in the interregnum, treading water, all of us occupying spaces we fashion for ourselves out of hope, stubbornness or myopia. This cannot last for much longer. Next year we are all to be thrust together, invited by history to cannibalise each other or form a latter-day laager from which to re-engage with a tough world. I'm still betting on the miracle.

SATURDAY STAR, 11 DECEMBER 1993

ON THE STUMP IN STANFORD

The momentous negotiating year was all but over; election year approached. FW de Klerk, very probably the last white president, decided it was time to start campaigning.

IT'S PEACEFUL, ORDINARILY, ON THE RUGGED EASTERN shores of Walker Bay round Christmas time. It's been like that since colonial days when Lady Anne Barnard would trek there by ox-wagon from Cape Town – several weeks' journey – to look at the shimmering dunes and swim in subterranean mineral pools in the fantastical caves wherein, she was convinced, lived tigers at the very southern tip of Africa.

The loose string of isolated fishing villages and clusters of holiday shacks now overhanging the glistening Atlantic waters – deep dark waters filled with great pods of breeding Southern Right whales – seem never to have been too disturbed by tumultuous events in the hinterland over the centuries.

This year it seems peaceful, too, but this is not an ordinary year. There is a buzz of excitement in the Market Square of Queen Victoria Street in the old village of Stanford. It is the afternoon of the 28th of December 1993, just after South Africa marked its last white Christmas, and the president is coming to town. We are informed of this in a pamphlet displayed in the local pottery shop: FW 'the Nobel Peace Prize winner', FW 'the man who gave us back our dignity' is going to address the burghers of Stanford.

FW de Klerk has a great affinity for this simple, slow, hypnotic stretch of the south-eastern Cape coast; he spends his holidays nearby. It is not the worst place he could have chosen to launch himself at the head of the National Party's arduous, uphill campaign trail.

The afternoon is blustery in the village square, ringed by quaint cottages in the shadows of the Klein River mountains, along Maanschynbaai, the Moonlight Lagoon. It is pioneering country and this modern Afrikaner leader is a pioneer again, in sight of an ancient stone church under heavy clouds. How the wheel of South African history is spinning and spinning.

The excited knot of people, a few hundred, that has gathered expectantly, is not predominantly white. About eighty percent of the crowd – perhaps more – is 'coloured'. There are posters, mostly written in Afrikaans, flapping in the wind: 'Stanford loves FW', 'FW our pride', 'FW fears nothing', 'FW makes the difference', and further variations on the theme. Young brown-faced children are gathered in groups, staring at the master of ceremonies standing on the rickety, makeshift stage perched on a truck that has seen better days. The MC, a portly, personable loudmouth, is trying to sustain the atmosphere of expectancy. (The president is a little late).

'Who's going to win the election?' he bellows in the distinctive Afrikaans patois of the Overberg. 'FW! NP!' shouts the crowd happily. Then he leads them in a song, the trick being to repeat the chorus with gusto. *'Die NP het 'n donkie kart wat op Mandela ry!'* (The NP has a donkey cart, that's driving over Mandela), they bawl, and *'Mandela waai! Mandela waai!'* (Go away Mandela, go away Mandela). They're laughing all the while, so there's little menace in the scene, and in the original Afrikaans the ditties are quite melodic and funny.

343

There is a frisson as a convincingly smart-looking car turns the corner, but the MC cheerfully announces that 'it's the wrong car. Sorry'. Eventually the right car, part of an imposing motorcade, does pull up. De Klerk, in an open-neck shirt and slacks, begins to work the crowd. A middle-aged coloured man says under his breath: *'Ek gaan hierdie man se hand vat'* (I'm going to shake this man by the hand). And after he has done so he is obviously moved.

De Klerk, flanked by his severe wife Marike, clambers onto the back of the truck as the colours change on the magnificent, looming mountains. 'I am not here today as the president,' he booms. 'I am here as the leader of the National Party, which is going to win the election.

'You are all worried,' he says, warming, 'because you are told that the ANC is going to do very well. But that will only be if we throw our hands up. If every reflective, calm South African joins hands, it won't happen.'

De Klerk fixes his gaze on a few grizzled, sun-dried faces in the crowd. 'The man that catches fish on the rocks – all of us, we must now start to speak politics. The ANC is a dangerous party . . . This election is not about the past, it is about the future. Become a worker in the election battle. I personally invite you to. Think politics, talk politics. Our political enemy, our chief opponent, is the ANC. We must cut them down to size. Ask the children: who will win?' The shouts of 'NP, FW, NP, FW' ring around the square.

Later, as the motorcade moves off, a man with jet-black skin – rare in these parts – leans against a fence, watching. A sardonic smile plays about his mouth. On his T-shirt, against ANC colours, is the legend: 'Hamba kahle (go well) Chris Hani, 1942-1993'. Then Stanford returns to its usual apolitical, aesthetic quiet. How the wheel of South African history is spinning and spinning, and how unqualified are we to know where it might stop.

UNPUBLISHED, 28 DECEMBER 1993

THE SCHOOLYARD TEARAWAY,
SOON TO BE A PREFECT

April 27, election day, was approaching like a bullet train.
The decisive new year brought with it a change in the ANC's
approach – from opposition to preparing to govern.

———————

NINETY-FIVE DAYS TO GO. THIRTEEN AND A HALF WEEKS.
Just over three months. No longer than a single school
term, one-third of a pregnancy, an old national service
army camp, a period of notice after resignation, the length
of a foreign sports tour, a mere bat of an eyelid in the life
of a nation. The Big Year is already upon us; the Day
around the corner. What history always told us would
have to happen one day in South Africa is about to happen
and will be over before we have drawn breath. April 27
approaches like a bullet train.

There is, unsurprisingly, and entirely new mood abroad
in political circles in our country. The election campaign
has started. It is to be found on city lamp-posts, every
corner bellowing an exhortation to vote for the party that
killed apartheid, not people; the one that holds the silver
key to the future; the one that says the time is now. It
is to be found in unlikelier places, with the prisoner-
turned-putative-president in a factory promising workers

that they will matter more, the president-turned-putative-partisan in a harbour town warning fishermen that only he will protect their right to fish. It will all escalate alarmingly. The thing is under way and cannot be stopped; we cannot know what it will bring, though the polls tell us the results each week; the polls that have lied from Canberra to Kansas to Cardiff.

But there is more to it than the ordinary, uninspired election paraphernalia. The smell of power to be gained and power to be lost is in the air. It is a sweet-sour smell of excitement and fear, growing more pungent by the day. The politicians are going into that special trance which shuts us out and is compelling at the same time.

Within all of this there is a fascinating new dynamic. This is the year in which the ANC and its allies are squaring up to the profound prospect of being in government – part of the system – after eighty years of endeavouring to break the system down. The opposition is preparing to become the system, the system preparing to become the opposition. It is a bemusing prospect for both, but for the ANC it requires the more radical alteration in world view. The movement, which fully expects to receive its liberation dividend for having been right in 1912, is trying to reshape its personality like a schoolyard tearaway who has just been told he is to be made a prefect.

In the past week the ANC has not spent its time planning a fresh mass action campaign against this or that. Quite the opposite. In the past week it has been promoting its 61-page reconstruction and development programme; explaining what it wants to do with South Africa's health system, calling on township residents to break the long-ingrained habit of rent boycotts, preparing volunteers for service in the National Peacekeeping Force . . .

Prominent ANC figures Jay Naidoo, Cheryl Carolus and Trevor Manuel were in Johannesburg on Wednesday to explain and defend the reconstruction plan to representatives of the media. The rhetoric levels lowered, the mood was serious, and Carolus spoke in an almost awestruck tone: 'Last February', she said, when plans for governance began to be drawn up, 'we realized that for the first time the organisation would be responsible for what was happening in the country.' She added: 'We have a huge legitimacy problem where government is concerned. (The institution of) government is not respected by the majority . . . there is an almost anarchic attitude, lawlessness . . .'

The responsibility that comes with power, umbilically linked, has been recognized. Quite aside from the problematical and the positive elements of the reconstruction document itself, the approach to life is changing. Here is Jay Naidoo: 'We have to acknowledge that we are not going to solve the problems in the first year of the new government. We are now making a quantum leap from our previous position – from making demands – a leap from opposition to looking at being in government.' He speaks, with reason, like a man who will shortly be in a position of great influence, and accountable for it. The priority now is to get maximum consensus for what is to be done, or face the consequences uncomfortably soon.

Many South Africans are beginning to wonder just what it will be like immediately after the election, at the beginning of May. Will the physical world swirl and mutate in front of our eyes, as in eastern Europe? That seems unlikely. Firstly, there will be a short interregnum with the De Klerk government still in power while the government of national unity assembles itself. Secondly, as Naidoo sees, that government of national unity cannot and will not move precipitately, at least until 1995. But – and this is a big but – the pyschological effect, the feeling of our country, is going to change in a way that we cannot even guess at. Now, in January, the ANC is starting to feel its way towards that new feeling.

SATURDAY STAR, 22 JANUARY 1994

TODDLERS IN DEMOCRACY'S KINDERGARTEN

As the election campaign gathered speed, so the ferocity of exchanges between Mandela and De Klerk increased. The public wasn't sure whether it was hot air, or cause for real concern.

WHERE HAVE ALL THE POLITICIANS GONE? ON THE STUMP, every one. For those who expected the election campaign to get under way stutteringly, this weekend should disabuse them of the notion. Mandela is launching the ANC's election manifesto near Soweto today, moving on to Rustenburg and beyond tomorrow. De Klerk has whizzed through Middelburg and Witbank and makes his way to Bethal and Standerton today. Buthelezi has gathered his faithful in Ulundi, promising to come closer to reaching a decision on participation in the election.

In Pretoria, the Afrikaner Volksfront is naming its 'shadow government'. Scores of lower-ranking party activists are beating on doors elsewhere across this country. The noise is deafening, though the crescendo is still far off.

It's a good time as we emerge from the three-months-to-go starter blocks, to make a general point about the election campaign, before it gets so loud and furious that we can't think straight.

We need to keep reminding ourselves – white as well as black – that our path to democracy has no precedent, that we really know nothing of true democracy and its robustness, and that we are in for an unsettling experience. The point concerns personal relationships between political leaders during a campaign of this importance. An example might help. Within the space of a few days we have heard Mandela go so far, if taken literally, as to accuse De Klerk of planning murder – and then we have seen him sitting, gracious and magnanimous, on a shared podium with the very same National Party leader in Gaborone.

Not only that, but in post-press-conference banter, the ANC president smilingly remarked that he intended to be a 'dove' during the campaign, leaving De Klerk to play the role of hawk. Little wonder that De Klerk responded with a bemused smile. One could almost read his thoughts: 'If what you've said about me last week is dovish, Mr Mandela, I shudder to imagine what is still to come . . .'

On the surface the situation is enigmatic, to say the least. How do we square these two seemingly contradictory forms of behaviour? Well, we should start with the observation that there is no sense of contradiction or inconsistency in Mandela's own mind. Two inextricably linked levels of politics are operating simultaneously in this transitional South Africa. The first finds expression in the Transitional Executive Council and its myriad spin-offs, like the Independent Electoral Commission, the National Peacekeeping Force, the Independent Broadcasting Authority and the like. This is the consensual side of our politics where, as at the Botswana meeting, it is simply understood that co-operation among rivals is a necessary condition for progress.

Then there is the campaign itself, where parties whose representatives were amicably sipping coffee together in the morning are at each other's throats in the afternoon. This is another matter entirely – the country's conflictual face – and we are not well equipped to take it in our stride. Election campaigns are not elegant, nor are they pretty.

This is not unique to South Africa. They are muscular events, not for the thin-skinned, and they almost always give rise to a kiss-and-make-up session when they are over. We have to grow used, like the Australians, to politicians saying the most awful things about each other and then agreeing to work together without a blink or a blush.

A colleague of mine says we have to 'thicken the public skin'. He is right – we need to grow some calluses, to develop a tolerance for tough talking. It comes from all sides, depending often on the audience to which the politician is speaking. De Klerk sharing his opinion of Mandela with leaders of the Frontline states is very different to De Klerk addressing farmers in the Free State . . . It is the name of the game, and unsurprising.

From time to time there have been suggestions that an 'election rule book' should be drawn up, but if this attempted to be too detailed regarding what may and may not be said it would backfire – and it certainly would not ensure gentility on the hustings. My own preference is that politicians should avoid calling each other murderers unless they really have to, and can produce proof of the deeds. But even if they cannot resist the temptation, we should try not to get unduly excited. During an election campaign more hot air is released into the atmosphere than normal, and that can make the climate uncomfortable. It need not be unbearable, though, if we recognize it for what it is.

SATURDAY STAR, 29 JANUARY 1994

ALL ABOARD THE MANDELA EXPRESS

For the launch of the ANC's election manifesto, Nelson Mandela took a train ride from Johannesburg's Park Station to Nasrec near Soweto. It was a benign event in a hard country.

THE WHITE POLICEMAN WAS BURLY AND MOUSTACHED, AND in his cradled arms the pump-action shotgun looked no bigger than a water pistol. He was standing in a line with blue-uniformed colleagues on the station platform, ready to make sure that there was no nonsense when Nelson Mandela's train came through the station.

It soon approached, tooting away merrily, ANC flags flapping out of the windows, music blaring from the front coach. The line of policemen stiffened at first, and then suddenly, fleetingly, got caught up in the spirit of the thing. The man mountain, flanked on either side by black policemen, half-waved coquettishly as the ANC president's coach flashed by with Mandela's smiling face framed in a window. Then he brandished his shotgun again and assumed the regulation glower. Was it a touch sheepish? The instant had passed too quickly.

By no stretch of the imagination could one believe

that this grizzled tough guy cop is fond of the politics of the ANC. That is one acronym alongside which his April 27 cross will most certainly not be placed. But his spontaneous reaction spoke volumes about the unexpected atmosphere that surrounded Saturday's launch of the ANC's American-influenced, razzmatazz-driven phase of its election campaign.

It was kind of, well, fun. The clever gimmickry – having Mandela travel by rail to Nasrec where the ANC's manifesto was launched US party convention-style – lent a benign character to otherwise serious proceedings. It was possible to conjure up a naive picture of an election campaign in which the only violence was verbal and everyone played fair. Of course that is too much to hope for, but the weekend's events do hold out the possibility that the next three months are not going to be all viciousness and nothing else.

Happily, President de Klerk's alternative roadshow appears to have headed off in a direction which also includes occasional moments of levity. There he was over the weekend at the royal kraal in Badplaas, donning a traditional Swazi skirt over his suit trousers and yanking off his tie. These are good, harmless publicity stunts which amuse the public and lower the temperature of a campaign which is going to become dangerously hot.

If the various parties' election strategists are constantly monitoring the success or otherwise of their campaign stunts, they should be putting in some overtime on a case study of the 'presidential train ride'. It added spice to an otherwise relatively bland though worthy and important affair. The actual launch of the ANC manifesto, in a cavernous hall decorated with outsized portraits and giant balloon columns in ANC colours, had to it a going-through-the-motions, stage-managed quality. It was perfectly well organized and executed, but in the end it was predictable – as election manifestoes themselves commonly are. The train ride lifted the event and lent it distinction.

Mandela and his senior lieutenants seem to have taken to

352

the glitzy side of electioneering quite readily. The beaming ANC leader happily acceded to a request from a television crew to be interviewed by a 'voter education puppet' (as did Joe Slovo and Jay Naidoo), babies were dandled and kissed, there was dancing and singing and backslapping. The focus was on the possibilities of the future, not the horrors of the past.

I have a sneaking feeling that the South African public, drained and jaded after the much-interrupted political marathon of the last four years, will respond far more enthusiastically to these kinds of electioneering ploys - which they have seen happening, on television, in other countries – than they will to the flipside of the campaign, which is the mutual savaging of opponents. There is a weariness with negativism, possibly induced by a growing realisation that coalition government means the guys you don't like are still going to be around after April, and probably forever.

THE STAR, 1 FEBRUARY 1994

PROCEEDING IN AN
UNPRINCIPALLED MANNER

Efforts to woo the conservative black and white parties of the 'Freedom Alliance' dragged on frustratingly. Part of the problem was that the leaders themselves weren't there.

———

ON THURSDAY IN PRETORIA THE VERY LAST ABSOLUTELY final no-going-back decisive eleventh-hour crunch crossroads end-of-the-line meeting took place between the ANC and government and the Freedom Alliance. Ha ha ha. Now we are told that Monday will be the very last absolutely final . . . etcetera. We shall see. I doubt it.

Were the participation in the election of the odd alliance not a matter of such importance, this long-running pantomime would deserve to be lampooned out of town. The alliance is increasingly resembling a femme fatale who has no intention of succumbing, stringing along a pair of hapless suitors who are hanging on in the faintest hope that what their eyes tell them is not true. Men often use a more vulgar, sexist phrase to describe such a person.

The will-they-won't-they saga of the Freedom Alliance took an extraordinary turn this week, with a flurry of excitement about a new ANC enticement package, and then anticlimax as the negotiators didn't make it even so far as to put the thing on the table. We'll show you ours if you show us yours. No, you show us yours and we'll show you ours. Stalemate, frustration: for crying in a bucket . . . it's 'back to the principals'!

Now I am one of those who has believed for a long time that the Freedom Alliance needs to refer to its dictionary for a definition of negotiation. This is not to say that its opponents haven't been ducking and diving too, but I harbour the suspicion that the recalcitrants just might not want a settlement after all, and are extracting concessions only in order to demand more.

But this view is irrelevant in the face of the more obvious fact that everything – and more – must be done to make the election inclusive. Whether one believes that the interlocutors are ingenuous or not, the talks must go on. But what about the poor confused public? How long can they go on? Where are some deadlines we can trust – dramatic deadlines that cannot be miraculously and unblushingly moved by the politicians when it suits them?

I'm tempted to say we should decide forthwith to ignore these self-proclaimed D-Days and concentrate on constitutional and other logistics. So, a final yes or no from the FA might or might not be forthcoming on Monday, but that's not the point. The election campaign moves ahead apace and we will know before April 26 whether the alliance is serious about its boycott threats. Journalists – this one included – have had their fingers burnt by taking the politician's self-proclaimed deadlines at face value, and we must stop it. As far as I am concerned, when the trilateral talkers finally do or do not have a deal, they should call us.

A last point about the courting of the FA. Hindsight is a frustrating thing, because invariably the illumination it provides comes too late to be immediately useful. As final meeting stumbles on to final meeting, I am reminded of a very pithy observation made to me by a prominent politician in June of last year.

He said: 'One thing concerns me about this negotiating

355

process. In South Africa the leaders are absent, and that is unique. I've never come across discussion of the constitution of a country in which the leaders were not the ones who were negotiating.

'If we had De Klerk, Mandela, Buthelezi and others actually present, you wouldn't have reporting back, misunderstandings, new instructions and so on. This is what's happening. You don't know what report has been given and whether it is an accurate reflection.'

He added: 'I have mooted the attendance of the leaders on several occasions, even to Mr de Klerk himself. I said we may pay a heavy price this kind of second-hand negotiation. The principals could listen to the debates, be convinced and make swift decisions. Ours is a very dangerous way of negotiating and I don't think it will change, because people seem to be set in this way of proceeding and don't seem to realize the effects.'

And who was this acute observer? Why, it was Joe Matthews, chief executive of the Inkatha Freedom Party. What he was saying was that there is a grave danger in acting in this unprincipalled manner.

SATURDAY STAR, 5 FEBRUARY 1994

A LIGHTNING-ROD CALLED SIBONGILE

The big two parties were hogging the headlines as their high-profile campaigns gained impetus. But the smaller fry, notably the liberals of the Democratic Party, weren't giving up.

THE SCENE: THE CARLTON HOTEL BALLROOM, Johannesburg, on a wet and gloomy Sunday morning. Several hundred enthusiasts have gathered inside, an Afro-Disney version of those gigantic American party conventions one sees from time to time on television.

Complete with polystyrene boaters, tall, thin signboards indicating the regions from which the delegates have come, choirs, balloons, video screens, and outsized loudspeakers booming out a medley ranging from 'Eye of the tiger' through 'Take a chance on me' to 'Michelle ma belle' (the last for former Miss South Africa Michelle Bruce, now an election candidate), the genteel gathering is colourful and happy. But is it meaningful in the context of massive public outpourings of support for a man like Nelson Mandela?

On Sunday the Democratic Party set out to demonstrate that reports of its demise were premature. The occasion was the launch of the PWV region's election campaign,

357

an important test of the current and future health of the small party.

The PWV region, led by the feisty Tony Leon and his terrier-like lieutenants, is a bedrock of the DP: if it cannot make any impression on the election campaign, then the national game is probably up.

The Leon of the North knew this, and the party which was once seen as the voice of the mink-and-manure belt (but is now, ironically, probably one of the poorest of all contenders) sought to reinvent its image if not its principles. As is only to be expected in the fast-running river that is transitional South Africa, the zesty exercise by these outright underdogs was partially but not wholly successful. The successful elements, however, were invigorating for the most exhausted of old campaigners.

But let us first dispense with the drawbacks. There was still on display the albatross of elitism which has always weighed down this vessel of articulate liberalism. Cynics were afforded opportunities aplenty for cheap shots. The DP is still very white, especially at leadership but also at branch level, although it has achieved more than a token black presence. (Its signwriters wrote 'Soshanguve' as 'Soshanguwe', suggesting they had never been to the place.) Some of the older leaders spoke as if this was another good old 'general' election involving a fraction of the population, and told inappropriate outdated jokes with no resonance whatsoever for the black delegates who were displaying considerable courage just by being there. Some were silly enough to proclaim the DP was 'going to win', though they sensibly stopped short of the absurd suggestion that this might mean actually taking power in April.

But this was the predictable stuff. It was on the unpredictable side that optimists within the DP could find morsels of hope for some long term influence in South African politics. The DP has several outstanding, unshakable qualities, which deserve incessant repetition because they could be so vital to the future body politic. These include its coherent, anti-opportunistic set of principles, its energy and talent, and its blamelessness in the matter of violence.

We don't need polls to tell us, however, that these admirable abstracts do not automatically translate into millions of votes – especially in South Africa's 'liberation election'. Some other conduit is needed to transfer some current, and two such lightning-conductors were unexpectedly in evidence on Sunday. Their names are Sibongile Mahlangu and Patricia Zwane. Let me explain.

Half way through the proceedings, 10 DP candidates were invited to the podium to tell the faithful why they had agreed to stand for election. All were good – the convincing labour consultant Andrew Levy, the personable Kate Prinsloo who vowed to protect the right of Pretoria's citizens to wear grey shoes if they wanted to in the new South Africa, the impressive gay rights campaigner Craig Oakley-Brown – but Mahlangu and Zwane were brilliant.

Mahlangu, an SABC news archivist from Tembisa, and Zwane, an office worker from Daveyton, brought the DP down to earth – where parties belong in these times. They are at numbers three and fifteen respectively on the DP's PWV regional list, but should be elevated immediately to the party's inner sanctum and its public face.

Mahlangu introduced herself thus. 'I am Sibongile Mahlangu, divorced mother of four beautiful children. Here are they. We are heading for the first election in which I will be allowed to vote. Now that all South Africans have got the right to vote, we all have the right to vote for whoever we want to.

'Last night I was woken up by a rock through my window. To all those who want to intimidate me, I want to say this: it is my democratic right to stand for the party of my choice. I have waited all my life for this moment. Don't try to take my choice away. I will stand for the DP. I am just an ordinary person. I don't live in a fancy house or drive a fancy car. When I am elected I will represent the voice of the ordinary people. I am proud of who I am. I am Sibongile Mahlangu.'

Zwane delighted the delegates with her impish delivery: 'The DP is a party of all races, blacks, coloureds, Indians . . . and even whites.'

In these two strong women, and others like them, the DP could be on to something. It was not so much a breath of fresh air, as a hurricane. If the party is to have a presence in the new South Africa's parliament it might consider a dose of from-the-gut Mahlanguesque straight talking, along with its valid points about the advantages of proportional representation, the need for watchdogs, and so forth.

THE STAR, 8 FEBRUARY 1994

BRACING FOR THE UNWANTED BOYCOTT

Suddenly, South Africans began to take seriously the prospect of the election going ahead in the face of a boycott. A taboo was broken, and the country stared at the consequences.

TABOOS SEEM TO DEVELOP WITHOUT MUCH DISCUSSION OR reflection. Then they're broken just as arbitrarily. This happened in our country this week, and it will take some time for the implications to sink in.

As the election stopwatch moved to eleven weeks and counting, the political lens shifted with a clunk. Until now, the election paradigm has ended with the question: How will the Freedom Alliance be brought into the transition process, and when will this happen? No-one chose to stare into a future beyond that. But after the umpteenth failure of three-way Government-ANC-FA talks in Pretoria, a new question announced itself unsettlingly, breaking the taboo: What, exactly, will happen all over South Africa in April if the likes of the Inkatha Freedom Party and the Conservative Party actually go through with their threats to boycott and resist? People began to imagine the raw, practical consequences.

It is now well known that important National Party

and ANC figures feel instinctively that the FA, or at least big parts of it, has decided to boycott the election come what may. This moves us into the realm of political will, which is not necessarily influenced by rationality or last-minute compromises. Hence contingency plans are having to be made for that unhappy eventuality. Time is short – too short for taboos. How would you place ballot boxes around Bophuthatswana in such a way that those who want to vote can do so without risking their lives? Will the Bophuthatswana Defence Force, that timorous, fickle band that succumbed humiliatingly to thirty-four SADF soldiers in 1988, really open fire if balloters cross the imaginary border in April? Will the KwaZulu Police throw up barricades? Will the well-armed and well-trained zealots of the white Right use real guns this time; was Fort Schanskop a trial run rather than schoolboy buffoonery? Will the security forces hold the ring on behalf of the new society? In short: can the election succeed under these circumstances?

Computer screens are flickering late into the night as those charged with administering this election grapple with these and a dozen other apocalyptic questions. Political insiders are now working with the probability that at least a partial boycott will come about, and the knowledge that although the constituent parts of the FA probably represent a fraction of all voters, their potential influence on proceedings is much, much more than the sum of their support.

Of course it is true that it ain't over 'til it's over, and this saga will twist and turn for a long time beyond today's 'final' deadline, which will pass inconclusively. But in the meantime the ground has shifted beneath our feet. Unless they are indulging in an astoundingly risky poker bluff, we must accept that the two big brokers of the World Trade Centre deal will not put off the election under any circumstances. They fear an uncontrollable outburst of black anger, and they fear that if they bend on this issue of issues, the transition might be held hostage indefinitely. So the options are clear, and severely limited: keep the door open to the FA, keep talking even when it seems hopeless, but at the same time move unerringly toward the April catharsis.

The mood of the Government and the ANC has hardened in tandem with that of the Conservative Party, the IFP, the KwaZulu Government and the Zulu king. There is a sense in which all sides appear to be continuing to try for an inclusive settlement primarily because they wish to be judged well by history – 'We did all we could, and more'. Certainly, in some ANC quarters the main reason for the dogged engagement of the Afrikaner Volksfront is based on a historical lesson rather that real hope of success. The MPLA government in Luanda is today paying a heavy price for having ignored the maxim that you continually engage your enemies in order to fight them more effectively: the MPLA refused to talk to UNITA for all the earlier years of Angola's civil war, and the result is there for all to see. It is the same within the NP. President de Klerk says the door will remain open to the FA even after the election, while his negotiators say privately that the exercise will be fruitless.

It seems now that only a change of heart – of political will – from the FA's constituents, jointly or severally, can stop a full-scale boycott. The current auguries are bad, with FA members seeming to take strength in numbers rather than fracturing. In the Afrikaner Volksfront, General Constand Viljoen looks increasingly lonely and marginalised – although he, who knows war so well, has warned against it so often. In the IFP, the doves have fallen silent, timid and trembling, and impotent. The boycotters must recognize the profound consequences of their stance – not least among them the obvious fact that they will be pouring millions of votes down history's drain in April – but that does not look like being enough to make them change their minds right now.

It will be a great and unnecessary tragedy if the April poll takes place without the black and white conservatives of the new South Africa. This is not the same as saying the poll must therefore fail, but no-one should doubt that our prospects for a miraculous, stable outcome will be greatly diminished. We should be praying to our various gods for wisdom to descend on the Freedom Alliance.

SATURDAY STAR, 12 FEBRUARY 1994

ACROSS THE WATER, TO SETTLE
A SCORE

Four years after his release from prison, Nelson Mandela went back to visit Robben Island with his fellow lifers. The wheel of South African history turned full circle that day.

———————

THE GRUFF VOICE OF THE PRISON WARDER ON THE BUS betrayed not a trace of irony. 'Ladies and gentlemen,' he said, 'please make way for the VIPs.' A smiling group of elderly men clambered aboard, chatting excitedly. This time they wore dark suits and airs of authority; thirty years before they had been in prison overalls and chains.

As the ancient bus clattered through the harbour gates and made its way across the island, the warder provided historical commentary. 'On your right is the maximum security prison,' he said, 'built from stone which was quarried here on the island . . .' One of the veterans piped up: 'Yes, by us!' The commentator fell silent.

It was Andrew Mlangeni who had spoken. He and four other Rivonia trialists - Walter Sisulu, Govan Mbeki, Ahmed Kathrada and Denis Goldberg – were on their way to join ANC president Nelson Mandela in a historic, pathos-filled homecoming to the windswept island jail in which most of them had spent the better parts of their adult lives. It was a stage-managed piece of electioneering, of course, but also much more than that.

Robben Island changed yesterday from being the symbol of brute white power, to the redoubt of those about to defeat it, in the latter years of their lives. The prisoners took over the penitentiary, and the respectful solicitousness of the warders offered just one glimpse of the overpowering symbolism of the occasion. The men who had once arrived on Robben Island as the wretched of the earth now returned as a feted elite.

Old man Mbeki bubbled with youthful humour: 'You know, we built that prison with our own hands. And the great irony is that we made it maximum security, so we couldn't escape.'

Yesterday's display of the turn of the wheel of South African history had its bizarre moments. A beaming Mandela stood to receive prison officials and journalists in the modest colonial splendour of the island's guest house, directly beneath photographs of FW de Klerk and Adriaan Vlok. Once those official portraits would have signified the unshakable force of the State, but now they looked decidedly temporary – just pictures on a wall, easily removed.

The return to Robben Island reintroduced history into the election campaign, a terrain on which the National Party cannot hope to compete with the ANC. Mandela-as-presidential-candidate returned to the status of Mandela the martyr, as he and his fellow lifers retraced the steps of bitter decades. 'I find it difficult to personalise the collective experience of prison,' Mandela said, 'but my advisers tell me that on this occasion I should talk about myself and not be shy.' The world's most famous ex-prisoner spoke of the 'shattering' experience of those years – of seeing his mother depart from the prison harbour for the last time in 1968, of hearing of the death of his son, of the hardship of the lime quarry, of psychological persecution, the isolation of his claustrophobic cell. 'Of course the wounds that cannot be seen are more painful than those that can be treated by a doctor,' he mused. 'I did not share my pain with anyone.'

But each time he checked himself, and returned to his favourite theme – of the camaraderie and strength in adversity among the prisoners, and of the luxury of time to think about issues, a luxury taken away from the moment of his release. The story of Robben Island is more than anything else a human epic. The tour took in the eerie, cavernous lime stone quarry, where the prisoners had broken rocks as younger men with the maddeningly enticing vista of Cape Town across the bay. The old men, hair ranging from white to greying, wandered briefly and alone into the quarry, lost in reverie, but returned laughing about spare diets and the political debates they'd had there – one, between Mandela and activist Neville Alexander, had lasted thirty-one days. Then they falteringly sang an old working song for the television cameras.

Later Mandela stood at the steps to the main prison. How did he feel? 'Well, today I know what I'm walking into, and I know that I'll be able to go home at the end of the day.' On, through the yellowing corridors of the empty 'political' jail, and soon Mandela and Sisulu were standing again in the concrete courtyard that had been their recreation area throughout the 1960s and 1970s. Mandela reached his cell, number seven, and waved – grinning broadly – through the bars. Had he ever despaired of escaping that space of barely more than two square metres? 'It would be easy to answer that we always hoped to return. But there were moments when your spirit was down, moments when I confess that I was not so certain.' He laid yellow flowers in the cell, and left.

As the extraordinary day drew to a close, the Rivonia veterans began to forget the presence of the journalists, and happily succumbed to private reminiscences among themselves. It had been a long journey from the jail-house doors to the gates of the new South Africa, but an old score was now settled.

THE STAR, 14 FEBRUARY 1994 (WITH MICHAEL MORRIS)

THE FREEDOM ALLIANCE
HAS A FAULT-LINE

There were tremors in the foundations of the Freedom Alliance. It was time to take the plunge, and predict which of the conservatives might join the election after all.

IMAGINE AN ELECTION IN WHICH PARTS OF THE AFRIKANER Volksfront, but not Ferdi Hartzenberg, participate. In which some members of the IFP, but not Chief Mangosuthu Buthelezi, participate. In which some Bophuthatswana government politicians, but not President Lucas Mangope, participate.

This complicated scenario is now a possibility following the latest in a long line of 'reassurance packages' offered by the ANC and the Government to the Freedom Alliance. Many observers now believe that a unified, comprehensive answer from the FA – a straightforward 'yes' or 'no' to the election – will not be forthcoming, no matter how many more surprises, crisis meetings, compromises and deadlines we live through in the coming weeks.

What might happen, though, is that the constituent components of the Freedom Alliance – and sub-components within these – could begin to respond differently to the advances of the ANC and Government as the election vice

368

tightens and the pressure becomes unbearable. There need not be a formal split in the FA, a dramatic collapse of this political house of cards at an appointed time, for this to occur.

The alliance has always been more certain of what it commonly opposes than what it commonly supports, and the initiatives emanating jointly and severally from the ANC and the Government are clearly placing unprecedented strains on FA unity regarding the latter.

The AVF, IFP and Bophuthatswana government have different interests, although the focus of their hostility remains the same. It is worth looking at the differences, which history could prove to be irreparable fault-lines.

Within the AVF, powerful pressure groups support General Constand Viljoen's approach – which is, in essence, to cut a deal that guarantees serious consideration of volkstaat proposals by a new government, in return for participation in the election. Viljoen genuinely does not want war, and nor do the established Afrikaner interest groups that back him. He knows it is unwinnable and he understands that the election is unstoppable; the best hope of protecting the interests of the volk under the circumstances lies in extracting concessions, not in a firefight.

The Conservative Party, the AVF's biggest constituent – and its loudest – does not or will not understand this reality. The Conservatives believe they can get their volkstaat before elections, and are, to varying degrees, serious about sacrificing everything in another war of freedom.

The latest ANC offer – in whose genesis the Goverment has played its part – is therefore tempting for the Viljoenites, but not for the hardliners. The proposed new principles on self-determination might be enough to draw Viljoen and his supporters into the process on the basis that this is the best they can hope to get – and they could do so even if the CP stays out.

The IFP's situation is still less tractable, but as intensely pressurised. Chief Buthelezi seems irrevocably set against participation, but this does not mean that each new offer – the latest and most important being a constitutional principle which guarantees that regional powers cannot be undermined – has no resonance for other IFP officials. Some, like former DP MP Mike Tarr, have already gone public with their frustration about the boycott tactic. Others, like Kwazulu Cabinet Minister Chief Simon Gumede, have taken the option of resigning from active politics. Put another way, Buthelezi might not take the IFP into the election, but he might not be able to keep all of it out.

Bophuthatswana appears to be the most susceptible of all to the latest approaches. Mmabatho's response to the new package, in contrast to Ulundi's, leaves the door to accommodation wide open. This, along with intensive bilateral discussions with the ANC at the moment, suggests the possibility of an understanding being reached with the Bophuthatswana government.

A related element is the fear among some officials that a future government might seek to have them punished for repressive acts in the past: it is possible that these figures might seek and receive assurances about their personal futures, and undertake not to take part in active resistance against the election.

Some might find other political homes, and it would surely be a rational option for President Mangope to retire gracefully from politics rather than face a bruising battle against the ANC in his region – provided that his personal and financial security was guaranteed.

In this context the Mandela package, offered just before the ANC leader's departure for Europe, is a deeply serious initiative, its swift rejection by Ulundi notwithstanding. It includes significant movement on the matters of regional powers and self-determination (not precisely what the FA wanted, but significant movement nevertheless) and, crucially, it was presented without strings attached.

It is on the table whether or not the FA gives any assurances about participation, and this makes it much more difficult for the FA to ignore. Give or take a few refinements still to come, the document could yet prove to be the political straw that broke the FA camel's back.

SATURDAY STAR, 19 FEBRUARY 1994

THIS POLL'S ABOUT PERSONALITIES

South Africa carried on as if preparing for an old-style contituency-type election. But in fact the battle was between the personalities of two men – and one had the easier task.

NINE BREATHLESS WEEKS STILL TO GO OUT THERE ON THE campaign trail, but stylistically the differences between the government-in-waiting and the opposition-in-waiting are clear for all to see.

And, whatever the contrary blandishments on offer, both the ANC and National Party campaigns have become heavily personalised in the figures of their leaders Nelson Mandela and FW de Klerk. In very large part, supporters of both are being asked to vote for the man at the helm, with the parties thrown in – not the other way around. This places heavy burdens on two pairs of shoulders; to different effect, as I will argue.

But first it is worth noting a curious feature of our first democratic election – possibly also another indication of our country's generalised political immaturity – which is that the parties took so much trouble to get 'celebrities' on to their electoral lists. In fact proportional representation (PR) means that the leader and the party image, rather than the individual candidates, are what matter. PR allows a party to have a few heavyweight politicians at the top for glamour, and experts in various fields for the rest. This, in theory, is what is best for the quality of future governance.

But in South Africa's election '94 most parties have behaved as if there are going to be tightly fought constituency battles, where a Naas Botha or a Miriam Makeba or a Melanie Walker – each of whom has made a name in somewhat different fields – would tip the scales in their favour. It is difficult to fathom any other reason for the inclusion of the 'celebs': certainly they are not going to draw votes on the basis of their proven political acumen, bureaucratic brilliance or technical talent. It is a silly feature of this all-in election, and one which will hopefully disappear next time around.

But the main point to note at this stage of the election battle is that, whether the parties have realized it or not, it is the big name at the top which dictates the focus and content of their campaigns. This has been obvious since earlier this year when the Mandela and De Klerk roadshows got under way, and it is a fact which makes life much more difficult for the National Party leader.

Watching Mandela's triumphal tour of black South Africa has been reminiscent of the ecstatic outpouring of adulation by Zimbabwe's voteless masses when Robert Mugabe made his return – except multiplied by a factor of ten. Not even the televison pictures or reports of huge crowds can get across to those who have not witnessed it, the scale of support for Mandela, or its emotional intensity. He is the living embodiment of eighty years of struggle against apartheid and there is no force on Earth that can take that away from the ANC, especially in this cathartic 'liberation election'.

A flipside is that although Mandela has made conscious efforts to reach out to minorities and even sub-minority interest groups, his messiah-like reception in the black townships has not been mirrored there – nor should one expect it to have been. The tidal wave he is riding does not cover every piece of the land and this, then, is one of his major pre-election tasks: he has the masses all but sewn up, but he needs in the coming weeks to delve into some important nooks and crannies.

De Klerk's challenge can be viewed in precisely the opposite terms. It is within the masses who make up the majority that he has to establish a foothold, and he has been trying doggedly to do so via donning various forms of traditional dress and making forays into townships where he thinks he can. His support among minorities who are leery of an all-powerful ANC is considerable (though his strategists are not foolish enough to rely on it to turn itself out at the polls without active wooing), but his most formidable task is to convince a reasonable number of the majority black South Africans that he is a better choice than Mandela. And he, unlike Mandela, cannot rely on their instinctive sympathy.

The starkness of the task makes the tactics his advisers have adopted all the more baffling. To a great extent they have opted to fight the ANC on the terrain of the past, rather than the future. Thus we have arguments at the hustings and in newspaper advertisements over who actually did the liberating in 1990, about the short-comings of the ANC, about which is the more moral party.

On this terrain De Klerk is on a hiding to nothing. The finest advertising minds cannot copy-write their way around the fact that the ANC was right in 1912 – it envisaged a non-racial democracy – and all other major parties were wrong. Debates about tactics like the armed struggle notwithstanding, De Klerk's spin-doctors cannot hope to convince even a fraction of the black majority that the NP was not responsible for the horrors of apartheid. Each time the NP picks a fight about the past, it will get a bloody nose.

De Klerk's potential strength lies in what his new National Party can offer for the future, and it seems extraordinary that this has not been fully recognised.

An approach which said: we messed up in the past, we are sorry, but now we are changed and we have considerable skills to offer in the future, would be infinitely more resonant. ANC strategists know this, and must be gleeful at their easy ride thus far in the propaganda war.

Perversely enough, the strongest card held by the NP and other parties is precisely the overwhelming reception the ANC has received. Conversely, this is one of the ANC's main points of vulnerability. Mandela is, blindingly obviously, the messianic figure for the masses, and no-one else should try to compete with that. What they can do is to argue incessantly that variety in the government of national unity would enhance quality and increase the chances of a stable transition. It will be interesting to see whether this approach, rather than futile anti-ANC mudslinging, is adopted in the nine weeks of campaigning which remain.

THE STAR, 24 FEBRUARY 1994

ARE YOU MY MOTHER?

There wasn't much life left in the old South Africa. Some whites – well, this one anyway – began to wonder why they weren't being called Africans, like their compatriots.

EXCUSE ME, SORRY TO INTERRUPT WHILE SO MANY OTHER important things are being decided, but there's something I'd rather like to know before the foundations of this new South Africa set solid. Am I going to be able to call myself an African in future, as I always have in the past?

The reason for asking is that no-one else seems to be calling me that. It's worst during an election campaign like this one, when everyone has a rush of ethnic terminology to the head. Take the ANC as an example, because it seems safe to assume that it is one organisation which will hold a great deal of sway over our destinies.

I think (though it's difficult to keep up), that the state-of-the-art preferred nomenclature in describing our ethnic cornucopia is: whites (small w), Indians (big I), coloureds (small c) or Coloureds (big C) or 'so-called coloureds', and Africans (big A, occasionally small). Phew. And this list doesn't even begin to look at the Khoi, the Chinese, and a variety of other compatriots.

Now of course we've all been here in our home on the

southern tip long enough to know what is meant by these terms, some of which predate considerably the disastrous scholarship of Dr Verwoerd. But are they the terms we want to take with us into the new society? Just as a crazy Government used to veer from native to bantu, bantu to plural, plural to some other nonsense, the forces of resistance have played nomenclatural hopscotch along the way.

There was a time I remember when – in response to the look-down-the-nose-with-a-dismissive-sniff term 'non-white' – most people who weren't 'white' wanted specifically to be termed 'black', to indicate what they were on the bum end of the apartheid equation. This seemed to make sense at the time, and many of us took great care to use Coloured (or coloured) only when it was entirely unavoidable (which was surprisingly often), Indian only when 'Indian' people used it themselves, and mostly ended up mumbling into our collars in confused embarassment. I think we're still in a discomfiting mess, though apartheid is about to be tossed into the Atlantic.

Please accept that I don't have an easy formulaic solution, but it seems a good time to raise the problem and ask greater minds to advise. Okay: so I'm still white with a small w (pinkish is more accurate, as Steve Biko pointed out, but let's not confuse things any further), but I'm also still an African. Except that surveys tell us that category belongs to other people: I know for example that my opinion is always recorded in that little survey bar graph for 'whites' only, while many friends and colleagues go in the big one for 'Africans'. So if that implies I'm not an African, then what the hell am I?

'White' on it's own doesn't mean a thing; it's an ethnic construct so malleable that even grand apartheid in its heyday wouldn't have dared to try to fit it into a homeland. 'Non-black' doesn't help either, because an inversion of an old insult doesn't make a compliment. And what do c/Coloureds and Indians want to be called? It's enough to make your head spin.

Most 'Indians' I know have never been to India, just

as most 'Europeans' (whoops, there's another term for whites I forgot about) have never been to Britain, Holland or anywhere even close. If there are such things as genetic banks (a risky subject to get into, I know, but I'm stuck now), then I guess mine would be classified as having been European in origin in some century or other. The problem is I'm sure the bank account was overdrawn years ago; my Transkeian roots are what I remember.

All I ever knew about Europe was what I read in books, until I visited the place as a foreign adult not all that long ago. The Europeans, at least, were refreshingly unconfused about my antecedence: to them I was a foreigner, an African – my sentiments precisely. It's only when you come home that things get complicated.

I'm being flippant, but not entirely so. Do we need to develop a new lexicon? Can we? Should we, when we absolutely have to be defined, call ourselves black South Africans, white South Africans, coloured South Africans, Indian South Africans and so on? There must be a way of making it clear, at least, that we're all South Africans first and foremost.

I'm more confused now than when I started. But I do know I'm unhappy with this meaningless 'white' business if that's all the genealogy I'm to be allowed. I want to be known as being from my continent and my country, the only continent and country I belong to, and the only ones to which I owe my loyalty. (I hope the PAC heard that bit.) This is a plea to some professor out there – any old kind of African will do – to break through my befuddlement.

SATURDAY STAR, 26 FEBRUARY 1994

WHEN WE LOSE
OUR CULT STATUS

A journey to the other side of the world served to remind that when apartheid was over, we'd have to prove our worth like any other country – political superstardom wouldn't last long.

NO WORDS ARE NEEDED TO DESCRIBE THE TRUE IMPORTANCE of Africa, and South Africa, in the international scheme of things as viewed through Japanese eyes. All that is required is a visit to the office of the Second Africa Division at Japan's Ministry of Foreign Affairs building in downtown Tokyo. Your eyes will tell you the story.

The office, to put it mildly, is neither expansive nor opulent. In this claustrophobic, thrilling Asian metropolis of some 12 million people, half of the continent of Africa is dealt with in a busy and cluttered room the size of a Hillbrow bachelor flat. The other half is handled next door, by the First Africa Division, whose accommodation looks similarly spartan.

My face clearly betrays my surprise, because the first thing that a smiling Hisao Yamaguchi says is: 'You will notice that we are not given unlimited resources.' I say I have noticed. Yamaguchi, experienced director of the

Second Africa Division, nods at the mutual understanding we have achieved.

I begin quickly to shed that carapace of self-importance that most of us South Africans automatically adopt when discussing the affairs of our country with foreigners, assuming our homeland to be unquestionably the most interesting subject on Earth. Japan puts you in your place in world politics.

What is the obvious point? It is that within a matter of months, South Africa is going to begin to lose its curious cult-figure status in the world, and I don't know that many of us are prepared for this.

The great irony of our history is that the horror of apartheid elevated us to a status that neither our demographics nor our economics warrant, and we have become very used to being a centre of attention.

In fact we are a middle-to-lower ranking country in the global league table, with a lot of potential for promotion. We are of abiding interest to others primarily because of the possibility of achieving unprecedented racial reconciliation, but that is an abstract and fickle attraction in a world tied up in economic knots. If we do not now recognise the folly of cannibalising each other when we need to weld our energies together in reconstruction, then we will be made to feel it within a very few years. The world is watching with sympathy, and it is even prepared to help pay for the performance, but its attention span is limited.

Koji Kakizawa was, until Japan's change of government last year, Vice-Minister of Foreign Affairs in this pressurised, powerhouse island nation. He speaks for most Japanese, and certainly the intellectual-political classes when he says, 'I really appreciate the courage of Mandela and De Klerk. The changes are truly revolutionary and brave.'

But he is also bluntly unsentimental: 'After the elections, there must be economic recovery and development. Your politicians must be speaking the political and economic language of the 21st century.

'I see opportunities for greatly increased Japanese aid to South Africa, and I have made a concrete proposal to involve Japan in infrastructural and other development. But if you cannot stabilise, then, well . . . ' His voice trails off, but the sentence finishes itself.

Yamaguchi is also diplomatic and encouraging, but no less direct in his meaning. Africa is far away from Japan, he says, and in the past much of Japan's involvement on the continent was simply aimed at 'raising the flag of friendship'. It will stay that way unless South Africa can prove an exception to the continental rule. 'Many Japanese business delegations have travelled to South Africa recently,' he says, 'and all have given the same reports. There is great potential, but they will have to wait and see what . . . '

The inordinate number of newspaper columns and television minutes that are being devoted to our country here in Japan and elsewhere in the world at the moment are deceptive. Like Lillehammer, we are enjoying our time but soon it will be someone else's. There is a suspension of judgment for the moment, manifesting itself in a combination of international solidarity and scepticism. The verdict will be delivered soon after our election, as harsh or constructive as we allow it to be. If we look like re-enacting the disasters of our continent, the office of the Second Africa Division of the Ministry of Foreign Affairs in Tokyo will certainly not be making any plans to expand its operations.

WEEKEND STAR, 5 MARCH 1994

THE BREAKING OF
BOPHUTHATSWANA

History's tidal wave crashed over Bophuthatswana, as it had threatened to years before. Lucas Mangope was engulfed; he had not heeded the warnings. Would other leaders learn from him?

IT WAS SIX YEARS AND ONE MONTH AGO. THERE WAS NO doubt in anyone's mind as to where power lay: in the tip of the finger of the bespectacled white man with the black hat.

A laughably small force of South African soldiers had put down a farcical coup attempt against Lucas Mangope. When night fell, then-President PW Botha had flown with several of his ministers to the South African embassy outside Mmabatho, where he presided over a pathetically grateful Mangope grovelling before television cameras. It was 1988, the old South Africa had some life in it yet, and the scene witnessed by a group of exhausted, grime-caked journalists was sordid and revealing. I still have my scribbled notes from that day and night of bantustan madness.

Mangope, shaken but lucid, had travelled to the embassy directly after giving a television broadcast reasserting his control. On seeing Botha, his first words were: 'Oh! I never knew friends could be so loyal.'

Botha explained with seemingly forced gravity – it looked like the former military man was having some difficulty in concealing his delight at the success of the 'operation' – that he felt he had owed it to Bophuthatswana to 'uphold good order and orderly government'. His official announcement to Parliament, made in deadly earnest earlier in the day, said South African security forces had been ordered to go to the aid of the temporarily deposed Mmabatho government in response to a request from Bophuthatswana's foreign minister.

This had been acceded to, Botha said, because the legally elected head of a sovereign and independent state had been deposed. There was a 'mutual assistance agreement' between Bophuthatswana and South Africa which covered the present situation, and the South African rescuers had been 'ordered to give priority to the safety of the SA embassy and personnel, President Mangope, his foreign minister, his Cabinet and their families'. Botha told the curious gathering: 'This is not only a unique occasion, but one on which we (South Africa and Bophuthatswana) pledge each other to remain true to each other.' He wished 'the president of Bophuthatswana to go and have a good night's rest . . . go and sleep peacefully knowing that your friends are on your side.'

Then he made his fateful slip, never to be forgotten by those who were there: 'Well, we had these problems. We are tonight back in full control . . . er . . . the president of Bophuthatswana is in full control.' Mangope was not, of course, in control at all, but there on the sufferance of the white power structure.

This week's bloody and decisive replay of the homeland's earlier crisis brought all these memories flooding back – but more than that. The humbling of Bophuthatswana is the most dramatic illustration yet of the power shift and partial hiatus during the transition. The tortured logic of the apartheid years made matters relatively predictable: the

Government created a fiction of 'independence' and stuck to it with a straight face. Thus receipt of an appeal from a 'sovereign' state resulted in the forceable reinstitution of the satellite status quo. But that was then and this is now – now, in the dying days of the old South Africa, Mangope is being left hanging out to dry.

Foreign Minister Pik Botha, who used to extol Bophuthatswana as an African success story, recently took to warning that the statelet had no chance of surviving on its own. Mangope failed to take the hint that the precious 'friendship' was inoperative until further notice. Power no longer resides in the finger of the old man in the Wilderness. Nor is it to be found with erstwhile strongmen Magnus Malan and Adriaan Vlok, who had flanked the Groot Krokodil at his gauche victory party that night. Moreover, nor does it remain within the gift of Pik Botha, the only one of those Ministers still active in politics. Power in South Africa is inestimably dispersed, compared to what the situation was at 9:15pm on Wednesday February 10 1988.

Lucas Mangope and his henchmen should have learnt better the lessons they endured six years ago. The bloodshed, hatred, greed and vengefulness of this weekend should not have come to pass at all, if the Bophuthatswana government had recognised the inevitable and agreed to allow its people to express their will at the ballot box. Bophuthatswana is finally in the election, as predicted in this column, but at an unnecessarily high price. Are other leaders, swimming desperately against the tide of history, listening today?

WEEKEND STAR, 12 MARCH 1994

CONSTAND VILJOEN'S
HOUR OF COURAGE

*General Viljoen hauled right wing whites into the election. It
was proof of the adage that it often takes one of the former
'bad guys' to really change the course of history.*

ON AUGUST 14 AND 15 1945 A FRATRICIDAL POLITICAL
battle was fought between Japan's leaders in Tokyo, on
the outcome of which hung the future of the entire
Japanese nation. The battlelines were clear, although the
manoeuvres and counter-manoeuvres were inordinately
complex.

On the one side were military men and politicians who
recognised that only surrender – admission of Japan's first-
ever military defeat and acceptance of the consequences –
could preserve the Japanese people in the long term, and
give the nation a chance to regroup and rebuild itself.
These men believed that the alternative was nothing
short of the total annihilation, obliteration from the face
of the earth, of the ancient culture of Japan and the
modern nation it had spawned. Although surrender was
an anathema to them, it had to be borne – in Emperor Hirohito's words, the time had come 'to bear the
unbearable'.

385

On the other side were military men and politicians who refused to countenance surrender in spite of overwhelming evidence that comprehensive defeat at the hands of the Allies was inevitable.

The most fanatical among them proposed effective mass suicide, whereby the entire nation would rise up, fight and die, retaining honour though consigning itself to oblivion. Others in the war faction held to the unlikely belief that one last massive engagement, on Japanese soil, would at least secure more favourable peace terms. The battle between the peace faction and the war faction raged throughout what historians have called 'Japan's longest day'.

Among those proposing immediate surrender in order that younger generations of Japanese might still be given the chance to flourish, the Navy Minister – retired Admiral Mitsumasa Yonai – was prominent. Yonai's military pedigree gave him stature in relation to the hotheads, particularly in the army, which civilian politicians could not enjoy.

The chief conspirator in a desperate coup attempt, aimed at installing the army in power and ignoring the emperor's request that surrender be effected without delay, was the fanatical nationalist Major Kenji Hatanaka. By the end of the 'longest day' Hatanaka was one of many military men who committed *seppuku*, ritual suicide, and the peace faction had prevailed. Japan surrendered, the bombing – atomic and incendiary – stopped, and shortly the islands of Honshu, Kyushu and Hokkaido were occupied, but never invaded.

Today, nearly fifty years later, everyone knows the Japanese nation has not only survived, but has performed a miracle – rebuilding has been so successful that the country is a world economic superpower.

So much for the history lesson. What do these events of long ago have to do with South Africa as it approaches its own date with destiny? A great deal if one reads the history for lessons from human generalities rather than detail.

We have, I believe, an Admiral Yonai in General Constand Viljoen, and a major Hatanaka in Eugene Terreblanche. The battle between these peace and war factions has begun, sparked by the denouement in Bophuthatswana. Viljoen, the reluctant and unschooled politician, has found courage that could secure for him an honourable place in future historical accounts of our transition.

There are many twists and turns still to come. But Viljoen, like Yonai, has realised that the waging of all-out war by his Afrikaner followers could lead to the utter destruction of his volk.

Thus Viljoen had broken with the Afrikaner Volksfront, which he could not win over to his view, and registered for the election. His Freedom Front provides a political conduit for people who would otherwise not have a voice in the election. He is taking the long view, thinking in terms of the generations of Afrikaners to come.

Terreblanche and others of the war faction, such as Dr Ferdi Hartzenberg, remain wedded to the Hatanaka world view. They urge the people on to final resistance, whatever the consequences. Some believe, like Hatanaka, that if the right wing can demonstrate its military capabilities (even though they recognise that those capabilities are not such that they can inflict defeat on their opponents), then more concessions will be wrested.

The 'invasion' for them is the election of April 26-28, and they propose to rise up and fight it in terms of a boycott, although they must know that they cannot stop it. It is a great drama that is being played out and, as in Tokyo half a century ago, the precise outcome will be known only at the end of the long day.

Viljoen the officer-turned-politician has, as Yonai did, taken a long time to make a decisive move. Now Bophuthatswana has forced matters, and Viljoen, along with allies such as Pieter Mulder and other Conservative Party MPs, has faced up to the inevitability of showdown.

The Japanese writer Ogata Taketora coined this aphorism:

'When a madman starts running, the sane run with him.'
Viljoen ran with the madmen for a long time, but now this
old soldier has taken probably the bravest step of his life
– by suing for the best peace he can get.

THE STAR, 14 MARCH 1994

THE JUDGE AND ONE HEAD
OF THE HYDRA

After years of claims and counter-claims, the most important allegations yet made about 'third force' activity were released at the Union Buildings in a sensational report.

LADIES AND GENTLEMEN, SAID A GRIM-FACED, TIGHTLY controlled Frederick de Klerk. 'The matter of the third force.' There was an intake of breath in an already tense room. 'I have no doubt,' he said, 'that immediately this report will be dubbed the third force report.' The president paused.

The atmosphere in the wood-panelled Union Buildings chamber was thick; Mr Justice Richard Goldstone sat impassive, earnest, on De Klerk's left. On his right, Law and Order Minister Hernus Kriel stared through the phalanxes of journalists.

De Klerk drew breath and continued. 'The history of the so-called third force, and the Government's attitude to it, is well known. But I think it is necessary that I restate it.

'I have always maintained that it might be possible that individuals within the (security) forces might be involved in political violence, and matters related to political violence, and that whenever evidence comes to the fore to that effect we will act strongly against it.

'I have also maintained that I have at no stage had any evidence of a specifically organised entity which might be termed a third force within the security forces. This was supported by a number of findings of Judge Goldstone.' De Klerk's audience almost willed him on to his conclusion.

'This is the first time that we have evidence . . . such *prima facie* evidence was laid before us, and I am now keeping my promise. That is to take immediate action.' I took this as an indirect admission by him, finally, that years of allegations of third force activity might not after all be just the work of malicious propagandists.

De Klerk then moved on seamlessly to stress, properly and with the concurrence of Judge Goldstone, that the sensational report which had led to this fraught gathering dealt with allegations about a relatively small group of rogue policemen.

Policemen including the second-most powerful in the land, yes, and policemen who were accused of fuelling despicable criminal mayhem, but a small group of them, nevertheless. It did not allege that the SAP as a force was fomenting violence, and thereby rebelling against the democratic transition.

De Klerk said: 'If, in the final analysis, these preliminary conclusions (in the Goldstone report) are found to be true, it does not mean that any other policeman or woman is thus implicated.' He concluded by saying that even if the allegations were proved, the wider problem of political violence went beyond the top policemen. Others were involved too.

Questions swarmed into my mind. There has been so much acrimony over the existence or otherwise of this thing called a third force. It has not done its proponents or opponents much good. We have never known precisely what it was, in how many manifestations it created itself. For myself, it had shaped itself as something – many things

– which intended to disrupt the transition by means of violence.

I take De Klerk's carefully chosen words to mean that if Judge Goldstone's allegations prove true, we will have found at least a part of the third force. He will probably not agree, will want to use some other term, but that doesn't matter much any more. It is time we stopped the fight over terminology and identified the common enemies of the majority, who yearn for a peaceful, just settlement.

Through Judge Goldstone we might have found one of the heads of the hydra, and that head might – if decisive action is taken – be chopped off. This opens up possibilities for enormous progress. It is simply true that sooner or later (and with the election six weeks away it is sooner), we South Africans need a police force that we all trust and support. This dramatic Friday night exorcism, if that is what it turns out to be, could mark the beginning of the achievement of that end.

There was another profoundly positive aspect to the terrifying story told by Judge Goldstone and his courageous investigators – a story De Klerk himself described as 'shocking'. It was that the President, unprompted, said he was inhibited from acting alone on this matter. He would have to work in conjunction with the Transitional Executive Council. He had already spoken to Nelson Mandela. The old ways of doing things in South Africa are gone forever. They were seen off finally by the bloody doings in Bophuthatswana. A new, co-operative, realistic method is beginning to emerge.

A new world is giving birth to itself; a world in which murderous thugs will not enjoy the enveloping protection of a morally degraded State. The third force is on its own, and the masses of decent people are finally coming after it.

WEEKEND STAR, 19 MARCH 1994

WHEN DECADES ARE
UNRAVELLED IN DAYS

*It all began to happen so suddenly: the onset of election day
placed unbearable pressure on some opponents of the transition.
Houses of cards began to collapse unpredictably.*

———————

THE RAPID APPROACH OF THE ELECTION – NOW ONLY 37
days away – is sharply forcing the pace at which the
outstanding questions of South Africa's transition are
confronted.

In rapid-fire succession the effective reincorporation of
Bophuthatswana, the Goldstone Third Force allegations
and the rocketing political temperature in KwaZulu have
caused profound realignments. Further shifts seem imminent, but they are unpredictable.

The unexpectedly decisive resolution of the
Bophuthatswana crisis has given rise to three new political
realities which strengthen the hand of the majority pro-
election grouping of parties. The realities are:

* The participation of Bophuthatswana's citizens in the
April poll is assured, and consequently the Freedom Alliance's bargaining power is weakened.

* General Constand Viljoen has parted ways with the Freedom Alliance and the Afrikaner Volksfront – particularly Eugene Terreblanche whose strongman image is punctured – and is contesting the election as the Freedom Front. This gives conservative Afrikaners an election vehicle and leaves the Conservative party and AWB in an isolated and reduced, though not terminal, state.

* The willingness of the South African Defence Force to obey constitutional authority in a crisis has been demonstrated.

Overall, the pro-election majority has emerged greater in size and more confident of being able to see through the transition even in the face of probable boycotts by the IFP and the CP-aligned rump of the white right wing.

But serious costs have been involved. The manner of Lucas Mangope's ousting appears to have hardened, not softened, Chief Mangosuthu Buthelezi's opposition to participation, to the extent that talk of outright physical resistance to the election is being taken seriously – especially at a grassroots level.

Ulundi is a tinderbox and Buthelezi has said that the declaration of a 'free and fair' election result would by definition mean that opposition to it had been unjustly quelled. Free polling in the area next month is difficult to imagine unless there are further realignments. The events in Mmabatho have had a similar hardening influence on the radical Right.

It is too early to predict the effects of Judge Goldstone's sensational report, but already the shock waves are being felt.

If it is proved that a relatively small group within the SAP was engaging in third force activity, the purged SAP itself might achieve full acceptance in the new South Africa more quickly than expected – this would increase the chances of a stable transition. If the matter is drawn out and murky, however, instability within and outside the force will deepen.

The election date is exercising its own irresistible magnetism on all parties, whether they are in or out of the transition deal.

Political battles which have been years, or even decades, in the making are likely to be resolved in a matter of hours once the catalyst emerges to bring them to a head. The Bophuthatswana uprising was just one such catalyst: more can be expected in the coming thirty-seven days.

THE STAR, 21 MARCH 1994

THE PRESIDENT
IN AN HOURGLASS

A sudden onrush of dramatic developments brought home the fact that exclusive power had shifted from the De Klerk government. The Transitional Executive Council had come of age.

───────────

IF SOME DAY SOMEONE WERE TO CHOOSE THE FORTNIGHT that has just passed and write about it to illustrate a slice of political life in the dying days of the old South Africa, would they be surprised at what their researches turned up? Hell, yes – but perhaps they shouldn't be. These are the cataclysmic kinds of things that one might reasonably expect to happen when close to 400 years of seething history begins to bubble over in the equivalent of a historical instant.

The election begins exactly one month from today. Those four weeks ahead are likely to be so intense that the dramas of the past two will seem like faded memories by May. Certainly, we will be obsessed by then about the election result, and what happened to the KwaZulu conundrum and the fissile white Right. This seems a good enough reason to stop for a moment and record some of the extraordinary episodes that have just occurred, before the next ones overtake them. So: here is what my overloaded eyes and ears told me.

There was a muffled crash as another homeland collapsed under the weight of its own absurdity and cynicism. The faintly ridiculous figure who had vowed to defend Ciskei's sovereignty to the death now smiled blithely as he tried to explain the sorry saga away as an inevitable trifle.

All that time – and money, don't forget the money – spent engaging King William's Town lawyers-for-hire to draw up a constitution to circumvent constitutionality; those pathetically cynical edicts making it an offence to impugn the dignity of a tin-pot head of a tin-pot state; all those corpses lying in the sun at Bisho. More: all those hours, days, months, years of bluster and filibuster at the World Trade Centre, based on the fiction that this was what 'the people' of Ciskei wanted their 'representatives' to do. All gone, in a puff. Gone, too, Gqozo's overconfident, overweight chief negotiator, a small-town lawyer who saw the gap and became briefly and ingloriously a 'Cabinet Minister'. All his talk of what 'his people' would and would not accept in the new South Africa – all gone, and at such great cost to those people's miserable lives.

I felt no satisfaction at the puncturing of the balloon, or in seeing early predictions of obvious opportunism and eventual irrelevance come to pass. Just dull acknowledgement. The people of Ciskei seemed to feel the same. No cheering crowds in the streets of Bisho, celebrating the lifting of the yoke that had been so onerously imposed by Lennox Sebe, and tightened by the diminutive brigadier. They stayed at home, too tired and drained to bother about expressing relief, let alone joy. It was over, that was all.

Elsewhere there was a loud crackle as the brushfire of discontent, fear, hope, sudden confidence and copy-catism leapt from Ciskei to other homelands. Within days the TBVC states had become the TV states: it didn't look as if it was going to stop there. It seemed the end of the bantustan nightmare was going to be played out on a stage filled with the props of violence; the end was going to be forced, just as the beginning had been. Everyone shuddered as the arc-light swung, inexorably, to KwaZulu; the big one, the different one, the unknowable outcome.

Away from the homelands, breathless and chaotic change too, some serious and some just plain amusing. There was Pik Botha intoning on television: 'I have spoken to Mr de Klerk and President Mandela about this.' His 'black president' remark from the mists of time has become reality even before the electorate has spoken. And Law and Order Ministry spokesman Craig Kotze actually declining to comment on something – an historic first.

There were Inkatha Freedom Party officials suggesting that they would actually like to be reasonable about facilitating a free election, but now they were worried about 'the anger at grassroots level' among their followers. 'We cannot guarantee what they will do,' the spokesmen said dolefully – the spokesmen for the very leaders who have consciously, actively and successfully whipped their constituents into a frenzy of fear and paranoia. Ah, the cynism of politicians and the malleability of people.

And there, in the midst of it all, F W de Klerk, the president-in-an-hourglass, holding the line, being attacked from all sides. My heart went out to him in these circumstances: he is being courageous in the face of a revolt by his senior policemen, and he is doing so from a position considerably weaker than it used to be. The ANC has demonstrated its tremendous power in the past fortnight. If there is anything that will affect directly the course of events in the four weeks ahead, it is whether Nelson Mandela's organisation can resist the temptation to destroy the partners it is going to need to make the government of national unity work.

WEEKEND STAR, 26 MARCH 1994

397

WAR IN THE CITY, TROOPS
ACROSS THE TUGELA

Central Johannesburg was turned into a war-zone on a Monday morning; the city emerged shell-shocked. By Thursday KwaZulu was under emergency rule – the electoral reckoning loomed.

THE RATTLE OF GUNFIRE IN THE CRISP HIGHVELD AIR, pitched high and alien above the familiar squeals and hoots and shouts of the testy, jostling downtown traffic jam. The boom and burst of gas canisters, like low hard punches to the stomach. The staccato whirl of helicopter blades in the blue sky, the rumble of bulky engines in sombre, ominous, aimless steel machines in the street.

The chaotic slap-slap-slap of a thousand fleeing feet, the strange absence of voices; no screams. The flash of a sharpened spear in the sun, the long shaking shadow of an unsteadily trained rifle barrel cast against the brown wall of a building. The flotsam of panic in the gutters: shoes, shields, sticks, hats, abandoned. The people hiding, breathing heavily, squirming into any recess anywhere. The man lying senseless on the corner, his blood coursing from the black bullet wound in his chest, steadily reddening and obscuring the dove of peace on his T-shirt. What place on earth is this?

This is Johannesburg, on a Monday morning in March, in the year of our reckoning. The small and pathetic and pointless war is swirling around the public library, of all unlikely institutions. It is being observed by hundreds of office workers peering dully from their raised vantage points. One gets a bullet through his head but the others don't know that and keep watching, mesmerised. Old history mixes with new in the seething tableau; all South Africa's colours, clothings, weapons and grudges are on display. It is the civilian, financial heartland of the country, but it might just as well be one of our many ancient battlegrounds.

Already Monday's grotesque events are blurring into a memory of another dramatic day, one among so many in these times. Who fired the first shots? Who knows. But we do know something else, something bigger. The Monday morning carnage was not planned, but nor was it accidental. It was a link in the intricate chain of cause and effect, effect and cause, that characterises our country in the final, spasmodic weeks of the first phase of its great transition.

Monday's causes influence Thurday's effects – and now we have a State of Emergency in a great southern swathe of our land. That fact will give rise in turn to its own profound effects, but we cannot know yet what they will be. That will become clear only when the only real deadline, voting day, is upon us.

What are we to make of this State of Emergency, a new South African variation on an old South African theme? Every instinct should make us suspect it first and foremost. Emergencies are admissions of failure to organise society by better means. Inherently they invite abuse, and they are tenacious things, easy to close around an area but difficult to prise open again.

There are compelling reasons for believing that this one was unavoidable, though one can question its timing. We need to understand why that is so, in order to judge its implementation and constantly put the question that must be put: when can it be lifted? The KwaZulu/Natal Emergency has been declared on the lesser-evil principle. It must be held to that. History will show that the document which gave rise to President de Klerk's announcement was the Independent Electoral Commission's report on the propects for free and fair elections in that region. A week ago the IEC demanded that political authorities make it possible for electoral arrangements to go ahead, after it had concluded that Chief Mangosuthu Buthelezi's administration would frustrate the IEC's efforts. This provided the legitimisation for the later decision, taken with the active support of Nelson Mandela's ANC. In addition we are told that intelligence reports point to plans for widespread violence around election time, but we cannot pronounce on their validity because none of us has seen them.

There is much confusion about the Emergency's purpose and its probable practical effects. Those who are prepared, conditionally, to accept its necessity, need to be clear on the first count. The legitimate purpose of the Emergency is to force a recalcitrant regional administration to allow those of its people who wish to vote to do so. It has nothing to do with pressurising Buthelezi or his party into participating, or with frog-marching those who do not wish to vote to the polling booths. Buthelezi has brought the battalions upon his own people because he has defied the IEC, not because he has spurned Codesa. The overwhelming majority of South Africans wants these elections, and he has tried to deny his people the free choice of whether to join that majority or not. Can he not see it that way? Is there not still time for this man, who now looks so deeply sad and troubled, to ensure that the battalions are not called upon to fire – to accept what is just and unstoppable, in the nick of time?

WEEKEND STAR, 2 APRIL 1994

AFTER THE ELECTION
IS THE REST OF OUR LIVES

*Less than three weeks till the election and the country fixated;
everywhere there was paralysis, an on-hold mentality, waiting
for the apocalypse. Some chose to stockpile for siege.*

I OWE THIS TO A FRIEND, WHO ATTRIBUTES IT TO BISMARCK:
'You never get more lying than during a war, after a
hunt, and before an election.' Amen to that, even if the
translation's imperfect. There can have been few periods
in South Africa's history when more parties were doing
things for ostensible reasons so divergent from their real
motives.

Try some of these; there are plenty more. The Inkatha
Freedom Party had absolutely nothing to do with the
recent spate of Zulu royalist marches. (Although Themba
Khoza and Humphrey Ndlovu were the main speakers at
the fateful Library Gardens gathering.)

The declaration of the State of Emergency had absolutely
nothing to do with putting pressure on Chief Mangosuthu
Buthelezi. (Although the Independent Electoral Commission, and the ANC, had called for political intervention to
bring his administration to heel.)

The proposed volkstaat has absolutely nothing to do with

discrimination. (Although 'foreigners' in this mythical land – for whom read ethnically unacceptable persons – will never be able to qualify as voting citzens.)

Police and army generals are retiring in droves purely on grounds of health. (Although their names are coincidentally linked to allegations of nasty doings.)

Police Commissioner Johan van der Merwe is merely going by the book in defending Generals Smit and Le Roux and questioning the wishes of President de Klerk. (Although he doesn't appear to feel as intense a loyalty to General 'Krappies' Engelbrecht.)

Feel free to add to this list; you'll find you're easily able to cite examples to the detriment of every party contesting this election, one way or another.

We are in a breathless period and should expect low veracity levels, I suppose, as well as short attention-spans. The tricameral Parliament, source of so much idiocy and ridicule, disappeared last week without even the requisite whimper. Not surprisingly so: the pace of events is such that even watersheds, like the collapse of the homelands, are bundled off the front pages by bigger and newer things within days. It will not let up until well after the election.

Which raises an important matter. Those last three words have become peculiarly laden, and assume a tremendously emotive charge, as the election train bears down on us ever faster. Everywhere you hear the phrase 'after the election'.

Local businessmen put plans on hold; foreign governments do the same; many South Africans, black and white, make arrangements to be out of the cities, or even the country; supermarket sales go mad . . . all in the name of 'after the election'. Well, we should think a little about this mania.

'After the election' is going to last a long time; a lifetime in fact. Yes, it is of seminal importance that the actual three days of polling pass off relatively smoothly, but they by no means mark the end of the new South Africa saga.

I am not one of those who share the apocalyptic vision of

the scare-list which has sent shoppers scurrying off to stock up for the siege (prompting amusing fears, among others, of a chronic shortage of Perrier water in Sandton). It seems very silly: just when we should be congratulating ourselves on having reached a stage where once-unthinkable elections are possible, panic has set in.

In the white suburbs in particular, this just doesn't make sense. People who have adjusted to so much so quickly are now being spooked by a phantom. (The learning curve undergone by whites should not be underestimated: remember that in 1990, the very idea of a President Mandela made whites' hair stand on end – now most accept the prospect and ask the entirely more rational question: what kind of government will he preside over?) Whites are changing, if fitfully. My friend Jon Qwelane, a lonely truth-teller for so many years, is now a mainstream talk-show host. Few whites still think him crazy; most now really listen to what he has to say.

It's time for us to decide to ride the lies and exhale the hot air of the election campaign; that's what these things are made of the world over. It's time, too, to stop fixating on the end of the month, which will so soon be in the past, and to look to the future. Following Bismarck again, this irksome 'before the election' period is all but over, thank goodness, and there's no need to assume further wars or hunts in the foreseeable future.

WEEKEND STAR, 9 APRIL 1994

UNDER THE JACKAL-BERRY TREE

Four leaders went deep into the African bush to speak of peace and war. The Skukuza summit produced nothing but hostility. Time was running out and only a dramatic shift in political will could now resolve the KwaZulu crisis.

ONCE UPON A TIME, UNDER A JACKAL-BERRY TREE ON THE banks of a lazy river in the steaming African plains, a king and his men sat down with rival potentates to speak of whether there should be peace or war in the land.

As it has always been with such encounters down the centuries, the great men's deliberations took place far from the ears of the subjects who would reap the rewards of their success or pay the price of their failure. The men talked and talked, through the day and into the night. At times the four of them were alone in the talking, at others they were surrounded by their trusted and powerful lieutenants. When the king spoke his courtiers said: 'Bayete!'

This was a very great meeting and each of the men carried on his shoulders the spirits of his ancestors whose earlier wars had brought them to this place. Each had travelled great distances from their traditional strongholds. This was the territory of wild animals, and the closest listener was a lone hyena who laughed loud in the night.

A short distance away from the jackal-berry tree, but well out of sight of the great indaba, a less exalted group of people waited in the dark orange glow of nightfall. These were the messengers who would tell the people of the land, and millions across the sea, what the men had decided. They waited and waited, seizing on whispers from the junior members of the leaders' retinues, who would from time to time come away from the jackal-berry tree to say that the talking continued.

Deep into the night it was over at last, and the talkers arrived, ready to report to the world. They said a great deal; especially that they had not failed. Their many words have been amply recorded but what was on their faces and in their gestures has not; and it told a truer story.

Seated in a clearing, at a makeshift table decorated with leaves from the bushveld trees, were the four men. Nelson Mandela, FW de Klerk, King Goodwill Zwelithini and Mangosuthu Buthelezi were stiff and straight-backed.

Mandela, looking grave and as if suppressing anger through a conscious effort of will, held his glasses in his hand and stared down at a pad on which he made notes. De Klerk, more animated, appeared to be battling to give off an aura of vibrancy and optimism. The king sat slightly withdrawn, his hand resting on a ceremonial cane, an enigmatic, non-committal expression on his face. Buthelezi, by contrast, leant far forward, hands folded on the table serenely, and directly faced Mandela and De Klerk with a faint smile on his lips.

The atmosphere, already tense enough to touch, worsened after Buthelezi read out his surprise supplementary statement to the joint communique issued by the four men. By the time Mandela came to speak it seemed an angry explosion was about to occur. But he delivered his rebuke through tight lips while Buthelezi's eyes bore down on him. De Klerk wrapped his arms tightly around his chest, hoping that the cataclysm was not about to come. Buthelezi continued to smile.

Standing behind the king, indunas from the royal party

scoffed openly as Mandela spoke. Separately, Joe Matthews and Frank Mdlalose stood still as statues. Behind De Klerk, Roelf Meyer and Kobie Coetsee looked drained, with jaws clasped. Off to the side Cyril Ramaphosa – ever ebullient – seemed fresh and undaunted, but the day had taken its toll on Joe Slovo and Mac Maharaj, who shifted on tired feet.

The tension dragged out interminably, with barely controlled altercations, interjections, and snapped answers to questions. Everyone listening seemed to want it to be over, for the men to try another time, because they could see and feel the failure and the futility of explaining the obvious again. But the men continued to talk in circles, though battle lines were affirmed over and over by an immovable Mandela: the election date was sacrosanct, whatever happened in working groups and further meetings, from which he expected little.

Still Buthelezi smiled, outwardly more sure of his position than he has appeared since the events of Bophuthatswana. The king spoke little; De Klerk interjected again with positive blandishments. The session seemed endless, swinging like a pendulum dangerously toward outright confrontation and then back to gritted-teeth decorum. Each fresh statement drew a fresh rebuttal, on and on. It was past 11pm, an hour had gone by, and still the hostility threatened to bubble over.

It was the king who first, inadvertently, signalled a tactical withdrawal from potential outright battle in this odd locale. 'Actually,' he said in response to a question, 'I'm so tired at this point in time . . .'

Mandela leaned over to him, solicitous, seeming to suggest that proceedings be brought to an end. Presently the men stood stiffly. There were attempts at smiles, some more successful than others, and handshakes for the cameras.

Mandela reached forward for Buthelezi's hand, and Buthelezi said: 'Madiba'.

'Good night, Mr Mandela,' said De Klerk, and the

engines of the nearby jets began to whine as the throng broke up.

A haggard-looking political leader from Natal – it doesn't matter which party he is a member of – said quietly: 'For the first time, I am not looking forward to going home.'

Those words spoke sufficient volumes about what had occurred at the Sabie River on Friday. With fewer than three weeks to go before the elections, the Skukuza summit failed to resolve the crisis that is the Kwazulu authorities' refusal to co-operate with the transition process.

Moreover, it failed to produce a convincing procedure for substantive progress in the week to come. It was not the last chance, but it was a big one to miss.

There is little time left and next week's second round, on a river bank or anywhere else, simply cannot end the same inconclusive way. Something has to give, through an effort of political will. The ancestors, if not the descendants, surely know this to be true.

THE STAR, 11 APRIL 1994

ADIEU, HENRY KISSINGER

The famous men led by Henry Kissinger and Lord Carrington, supposed to mediate between the ANC and IFP, came and went in a flash. The KwaZulu conundrum remained unsolved.

GOOD MORNING, SANIBONANI, GOEIE MÔRE, DUMELANG. (Sorry, FW). Dear compatriots, you have been enjoying a special week-long extravaganza staged by the State Political Theatre of the New South Africa. In keeping with the traditions of the finest dramatic institutions around the world, the SPTNSA offers tragedy, farce, morality plays, period pieces and, occasionally, comedy – all in a multimedia format.

It also seeks to bring you (even if necessarily briefly) veteran guest stars from far-off lands. We very much hope you appreciated the variety of this week's performances, the penultimate act in the long-running 'Transition' saga.

If South Africa was a stage this week – and it felt like it – then the tragedians dominated the plot, though farce got the best lines. With the main show likely now to transfer to the provinces (one in particular), the humour levels can be expected to drop.

There was an overwhelming sense of the absurd at Tuesday night's gala premiere in Johannesburg of the mediation roadshow. It was not prompted just by the sight of shoals of dignitaries lost in an ocean of VIPs swimming in concentric circles in search of someone to talk to.

All the right elements were present as the Top of the Carlton relived glories past: a guest list fairly bulging with transitional South Africa's glitterati, a visiting troupe of terrifically famous if ageing actors, a combination of our country's most experienced vaudeville hams and the new generation of understudies-about-to-get-their-big-break.

Had the likes of Henry Kissinger and Lord Carrington arrived in our neck of the woods two years ago, the show might have run and run. In the event it was too late and everyone seemed to know it, although they wouldn't say so.

The executive producers – IFP/ANC/NP Short-Term Investments Inc – sought to cut their rapidly mounting losses by closing the theatre more suddenly and more amateurishly than expected, but it had been a matter of time anyway. A flop is a flop.

Virtuoso performances like that of the gravelly-voiced old survivor Kissinger ('We can only marvel at the achievements . . . overcoming memories, doubts, suffering . . . extraordinary . . . great figures of our epoch . . . now we must close the remaining gaps') can keep up appearances for a while but that's all. So adieu maestros Kissinger, Carrington, Bhagwati, Higginbotham, Kevenhorster, Laponce and La Pergola – thanks for coming, but we're a rough audience and you had a bum script.

Which leaves us to ourselves, alone to decide whether it's time to abuse, accuse or amuse. Ten days to go before the old South Africa's grand finale (The Ballot Box Suite), twenty-four to The Greatest Show Pretoria Has Ever Seen, and a while longer before we are all signed up as extras in the as-yet unwritten epic: The Rest of Our Lives.

Are we going to make it on schedule? Or, more to the point, are we going to make it on schedule and in one piece? Thursday's long-awaited televisual set-piece has come and gone, an on-balance satisfactory but certainly not immortal performance turned in by our major co-stars.

Some good was salvaged when the bickering ended, but they did not succeed in reinspiring the nervous nation or in explaining how the off-stage drama occupying everyone's attention would be resolved.

Whither KwaZulu? Buthelezi? These questions frighten people wherever they live and whoever they support. We have not yet been given a plausible answer – not in summits, states of emergency, offers and counter-bids, or in mediation. There seems to be little time, at least before the election, to imagine an initiative which can deliver first prize for South Africa: inclusive transition, on schedule.

Logically the possibilities in the now desperately troubled region seem to boil down to some combination of some of the following, depending on which, if any, side makes a move: IFP softening, ANC softening, Government/TEC hardening, the status quo leading to unprecedented bloodshed.

The pro-election grouping clearly has the capacity to force through the poll, but everyone realizes that force has in-built costs and the bill will arrive later. We look very much like we are heading for an entirely predictable clash, but the leaders of the ANC, NP and IFP each appear curiously serene about, if not mute on, what might still be done to stop it.

It was important that Nelson Mandela and FW de Klerk held hands on national television; important for us and important for what others think of us. But we are crying out now for a special unscheduled performance: The Last-Minute Aversion of a KwaZulu Disaster.

THE STAR, 18 APRIL 1994

THE FINAL DAYS IN THE OFFICE
OF WHITE POWER

FW de Klerk was fighting the election campaign of his life. But there were few days left to him as sole ruler. What was going through his mind, in the privacy of his famous office?

THERE, IN A ROOM DOWN PAST THE VAST OIL-ON-CANVAS portraits of his predecessors lining the long corridor, sits the man some call the last white president.

He sits in an office seething with memories: an office soon, surely, to be someone else's, not wrested away by force but parted with through vision. Whatever one's feelings about this man, and in a divided country they are divided, he has drawn on to himself the bright light of history, forever.

On this sunny, autumn afternoon, in the Union Buildings with its sweeping view over the capital, Frederik Willem de Klerk is prepared to muse aloud about the past and the future.

An Afrikaner pioneer on the grand scale of his rugged forebears, he has only days left to him as sole ruler of South Africa and its multi-hued millions. His high-ceilinged, wood-panelled room, with its draped old South Africa flag, presidential seal and familiar memorabilia of office,

411

is cool and quiet. The world has seen before the pathos of presidents contemplating the loss of their position, but few who have played so vital and so active a role in bringing about that change. FW de Klerk, a small, smiling, wiry man, sits in chair where PW Botha once sat, and wrestles with the fate of this exhilarating, infuriating nation – and, too, with his own destiny.

If you push him hard enough, you will find that De Klerk has long faced up to the probability that Nelson Mandela will win the election next week. But that is not a prospect he is allowing to weigh him down. Conceding only that he is 'more tired than he expected' after the television debate with Mandela, his mighty interlocutor, he balls his fists and flashes his fiery eyes. There is a campaign to fight, now and long into the future, and his demeanour is that of a boxer who fully intends to stay the distance.

'I don't like all these assumptions about what's going to happen in the election,' he says with a warning grin, 'We mean to give you some surprises.'

De Klerk is not an emotional man, and is much more comfortable speaking about politics than his personal feelings. But this is an exceptional frozen moment in history, a time for making exceptions. Is he lonely?

Yes, he concedes, his is a lonely position. 'Look, I'm a team man. I interact quite strongly with my Cabinet and the party leadership. Without naming them, there are three or four people that I am very close to.

'But lonely, yes. People feel you are very busy and so they develop a diffidence, it just develops, with the result that people who you would like to just walk in and say: 'Do you have a cup of tea for me?' no longer do that. And because this is the place where the buck stops. Finally, some decisions are yours alone, after having consulted everybody. It is very lonely. Only you can take it, and your supporters also ask you to take responsibility.'

With the momentous changes about to take place, how long does he plan to go on in politics? He thinks a while. 'Well, I'm fifty-eight now. I don't intend to hang on until they drag me out or kick me out. I know you might say 'famous last words' because many other politicians have said it before me. But at the first sign of ill health, for instance, when I feel I don't have the capacity – or the health or the drive or the commitment – to do the job, I will resign. In political terms, fifty-eight is still young.'

How would he like to be remembered by future historians? Again De Klerk smiles his trademark smile. 'It's one question I constantly evade. But of one thing I am sure – that this timespan, this past four or five years, will be recorded as the most dynamic and decisive periods in our history. But I'm a lawyer, and I know that in the end the success or failure (of the great South African experiment) will determine how this period is evaluated.'

On the subject of history, De Klerk is passionately concerned to see that the genesis of the National Party is understood from his perspective. 'Can I tell you the history?' he says. 'The NP of '48 was quite different from the NP of '68. And the NP of '78, when I became a Minister, was already different from the NP of '68. And the new NP was really born in 1986, when we totally moved away from separate development. And at certain times NP policy of that time . . . was in advance of colonial thinking. The NP started to grapple with the problem of black political rights before the colonial powers.

'Maybe that's too stark a statement, but I want to make the point. So, with all its faults, I have always experienced the NP as a dynamic party. Each prime minister brought something new and while I didn't always agree with everything the NP said, I always found it internally very democratic, allowing debate constantly.'

De Klerk laughs out loud. 'Sometimes it was ten years too late, but the NP has constantly managed to adapt to new circumstances. It always tried to be a party based on principles. It looked on itself as more than a mere political party, there to get people in parliament, but as having a mission – always.'

What does he regard as the proudest moment of his

life? 'One should say of my public life. Because in my private life I think of when I became a father, a grandfather, when I got married . . . when you achieve your degree with honours, that type of thing – they are such proud moments in one's career.

'But in my public life I would say the day that I became the leader of the National Party. Because that is the day that the final responsibility was placed in my hands, entrusted. Not the trappings, the trimmings (like the presidential inauguration). The Nobel Prize, of course yes, it was important. But none of that would have happened had I not been entrusted with the leadership of the ruling party, which made me also the leader in this office.'

As we leave this office, probably never to meet FW de Klerk in these surrounds again, he is busying himself for another task in the endless business of State. But his face suggests he is still thinking more philosophically, about the time he is living through and the new world he is about to live in. His face shows the determination, infectious enthusiasm and care-wornness that has imprinted itself on history.

THE STAR, 20 APRIL 1994

OUR ONCE-UNTHINKABLE
REBIRTH

*The election's finality, and its miraculous inclusivity, dawned.
The vilified process was prevailing. The future was open to
South Africans, if they would embrace it.*

PLEASE STOP FOR A MINUTE. CATCH YOUR BREATH. LOOK
to left and right, backwards and forwards. We're there. It
is upon us, the fragile moment of once-unthinkable rebirth
that will forever cleave South African history in two, into
eras of domination and – we fervently hope – democracy.

Johann Kriegler, one of the judges who has been called
upon to help pilot the untested ship of the new society
into harbour, says this landmark election 'is not about
sandbags and machine-guns. It is a festival.' We will him
to be right, and do so with renewed conviction, electrified
by the news – wastefully late but wonderful, nevertheless
– that Chief Buthelezi's Inkatha Freedom Party is going
to subject itself to the will of the people.

This is a time for quiet self-congratulation, before the
job of making the new South Africa work begins. We are,
all of us, on the brink of participating – in spite of the
sputtering, sinful guns of Tokoza that steal lives we should
have treasured – in a sort of political wonderwork. With

the exceptions of the diehard Drs Hartzenberg and Mosala, we are all in this election now.

Let no-one say this is just a stitch-up by the NP and the ANC: let us rather say well done Cyril and Roelf, and all the others who doggedly pursued a compromise that gives no-one everything and no-one nothing. It is not a thing of beauty you have created, this constitution, but an instrument with which to make the start that had to be made. And it is no mean achievement to have drawn up, in four years, a political rulebook acceptable to forces as disparate as the PAC and the Freedom Front . . . and the Soccer Party too.

I still believe that all leaders should now be required, in public, to put their hands to their hearts and swear to abide by the election results if they are declared sufficiently free and fair by the Independent Electoral Commission and the international monitors. It is probably too late for that, but we should at least let the politicians know that that is what we expect of them.

What of Buthelezi's *volte face*, accepting conditions that had long been on offer? This is not the time to ask why it has come so late, at the cost of so much blood, although those questions will arise. But it is worth reflecting on what prompted the Monday morning miracle. At the heart of the matter, I believe, was a final, belated recognition in Ulundi that the election would go ahead on schedule, come what may.

Ironically, it was probably the failure of the Kissinger-Carrington mission that did it: their departure took with them the IFP's last hope of forcing a postponement. It might still have been too late, were it not for the good fortune which saw businessmen, a mysterious Kenyan in the right place at the right time, and FW de Klerk and Nelson Mandela taking responsibility.

The precise election result is more unpredictable than ever, all our opinion polls thrown out by the re-entry of the IFP. That is a good, democratic thing to be able to say. In just a few days we will no longer have to take the word of politicians on how much support they enjoy: we will have told them the answers.

I have said before and say again without apology that whether the future turns out to be a triumph or tragedy, or something between, will be determined by mortal men and women, not signed documents. It is the behaviour of those we elect that will determine our fate: if they act within reasoned self-interest, we have a great chance of success. But they retain the option of fouling it up completely if they so choose.

Last weekend I travelled the far-northern Transvaal, watching the ANC wrap up its election campaign in one of its safest strongholds. There I met a man few beyond the region have heard of. Ngoako Ramathlodi, a highly-educated, thirty-eight year-old former ANC exile who hails from Potgietersrus, is a dead cert to become premier of the new province. Some say the ANC could win ninety-seven percent of the vote up there. I said to him that such power had to be the dream of any politician. He disagreed.

'There's a great paradox up here,' he said. 'The only forces are the ANC and the white right wing. And, thankfully, we've never engaged each other violently. We are a poor province, and our only hope is to build together in peace and stability. We grew up together here, these boer boys and us. We all belong here. I would welcome them in my government. This must not be an ANC government, but a government of the province. I will seriously consider accommodating them (the right wing) even if they don't make it at the polls. Everyone who lives here must be able to look at that new government and see themselves reflected in it.'

If Ramathlodi puts that thinking into practice once he has tasted power, I will travel to Pietersburg to salute him. For all sorts of reasons, I am proud and excited – if still a little frightened – to be a South African at this time and in this place.

WEEKEND STAR, 24 APRIL 1994

417

TWINS, BUT POLLS APART

Cyril Ramaphosa and Roelf Meyer were the transition's Siamese twins: opponents, but essential to one another. It was time to travel alone with each, to compare and contrast and marvel.

RAMAPHOSA'S CONVOY SNAKES OUT THROUGH THE SUBURBS, past the comforting banality of cars being washed and hedges trimmed. People glance at the green Jetta, not knowing that part of their future is inside it, and wondering why the following cars are sticking so close at such speed.

The ANC's chief negotiator is on the great north road, heading to Malamulele and Turfloop in ANC country, to talk to some of the people who will catapult his organisation into power next week.

Ramaphosa concedes that the years have taken their toll – 'I feel quite run down' – but that is nothing compared to the unstoppable excitement that is welling in his chest and which sustains his ready, infectious smile. After all the compromises and innovations that fashioned the government of national unity deal, in the end it is Ramaphosa and the millions he represents who are about to receive; it was they who had nothing and it is around them, primarily, that South Africa's reformist revolution has revolved.

* * *

Meyer's appearance on the scheduled flight to Cape Town causes a buzz of excitement as passengers whisper and wonder at the presence of the famous face.

The National Party's chief negotiator is heading south, to Stellenbosch and Mossel Bay, to talk to some of the people who will next week decide whether his organisation can make its debut in the new South Africa strong and permanent.

Meyer has paid a physical price for the negotiating years – 'I've just had to get used to five hours of sleep a night and food wherever possible' – but does not have the appearance of an exhausted man; he exudes enthusiasm and energy to all who engage him. After the heart-stopping decision to change course forever and the roller-coaster ride that began, in the end it is Meyer and the millions he represents who are about to give; it was they who had everything, and the test of his work will be whether they are accepted and influential when power shifts.

Oddly, or perhaps not, the two young men talk about each other a lot. This is largely because they are asked to do so by their supporters – so powerful in the public mind is the imagery and symbolism of their politically symbiotic relationship.

Both are generous, but reserved: they are not friends in the common sense, have never visited one another's homes, but there is a fondness and overarching trust. The ebb and flow of the relationship is striking, now.

Meyer has much the more difficult task ahead as the direction inverts – incumbent and interlocutor are swopping sides as the days tick by. Both, it seems to me, quietly hope that their linked role will not be brought to an end by the unpredictable erection of the new scaffolding of power. But for now they are direct opponents: Meyer's party has the difficult task of consolidating existing support and creating beach-heads in unknown areas; Ramaphosa has the mighty impetus of the liberation dividend awaiting it but must ensure that it is exercised at the ballot booths.

Ramaphosa's convoy passes volkstaat signs, neatly executed in white and blue, at the entrances to old South African towns. He barely notices. Soon he is talking, at a rural hotel near Rustenburg, to his local lieutenants, checking their preparedness for battle at the polls.

There is a meeting of homeland traffic officers going on nearby, and Ramaphosa glides in: 'I haven't much time but I just wanted to say hello,' he tells an awed audience, sitting bolt upright. 'I can see you are working to be ready for the new dispensation, that will make this great North even greater.'

The officers murmur concurrence and then laugh uproariously as Ramaphosa turns on his famous charm.

'I want you to know that this man,' he says putting his arm around the regional ANC chief, 'will soon be your premier. But I'm not sure he has paid all his traffic fines. Please make him do so before the election.'

As he is chivvied to his waiting car, hotel staff and guests jostle for a sight, a touch, a word. In the this place at least, this is political superstardom at work.

Meyer is instantly recognised in the streets of Stellenbosch, by clean-cut students and shaggy early-morning bottle-store patrons alike. One of the latter produces, from some pocket, a badge bearing FW de Klerk's picture. 'Viva NP' he says in the twang of the Cape Flats.

Meyer spends some time with local NP youth leaders, encouraging and reassuring, willing them on to a victory they believe is fully possible in their area. It is a very different style of politics to that of his rival, somehow more old-fashioned but potent nevertheless, and Meyer also knows how to brandish the weapon of humour.

An earnest young man wants to know how powerful AZAPO is: 'I was talking to one of them the other day . . . ' Meyer interjects with a grin: 'You're lucky to have met one.'

Another question: We know the NP will be in the Cabinet, but what if you get a portfolio like Fisheries?

Meyer is whiplash quick: 'I wouldn't mind doing a bit of fishing.'

Soon he is welcomed by hundreds of cheering students – the younger women are squealing if the truth be told – and within an hour he has convinced them that the future is something to embrace, not dread. 'I think we're going to go through this election with much less trouble than we expected,' he says, 'We might have been through the worst already.'

The departing faces are shining. Ramaphosa's motorcade throws up red dust as it stops in front of the rickety grandstand of remote Malamulele's soccer stadium. The stands look as if they might collapse – or take off – under the pounding of thousands of thundering feet. There are few youngsters here of pre-voting age; here are poor, proud rural people who want to see this leader and want to vote next week.

In the village there is a gigantic billboard bearing the smiling face of Nelson Mandela: 'Sekunjalo!'

Ramaphosa makes his painstaking way through group after group of supporters with outstretched hands. MK cadres, in brand-new, still-starched camouflage uniforms, stand to attention. There is celebration and solemnity, and Ramaphosa delights in the temporary distance between himself and air-conditioned negotiating halls.

When it is time for him to be introduced – the demand is deafening – Ramaphosa smiles a diffident smile ('Shall I go out now?') and leaves the makeshift tent for the podium. The voice of the master of ceremonies booms through the loudspeakers: 'Now we are calling upon our secretary-general, Comrade Cyril Ramaphosa, to ascend the stage and give orders and commands to our people . . .'

Meyer's arrival at the Mossel Bay Town hall is noisy. Hundreds of supporters, perhaps a quarter white and the vocal majority from the nearby coloured township, are very serious about this visit of the Minister of negotiations. There is a sea of NP flags and already the shouts of 'Viva FW' have started, without Meyer's instigation.

'The new National Party, a new era' read the T-shirts, and shortly the pop music through the public address system gives way to Pastor Benjamin's revivalist-style opening prayer. This is indeed a world in one country, as the excitable crowd lapses into pious silence and bows its collective head.

'*Moenie bevrees wees nie,*' intones the pastor, '*moenie bekommerd wees. Alles is in die beheer van die Here.*'

Meyer pitches his delivery directly at the 'new Nationalists' in the hall and they love it.

'Many of you here would not have been enthusiastic about the National Party two years ago,' he says, 'You were not only anti-Nat but passionately anti-apartheid. And with justification. With justification. But in the meantime we have opened our hearts to each other and finally we are all becoming one family. Is it not wonderful?'

The response is a bellow, mixed with clapping.

Meyer notes impishly: 'I see the old Nationalists still clap their hands, while the new ones use their voices.' He winds up: 'We will be there in the new government of national unity after next week, and maybe the ANC will be there too, and a couple of others . . .'

Soon he is besieged by autograph hunters. Then the departing busloads sing into the night until there is just an echo.

It dawns only later that not a single rightwinger had bothered to show up to challenge this *bête noire* of white conservatism, so dramatically has that threat retreated.

Ramaphosa is moved and withdrawn as he looks around his old campus at the University of the North. Echoing across the valley are the voices of tens of thousands of ANC supporters packed into the stadium, awaiting his arrival since the morning in the cloying heat.

He walks quickly, for nostalgia's sake, to see his old

room, and confides that his biggest regret was never becoming Turfloop SRC president – he was kicked out for political activities. Then he quickly addresses a meeting of striking civil servants, urging them to return to work because the election is the most important thing.

But the rally is the centrepiece, the heart of the journey.

Ramaphosa enters on the back of a bakkie, drums rolling round and round the bowl of the stadium and intermingling with a solid, unbroken roar of greeting and calypso rhythms. If this stadium has seen shows of defiance and resistance, this occasion is a carnival. An aspirant people's poet booms: 'We have reached the crossroads of our freedom.'

Ramaphosa rises to speak at last.

'Heita, Nelson Mandela,' he says, 'Heita.'

He must wait some time for the response to die down, so that he can be heard.

For both men, whether by accident or design, these final election forays were cheering historical moments, to be treasured for the right democratic reasons. They were encouraging for those watching, too, because here in these places was an election under way that was demonstrably working. There was no menace or fear or hatred because the people were there of their own free will. The multi-hued monitors were welcome, but superfluous.

Eventually both men, from different corners of the land, headed for home energised – sure of what they were doing and why. The electorate will speak about their respective efforts next week.

Neither man doubts which will emerge the stronger, but both know that the other will be around after the democratic leap of faith. If multiparty democracy needs to be given real names to be clearly imagined, conceived in the mind's eye at work in our country, we could do worse than starting with these two: Cyril and Roelf, true South Africans in black and white.

WEEKEND STAR 24 APRIL 1994

THE OLD MAN WAITING
PATIENTLY FOR POWER

Nelson Mandela was about to be the most sought-after human being on the earth – South Africa's first black President. But he made time to drink tea and talk about the future.

THE FIRST BLACK SOUTH AFRICAN PRESIDENT-IN-WAITING wears light linen slip-on shoes and a fashionable red shirt hanging open casually round the waist. Unhurried and gracious to his guests, he seems not to have a care in the world, smiling his dazzling, world-famous smile and offering tea.

Outside in his suburban garden the southern African sun is shining but the bite of winter is already in the air. It is a tranquil, commonplace scene – save for the fact that in this august, lined, septuagenarian face resides the imminent resolution of nearly 350 years of brutal, foolish and heroic history.

Soon, so very soon, Nelson Rolihlahla Mandela's followers will begin to dismantle apartheid and the nameless discrimination that preceded it, bringing it down incrementally as they drop their folded ballot papers into steel boxes across the length and breadth of the country, one by one by one.

424

He, of all people, feels the gravity of that prospect, and the weight of presidential responsibility about to descend on his shoulders. He knows also that then he will be, for a while, the most sought after human being on earth – quite literally besieged.

But that is next week, and for now he is making time to talk with less elevated fellow South Africans about their country on the cusp.

Mandela sits in a lived-in, warm room, surrounded by trinkets given to him by admirers over the years, paintings, family pictures and books. There is a biography of Rajiv Gandhi and of Sukarno. There is a history of the Maori people.

One photograph of himself is framed and leans casually on a mantelpiece – it shows Mandela standing on a rolling green Transkei hillside, looking at his ancestral village home of Qunu. If he has kept the official pictures of meetings with the world's leaders, he has chosen not to display them in this homely, personal room.

Mandela's epic life story is one of the best known of the 20th century, and needs no repeating. But how is he feeling now, on the very brink of a dream – a dream that could finally blot out the nightmares of Bulhoek, Bethal, Sharpeville, Soweto, Sebokeng, Boipatong, Bisho and so many others?

It is notoriously difficult to persuade Mandela to talk openly about his own feelings, so insistent is he that it is his movement, not himself, that matters. But it is worth trying again at this extraordinary time, sitting with this 75 year-old South African icon who is days away from finishing the job that others started in 1912.

'It is a very exciting moment,' he ventures at last, 'It is a moment for which we and our predecessors have waited, but also for which men and women have suffered. I am thinking now of Oliver Tambo, Chris Hani and the many others who struggled very hard to see this day dawn.'

A look of deepest sadness comes over Mandela's face.

'I wish we could wake all of them, so they could enjoy the fruits of their labour.'

If he could live life over again, would Mandela do anything differently? Does he have regrets? 'It would be easy to say I would have done just the same. But we must be realistic. There have been moments when we doubted that the ideas for which we were suffering were going to triumph . . . but this is going to be our greatest moment, 27 April.'

'I hope I would do the same again, though it has not been easy. To see your family, your children being persecuted when you are absolutely helpless in jail, that is one of the most bitter experiences, most painful experiences, I have had.

'Your wife being hounded from job to job, your children being taken out of coloured schools, police breaking into your house at midnight and even assaulting your wife.

'So I wondered sometimes whether I had made the correct decision – I had not anticipated the repression in relation to my family. But at the end of the agonising I felt, no, it was correct. My commitment was proper.'

Shortly Mandela's face is wreathed in smiles again, as he answers a blunt question about when he might retire. 'This depends on my colleagues,' he says, 'if they think I have done what is expected of me, that it's time to resign, I'll obey them. It's their decision, not mine.' But he gives an indication, via an anecdote, that retirement is not imminent.

'Last week I was at a meeting in QwaQwa. There were many Afrikaans farmers there. One chap asked this question: 'Now look, you are 75. We fear that you are not going to be in position very long . . . What guarantee can you give me that what you have said today will be respected by your people?'

'My response was that we've got precedents in South Africa. Smuts was over 60 when he became prime minister. Malan was prime minister until he was about 80. I said, well, I'm still 75 . . . there's another five years.'

Citing many of his predecessors as among his greatest inspirations – including Chief Luthuli, Drs Moroka and Xuma, and Samuel Mapogo Makgatho – the ANC leader repeatedly dodges the direct question: how would you like history to record the role of Nelson Mandela? 'It would be a distortion of history to think in terms of an individual,' he says, closing the subject, 'because he is exploiting the achievements of those who went before him.'

Mandela's old-fashionedness comes through surprisingly often. He is kind about PW Botha, loyal to those opponents he perceives as having done the honourable thing. He is passionate in his reassurances to South Africa's scared minorities, almost pleading with them to stay and build the new country.

Does he believe we will be a happier nation by this time next year? 'Oh yes, oh yes. There can be no doubt about that. We are not looking for victors and vanquished. Nobody should be frightened and think that this process is going to exclude them, that they are not required. We require all our people . . . Let's forget the past now, and think of the present and the future.'

Those close to him do not call him Mr Mandela, nor do many opt for the pre-emptive 'president'. Rather it is – in his presence – Madiba or Ntata. Out of earshot it is 'The Old Man', spoken in tones that connote final authority. On this morning The Old Man is patient and calm, as only a prisoner of conscience could be.

Later in the day he will be addressing tens of thousands of the faithful at his Siyanqobo rally. Among all those around him there is the adrenalin-driven freneticism of waiting for the starter's gun, but as we leave him in his room The Old Man is still and calm as a statue.

THE STAR, APRIL 25 1994

ALONE WITH OURSELVES
IN THE BALLOT BOOTH

Election day, 350 years in the making, arrived. In the background was the echo of brutal bombs; in the foreground overwhelming exhilaration. What did the future hold?

THE BOMBS OF FUTILE DESPERATION GO OFF, EACH NEW report shaking us to the core. The window of peace that opened after the Buthelezi breakthrough has broken panes. The nation goes to the polling booths with a small knot of fear in its stomach. But that feeling is overwhelmed totally by the exhilaration of being alive now, of participating in this deeply just event which was 350 years in the making.

The bombs of the diehards will not stop the arrival of the future; they cannot. Tokyo Sexwale, a man who responds with extraordinary statesmanship in times of crisis, is right when he says the saboteurs have taken on too big an enemy. The vast majority, millions and millions of ordinary South Africans, want this election and will have it.

We may still lie frightened in the night, reluctant to turn on a radio lest it tells of more terror, we might feel panic as the logistical magnitude of the poll knocks the IEC's plans sideways, but the people will not be stopped from taking

428

part in what could be the greatest racial miracle the world has ever seen.

In all its editorial comment this newspaper has doggedly supported the process of transition from apartheid to democracy, insisting even in the darkest moments that the miracle remained achievable. We counselled courage and contextualisation, not naively or slavishly accepting what the politicians said about themselves, but in the sincere belief that this process – however messy – was our complex country's only salvation, morally and practically.

We are proud of our approach, though well aware of the enormity of the difficulties ahead and the glaring mistakes made by all of us along the way. We have been vilified by the hard right and the hard left, by liberal purists and countless others.

All we can do is pray that history proves us to have been wise on the balance. We rejected the prophecies of doom which conjured up an indefinite Zulu guerilla war of resistance in the hills of northern Natal, an engulfing right-wing uprising, and uncontrollable chaos.

These things have not come to pass and need not, ever. Yes, the bloodshed has been horrendous and unnecessary. It shames us and it is not over yet, but it has always been perpetrated by a fraction of our population. That is so still today. The majority, through its astoundingly diverse political representatives, has chosen to face the future together – we are all South Africans now – rather than fighting a nihilistic fractricidal war to the end. No one should forget what kind of war that would have been, had we blundered forward on the apartheid path.

Very soon we will be looking into and guessing at the future. It will be our daily lives. Many predictable disillusionments lie ahead. The new government, uniquely conciliatory as its composition may be, will provide countless disappointments. There will be stupidity, inefficiency, expedience and many other defining characteristics of politicians in power. This is the way of the world; we are not electing saints or polymaths.

Of course heaven will not descend on the southern tip of Africa when our first-ever representative government assembles next month; far from it. The maltreated masses could not be uplifted immediately, even if President Clinton made us a gift of his entire GDP. Time and wisdom, as well as money and goodwill, are needed to reverse the tide of centuries. As for the once-cosseted minority, one can almost hear the complaints already, as some artificially high and skewed euphemistic 'standards' do begin to drop – or at least be made more difficult and expensive to secure.

Those who think that life in the new South Africa can be just like the old was, are setting themselves up for distress. It cannot and should not be – but it can be a country in which everybody has the opportunity of fulfilment. And we have not recognised the possibility that we might have been through the worst already.

In some cases this new government might prove to be no better than that which erected toilets in the veld. The enthusiasm of the heirs-apparent is great – their belief that they can perform miracles even sincere and infectious – but the truth is more mundane and mordant.

Some of them will indeed be better than those who went before, some will turn out pretty much the same, some worse. The flesh is weak and there will be weaknesses, but we cannot lose sight of this great, overriding difference between what is coming and what is going. This new government will be of the people, sharing power and responsibility, and it will take its initiatives with the force of that profound legitimacy. A satisfactory preliminary structure is in place; now it is up to the men and women who take up their positions within it.

The transitional years are going to be bumpy. In some aspects this will be exciting – there is for example a strong possibility of interesting new political realignments between now and 1999. But if it is going to succeed – and success will be achieved if we reach the turn of the century with our population at liberty, intact, increasingly affluent, and protective of a heterogeneous multiparty system – then the transition has to be managed with great discipline and reason. The time for promoting unrealistic expectations is well and truly over.

As we stand in lines today and tomorrow waiting to make our little marks; if we should doubt that this is a great thing that is being achieved, perhaps we should glance at the people in front of and behind us. There, in a display of democracy we have never had before, might be a fellow South African preparing to vote for Clarence Makwetu, and another for Constand Viljoen.

This is an amazing outcome, however difficult the future might be. I am going to vote with all the hope I can summon, relief at no longer wielding unjust political privilege and, more than anything, immense pride at formal induction into the ranks of the new South Africans.

THE STAR, APRIL 27 1994

ALL TOGETHER NOW

April 27, the day that will forever mark the end of apartheid, finally arrived. It was unforgettable, for many reasons – but how would history record the day?

SOUTH AFRICA, WEDNESDAY, APRIL 27, 1994. IT CAN BE remembered in many ways, with many emotions. History will in time determine the abiding image. I'm not sure it can be that precise.

Was it fury and frustration as the magnitude of the election organisers' unpreparedness became apparent in the broiling sun? Fear of a thousand car bombs as the dread news arrived from Jan Smuts airport? Hollow disappointment as it seemed the IFP might again jump the ship of transition?

We felt all these things, powerfully – but the abiding image? No, none of these. The abiding image of the day that South Africa began to become one nation, all together, was in the orange autumn sun rising over a country teeming with extraordinary, renewed people. It rose over a country with a new flag, a new anthem, a new map, and a profound new human mood.

When the people began to form those lines they became a new people, spontaneously and unintentionally. The tiny

432

seed first glimpsed on the national peace day last year, giving life to the otherwise lifeless political slogan 'non-racial', burst into resplendent flower. Black South Africans learnt what whites already knew: how to vote. White South Africans learnt what blacks already knew: how to wait.

They did it together, in marvellous straggly multi-coloured queues in areas where the polling was working, and in lines of astonishing forbearance and determination in areas where it was not.

The old South Africa's final revenge lay in the fact that the predominantly black areas suffered most of the difficulties, but even this unbearable frustration was borne.

The intangible feeling of new South Africanness – it is difficult to capture it more closely – was reflected in a thousand different exchanges, vignettes, shards of conversation. The snappily dressed young black man trying to persuade the long-haired, young, white man to vote for FW de Klerk, not Nelson Mandela. The burly Afrikaans-speaker blurting out excitedly as he finally reached the door of the polling station: '*Ek kan nie my mind opmaak nie!*' (I can't make up my mind!).

The aged of the country, caring so much about voting that they waited and even died in order to declare on the future for younger generations. The initially forced, soon natural, camaraderie between different races in the snaking lines. The chic suburbanite, seeing the racial composition of the queue at the polling station and exclaiming, 'And we call these *white* suburbs!'

The erstwhile warriors of hostel and township in one line, swopping complaints about the IEC's failings as they waited to cast their ballots for their rival leaders. The extraordinary, quite extraordinary, lack of violence on the day.

It is worth recalling what we were conditioned to expect. There was a brutal bomb, yes, and it ruined some lives and brought the fear back. But there were no marauding hordes, no drive-by killers mowing down the defenceless voters in their queues.

South Africa's weapons of death fell more silent than they have for a long time – on precisely the day they were expected to resound the loudest.

Perhaps it was just too clear what the people wanted, and what they were prepared to risk in order to get it. If ever a message was delivered to the desperadoes who still believe they can shoot down this march to democracy, it was delivered on April 27 1994.

Towards the end of the day, when the euphoria began to be tempered by fatigue and frustration, it was clear that there were serious difficulties – in truth, the election was at risk. Some areas had been outrageously badly treated, and Chief Mangosuthu Buthelezi had a genuine grievance regarding the stickers-on-ballots foul-up.

But from this all emerged an amazing realisation: so far had we come that South Africa's biggest problem was now technical, not political. And the technicians spent the night fixing the broken machinery: it looked like they just might succeed.

More South African myths were punctured on the day. Right-wingers did turn up to vote, in numbers, in the election they had sworn to resist to the death. The almost infinite capacity of human beings to adapt to circumstances through the force of rationality was on display.

And the oppressed masses: they did not attack, loot and wreak revenge on the day of the wrong's righting. They grasped their precious votes, the repository of dignity, to their hearts and celebrated.

The essential upliftment of miserable lives is still to come in the future. Material desire was not the deepest emotion on April 27; white South Africa has always underestimated the depth of the psychological slur of disenfranchisement, apart from the social poison it unleashed.

Do we white South Africans understand what it meant to our compatriots to put those stubby pencil points to paper in the flimsy wooden ballot booths? We should be trying very hard, if we are going to build together on this near-miraculous new beginning.

Among the millions who made their first crosses on the day was a very gifted young journalist from The Star. He was to exercise the right that had for so long been withheld from his forbears. When he came to grasp the pencil in his hand and place his mark against the leader of his choice, his hands shook uncontrollably.

They shook with the enormity of the moment, and with the fear of making a mistake at the very instant of enfranchisement.

He succeeded in his democratic act, and beamed with relief and elation when he re-emerged into the Johannesburg sunlight.

'Look at these people,' he said, pointing to the taxi-loads as he hurried back to work, 'They've all got the vote!'

THE STAR, 29 APRIL 1994

THE MORNING AFTER

Nelson Rolihlahla Mandela was South Africa's first black president. The final election results weren't in, but that didn't stop the celebrations. Was the country ready to wake up after the party?

WE ALL KNOW THERE'S ALWAYS GOT TO BE A MORNING after, but in South Africa it didn't arrive on the morning after the night before. The night before, quite unexpectedly and unforgettably, Frederik Willem de Klerk graciously conceded defeat and Nelson Rolihlahla Mandela graciously accepted victory. The results weren't in – far from it – but it was all over bar the counting. The racist republic was dead . . . now it was long live the non-racial republic.

History-watchers might have expected that the catharsis, which saw thousands of black celebrants take to the streets after Mandela's televised speech, would lead in the morning to a country in which power passed brutally from light-skinned citizens to their darker compatriots. They might have expected some gloating from the formerly emasculated, now empowered masses.

Well, South Africa is full of surprises. In fact, on that chilly early-winter morning after, there was this familiar scene. On a Johannesburg street corner, a white traffic policeman had pulled over a black minibus taxi, and was ticking the driver off while ticketing him. The driver stood penitently, accepting his fate. The passengers in the jam-packed minibus were looking at their watches, worried about being late for the office. It was a very commonplace sight. Except for the fact that behind this little group, framing the tableau, was a newspaper billboard on a lamppost. 'It's President Mandela', read the banner headline.

Apartheid and all that – gone. Mandela had just won his lifelong struggle, and life was going on in the curious beloved country. Traffic jams were no more and no less orderly than usual. People were going to work, like any other day. Race relations were just fine – a little warmer, if anything. The place was happy, there's no better word for it. We are such an unpredictable bunch in this country that we even surprise ourselves.

The generosity and normalcy of the morning after, very probably had something to do with the spirit-soaring triumph of the night before. At the crucial moment FW de Klerk and Nelson Mandela rose up and displayed all that is best in human beings. Their respective performances were so powerful that for a time they even overshadowed the interminable delays and mounting chaos which had gripped the vote-counting process.

In Pretoria at National Party headquarters at 6pm, De Klerk stood to tell his faithful followers what they already knew – that they had lost, white power was a thing of the past. But he did so in such a way that they did not need to feel vanquished. In a speech which history will judge generously, the white president magnanimously conceded defeat while simultaneously vowing that his party's role was far from being played out. In an atmosphere of thick emotion he said of his black successor: 'His role was a leading and an honourable one. I thank him and congratulate him.' He looked forward to working together with Mandela in the government of national unity, De Klerk said, and then paused before uttering these historic words about the ANC leader, dubbing him a 'man of destiny'.

'Mr Mandela will soon assume the highest office in the land with all the awesome responsibility it bears . . . He has walked a long road and now stands on top of the hill . . . The journey is never complete, and as he contemplates the next hill, I hold out my hand to him in friendship and co-operation.'

Three hours later, in a Johannesburg hotel, Mandela returned the compliment to De Klerk and the country. To an ecstatic reception from supporters, the elegant grey-haired icon said: 'Free at last'. He and De Klerk had finished a 'good fight' in the campaign, and the time for quarrelling was over. What he liked about his adversary, he said, was his ability to exchange harsh words 'and then be able to shake hands and sit down to drink coffee.' Mandela congratulated the once-loathed NP on its electoral performance, and the people of South Africa for their conduct in the election – which 'set the tone for the future'. It was time to 'heal the wounds and build a new South Africa', he said, 'time to drink a toast . . . to the small miracle.'

Tears flowed freely at both of these momentous events. They were not just tears of sadness at how much the land and its people had had to pay in order to reach this just outcome; they were also tears of reconciliation and expectancy. At the ANC's victory party Ronnie Kasrils, one of the old regime's fiercest opponents, said of De Klerk's gracious concession: 'He was a mensch'. The sentiment was widespread, forgiving, and forward-looking.

When will the morning after come? It will, as surely as night follows day. It is true that South Africa has never before experienced psychological renewal of this power, but there has been euphoria before, followed by chronic depression. We are very bad at seeing the wood for the trees.

We need now to treasure this celebratory mood, to hoard it as fuel for the future, so that when we soon run into the rough challenges of reality, we are still feeling strong. Change has happened in our society's superstructure; it has yet to arrive on the streets where we live. The birth cannot be free of pain, and we – especially the privileged among us – should be prepared for that. It will help if we remember for a very long time that the fates could not have given us a much better start, the monumental misfiring of the election machine notwithstanding.

4 MAY 1994 (UNPUBLISHED)

ENDNOTE: APOCALYPSE NO

Another night turns to morning, Johannesburg's strange seasonal smell of frozen dust touches the nostrils of the mining town, a reminder of shivering cold brown days to come. Winter in the new South Africa, almost before us. So much, thankfully, behind us. We are here. We are alive. The foreign correspondents are leaving, feeling faintly cheated: Civil War Cancelled. Soon we shall be alone with ourselves.

It feels in these early hours that we are growing vaguely irritable as the delays in setting the seal on the election slip from frustrating to farcical. But wait: perhaps it is just us, whose profession demands that we hang on the final result, who are so impatient and unforgiving. The nation – the new young boisterous polyglot nation – is asleep at this hour, dreaming dreams. Perhaps it is time to sleep, and let the big thing we are doing take its course like a great river that will not be dammed.

I had hoped to close this book, containing its thin slice of peculiarly coloured history, with a solid thud. 'Here is the precise outcome of South Africa's founding democratic election . . . ' But no, if I needed reminding that our continent doesn't work like that, it has been provided. Five full days have passed since the last ballot was cast in the miraculous election, and still we know little more than the fact that Nelson Mandela has achieved his destiny, and ours. This book must go to the printer.

Perhaps the percentage points do not matter, really. And perhaps the Old Man will be inaugurated on time, perhaps he will not: the tide has turned and we are about to start swimming, that is what matters.

Of course we know that the intoxication of liberation – uniquely enough, it is potent and heady for white as well as black – will wear off, probably quite soon. But these days can never be taken away from us and we would be fools indeed to squander them. Nobody told us there'd be days like these. If they had, we might not have believed them.

Reconciliation has been provided to be possible in the most race-poisoned country in the entire world; it will be permanent if we can achieve reconstruction as well. April 1994 has shown us how to unleash again the stoic, pioneering spirit of the rainbow nation's disparate ancestors. Nelson Mandela, the most fitting founding president any country could wish for, has already said it is now time to get South Africa working again. That work will bring back the reality of the terrible wrongs we have wrought, and there will be bitterness and anger at the inevitable failure to right them immediately. But our politics will be those of an incrementally normalising democracy, the primary injustice done away with.

As the year's pass, if we are sensible, we will recreate the *laager* of old – except that we will all be inside it, fighting shoulder-to-shoulder for something that belongs to us all. The new flag is already creeping into the hearts of those who tried to hold on to the old one. It will soon appear in the grandstands of Ellis Park. The beautiful new anthem will soon have us standing in solemn respect and pride. Travellers will not hide their South African passports at foreign airports – they will flaunt them. It is a time to have faith and to be romantic, even as we look up at the mountain we must climb.

I asked myself a long time ago, when I first came across his riveting entry, whether William Ten Rhyne might have been right about us South Africans. Ten Rhyne, 'Native of Deventry, Physician in Ordinary, Member of the Council of Justice to the Dutch East India Company', assessed the character of our fledgling nation in 1709. In a chapter headed 'Their manner of making war', he remarked, 'Nothing is more barbarous than this country, where the rugged climate and rocky mountains seem to have produced men of their own kind'.

I have always hoped we could prove him wrong. I think we might be doing so now, nearly three centuries later, free at last.

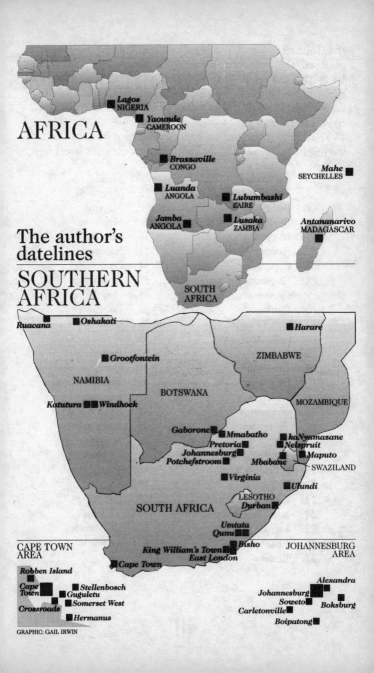

AFRICA

Lagos
NIGERIA

Yaounde
CAMEROON

Brassaville
CONGO

Mahe
SEYCHELLES

Luanda
ANGOLA

Lubumbashi
ZAIRE

The author's
datelines

Jamba
ANGOLA

Lusaka
ZAMBIA

Antananarivo
MADAGASCAR

SOUTHERN
AFRICA

SOUTH
AFRICA

Ruacana   ■*Oshakati*   ■*Harare*

■*Grootfontein*   ZIMBABWE

NAMIBIA   BOTSWANA   MOZAMBIQUE

Katutura ■■*Windhoek*

Gaborone■ ■*Mmabatho*   ■*kaNyamasane*
Pretoria■   ■*Nelspruit*
Johannesburg■   ■*Maputo*
Potchefstroom■   *Mbabane*■
                SWAZILAND
■*Virginia*

■*Ufundi*

SOUTH AFRICA   LESOTHO   *Durban*■

Umtata■
Qunu■   *Bisho*■
King William's Town■
East London

CAPE TOWN
AREA   JOHANNESBURG
                    AREA

■*Cape Town*

Robben Island■

Cape ■ ■ *Stellenbosch*   *Alexandra*■
Town ■*Guguletu*   *Johannesburg*■
■ ■*Somerset West*   *Soweto*■   ■*Boksburg*
Crossroads■
    ■*Hermanus*   *Carletonville*■
                        Boipatong■

GRAPHIC: GAIL IRWIN

MAP: PLACES REPORTED FROM AND ON

1. Alexandra
2. Antananarivo
3. Bisho
4. Boipatong
5. Boksburg
6. Brazzaville
7. Cape Town
8. Carletonville
9. Crossroads
10. Durban
11. East London
12. Gaborone
13. Gansbaai
14. Grootfontein
15. Guguletu
16. Harare
17. Hermanus
18. Honeydew
19. Jamba
20. Johannesburg
21. kaNyamazane
22. Katutura
23. Kempton Park
24. King William's Town
25. Lagos
26. Lumumbashi
27. Lusaka
28. Mahe
29. Mangweni
30. Maputo
31. Mbabane
32. Mmabatho
33. Nelspruit
34. Okankolo
35. Ondangwa
36. Ongwediva
37. Oshakati
38. Oshivelo
39. Potchefstroom
40. Pretoria
41. Qunu
42. Robben Island
43. Ruacana
44. Somerset West
45. Soweto
46. Stellenbosch
47. Swanieville
48. Tumahole
49. Ulundi
50. Umtata
51. Virginia
52. Windhoek
53. Yaounde

GLOSSARY

Amandla: power
Assegai: spear

Bakkie: pick-up truck
Barend Strydom: mass race-murderer, convicted in 1985
Biltong: salted, dried meat
Boere: township word meaning whites, Afrikaners in particular
Boerewors: farmers' sausage
Boma: bushveld eating place
Bosberaad: bush conference
Braaivleis: barbeque
Broederbond: secret Afrikaner society
Brown Nats: 'coloureds' who joined the National Party
Buiteland: foreign countries

Casspir: SA Police armoured vehicle
CCB: Civil Co-operation Bureau, a secret military unit
Clare Silberbauer: child killed in 1993 terror attack

Dagga: marijuana
Die Stem: official national anthem of South Africa
Dompas: passbook restricting movement of blacks

Dopper: member of the Reformed Church
Dumelang: a Sotho greeting
Durban July: premier South African horse race

Fahfee: popular form of street gambling
Flinkdink: quick thinking
Foefie: dodge or stunt
Freedom Charter: 1955 policy statement of ANC and its allies

Garona: government building in Bophuthatswana
Gold Reef City: Johannesburg theme park
Goniwe signal: alleged instruction to assassinate activist
Great Trek: 19th century Afrikaner migration inland
Groot Krokodil: Great Crocodile, nickname for PW Botha
Grys: grey

Heita: slang township greeting
Homeland: ethnic enclave created under apartheid policies
Hoor hoor: hear hear

Indaba: discussions, meeting

Induna: a chieftan's adviser

Inkathagate: scandal surrounding IFP government funding

Johnny Clegg: South African pop singer

Kaffir: derogatory term for blacks

Kaffirboetie: white who sympathizes with blacks

Klipdrift: South African brandy

Knobkierie: knob-stick or bludgeon

Kruithoring: gunpowder horn, symbol of National Party

Kumquat: small fruit

Laager: boers' circular protective encampment

Lost City: hotel and entertainment complex in Bophuthatswana

Mala Mala: exclusive game reserve in eastern Transvaal

Mass Democratic Movement: former informal political movement

Mealie-meal: maize meal

MK: *see* Umkhonto we Sizwe

Munts: derogatory term for blacks

Nartjie: citrus fruit

Necklace: brutal murder method, using tyres and petrol

NGK: Nederduitse Gereformeerde Kerk, Dutch Reformed Church

Nkosi Sikelel' iAfrika: hymn, anthem of black South Africans

Ntata: Father

Overbergers: people living in Overberg mountain region, Cape

Panga: machete

Pap: traditional African maize porridge

People's courts: illegal township courts

Percy Qoboza: late former South Africa newspaper editor

Pickard report: report on corruption inquiry

Pieter-Dirk Uys: South African actor, comedian

Potjiekos: traditional Afrikaner dish

Ratel: SA Defence Force armoured vehicle

Regses: rightists

Rinderpest: 19th century cattle plague

Robert McBride: convicted Umkhonto we Sizwe bomber

Saamwerk: co-operation

Samp: traditional food
Sand River Convention: Afrikaner-British agreement of 1852
Sekunjalo: Now is the time – the ANC's rallying call for the election
Sanibonani: a Zulu greeting
Shebeen: township bar
Sjambok: whip
Skande: scandal
Skiet: shoot
South Westers: term for whites of former South West Africa
Springbok: official emblem for national sports teams
Susterbond: sisterhood (play on all-male broederbond)

TBVC: the so-called independent homelands – Transkei, Bophuthatswana, Venda, Ciskei
Tjoepstil: quite still, quiet as a mouse
Toenadering: rapprochement

Toyi toyi: township dance common at political events
Trekboer: migrant farmer
Tsotsi: villain
Tuynhuys: official residence of head of state, Cape Town

Ubisi: milk
Uitgekak: severely reprimanded
Uitlanders: foreigners
Umkhonto we Sizwe: lit: Spear of the Nation, the ANC's armed wing
United Democratic Front: former ANC-supporting organization

Verligte: enlightened
Volk: nation
Volksraad: parliament
Volkstaat: nation state
Voorkamer: front room, parlour
Vrot: rotten

Wors: sausage

ACKNOWLEDGEMENTS

MANY PUBLICATIONS, AND PEOPLE, MADE IT POSSIBLE FOR me to be in all these interesting places over the past seven years or so. My thanks first to the publications in South Africa and abroad from which this collection has been drawn: The Star, Saturday Star, Weekly Mail, The Daily Mail, The Guardian, The Times, The Independent, The Sunday Correspondent, New Statesman and Society, South China Morning Post, The Argus, Time Out, Vula, and Penthouse magazines.

Special thanks to the following people. My wife Stefania, Glenda Parker of Trans South Africa Book Distributors, and her star team of Gavin Perrow, Russell Barnes and Sanjay Seeth. John Blake and Nuala O'Neill of Transworld. John Carlin, who edited the first edition. Doug Band, whose belief in the book turned the project from fantasy into fact. At The Star – Richard Steyn, Peter Sullivan, and Graeme King, who were wonderfully supportive.

Without my mother Joan, there could have been no book: for years she painstakingly kept cuttings. (I did not.)

The eminent persons who endorsed the book after reading an early draft of the manuscript were courageous and kind. Clem Sunter made special efforts.

Thanks also to the booksellers who embraced the first edition and made it such a success.

Finally, my thanks to the many readers, particularly of The Star, whose letters over the years convinced me that perhaps some of my writing was actually worth republishing.

Here's to the new South Africa . . .

The Death Lobby
How the West Armed Iraq
Kenneth R. Timmerman

'A devastating and persuasive indictment of Governmental stupidity, bureaucratic incompetence and corporate greed' *Frederick Forsyth*

Months after the triumph of Operation Desert Storm, the questions remain: what is Iraq's military capability? Where did Saddam Hussein get the armaments to provoke the Gulf War? What did he have, and what does he have left? *The Death Lobby* answers these questions and exposes the truth behind the bribery and subterfuge that brought about deals with companies and commercial contracts for arms and embargoed technology – and the conspiracy of silence in London, Washington, Paris, and Bonn, where repeated warnings of Iraq's true intentions were ignored . . .

Through his exhaustive research, Kenneth Timmerman proves that Saddam Hussein could never have brought about the Gulf War without the co-operation of Western governments and the decaying Soviet empire. His remarkable investigation has prompted questions in Parliament and has, at last, focused world attention on the insatiable greed and ambition that compromised world peace.

The inescapable truth today is that yesterday's lessons have still to be learnt . . . world peace still hangs in the balance . . . the warnings can no longer be ignored.

'Filled with carefully researched information about how greed for profits leads companies to support an unscrupulous dictator' *Simon Wiesenthal*

'Essential reading . . . *The Death Lobby* is in a class by itself' *The New York Times*

A Bantam Paperback
0553 406248

Princess
Jean Sasson

'Anyone with the slightest interest in human rights will find this book heart-wrenching. It is a well-written, personal story . . . It had to come from a native woman to be believable'
Betty Mahmoody, bestselling author of *Not Without My Daughter*

Think of a Saudi Arabian princess and what do you see? A woman glittering with jewels, living a life of unbelievable luxury. But in reality she lives in a gilded cage. She has no freedom, no vote, no control over her own life, no value but as a bearer of sons. Hidden behind the veil, she is a prisoner, her jailers her father, her husband, her sons.

'Sultana' is a member of the Saudi Royal Family, closely related to the King. As she tells of her life – from her turbulent childhood to her arranged marriage – she lifts the veil and reveals a history of appalling oppression and shocking human rights violations such as forced marriages, sex slavery and summary executions.

Princess is a testimony to a woman of indomitable spirit and great courage. By speaking out, 'Sultana' risks bringing the wrath of the Saudi establishment upon her head and upon the heads of her children. For this reason, she has told her story anonymously.

A Bantam Paperback
0553 405705

It Doesn't Take a Hero
General H. Norman Schwarzkopf

Rarely in public life does a figure emerge of such compelling leadership and personal charisma that he literally captures the world's imagination. Such a man – intelligent, forceful, engaging – is General H. Norman Schwarzkopf, Commander of the Allied Forces in the Persian Gulf, whom people everywhere instantly recognized as one of the outstanding leaders of our time.

Now, this eagerly awaited autobiography reveals the full story of General Schwarzkopf's life and career, in a book that is at once candid, outspoken, and certain to be controversial. Detailing an unusual youth spent in the Middle East and Europe, his complex family relationships, and a West Point education that led him into an army vastly different from the one he commanded in the Gulf, General Schwarzkopf speaks frankly about the events and emotions of his two tours of duty in Vietnam and of the 'dark years' that followed; about his 'outsider's' relationship with the Pentagon; and – revealingly – about the points of personal crisis throughout his extraordinary thirty-five-year career.

Here, too, are his inspiring thoughts on leadership and, for the first time, a behind–the–scenes account of the events and personalities of Desert Shield/Desert Storm, told from the general's unique perspective, that exposes the complexities and conflicts of command as no other commentary can.

A Bantam Paperback
0553 405519